Burdened by race: Coloured identities in southern Africa

EDITED BY
MOHAMED ADHIKARI

UCT
PRESS

Burdened by race: Coloured identities in southern Africa

First published 2009

© UCT Press, an imprint of
Juta and Company Ltd
PO Box 14373
Lansdowne, 7779
Cape Town, South Africa

ISBN 978-1-91989-514-7

Disclaimer

Project manager: Sharon Steyn
Copy editor: Wendy Priilaid
Proofreader: Fiona Potter
Cover photo: Eurafrican descendents of British settlers in Chingola 'coloured quarters', Zambia on Christmas day, 1965
Cover design: Marius Roux
Indexing: Sanet le Roux
Design and typesetting: Lebone Publishing Services
Printed and bound in the Republic of South Africa by Formeset Printers

Acknowledgements
The photograph used on the cover belongs to Mrs Sarah Adolph and was made available by Juliette Milner-Thornton.

FOR
RAFIQ AND ZAHEER

1. Not recognisable. **2.** Marjorie Stephenson, granddaughter of John Edward (Chiripula) Stephenson, British official in Northern Rhodesia; daughter of Omega and Lena Stephenson. **3.** Alison Milner, otherwise affectionately known as Sukey; great granddaughter of Dr Sidney Spencer Kachalola Broomfield; granddaughter of Joseph Milner; daughter of Japhet Milner and Nellie Broomfield; late younger sister of Juliet Milner. **4.** Carolyn Milner, great-granddaughter of E H Lane-Poole, Oxford graduate and colonial official in Northern Rhodesia; granddaughter of Joseph Milner; daughter of Michael Milner and Gertrude Mitchell; first cousin of Juliet Milner. **5.** Clement Adolf, great-grandson of a former British settler of Northern Rhodesia; son of Tommy Adolf (Cape Coloured) and Sarah Jones. **6.** Clarence Adolf , older brother of Clement. **7.** Morgan Jones, late paternal grandson of Mr Yule, a former British official of Northern Rhodesia; son of Phoebe Jones (Yule); nephew of Sarah Jones (Adolf). **8.** Juliette Milner, great-granddaughter of Dr Sidney Spencer Kachalola Broomfield; granddaughter of Joseph Milner; older sister of Alison Milner. **9.** Alexander Moore, maternal grandson of a Belgian official and paternal grandson of a British settler; son of John Moore and Ada, sister of Phoebe Yule. **10.** Clifford Adolf, brother of Clarence and Clement. **11.** Rodney Hodgson, grandson of A G O Hodgson, Provincial Commissioner of Nyasaland; son of Walter Henry Hodgson and Mary Gould. **12.** Owen Milner, older brother of Juliette and Sukey Milner. **13.** Francina Milner, older sister of Juliette and Sukey Milner. **14.** Marie Moore, younger sister of Alexander. **15.** Margaret Cardew, daughter of a British official in Nyasaland. **16.** Christina Moore, older sister or Marie and Alexander Moore. **17.** Doris Moore, younger sister of Christina and older sister of Marie and Alexander Moore. **18.** Priscilla Stephenson, older sister of Marjorie Stephenson. **19.** Jean Adolf, daughter of Sara Jones (Adolf); older sister of Clarence, Clifford and Clement. **20.** Elias Cardew, younger brother of Margaret Cardew. **21.** Moira Hodgson, older sister of Rodney Hodgson. **22.** Barbara Jones, older sister of Morgan Jones; maternal first cousin of Christina, Doris, Marie and Alexander Moore and paternal first cousin of the Adolf children (her father and Sarah Jones were siblings). **23.** Sarah Jones (Adolf). **24.** Eve Moore, younger sister of Christina, Doris, Marie and Alexander Moore.

TABLE OF CONTENTS

ACKNOWLEDGEMENTS

On more than one occasion, upon hearing that I was editing a collection of essays, colleagues remarked that the task called for the arts of persuasion and coercion. Although both were used, it was largely cheerful cooperation that marked the compilation of this volume. This, together with ongoing friendly communication with contributors, helped make the production of this book a most gratifying experience. Despite its eclectic nature, there is nevertheless a distinct bias towards historical analysis in this anthology. This is a reflection of my own background and the contacts I have built up over the years among postgraduate students working on aspects of coloured identity in southern Africa.

All of the contributors are young researchers and academics who have either recently completed doctoral dissertations or are still busy with PhD theses. All except one, whom I met at a conference, contacted me at some point during the last decade to discuss aspects of their research. This volume is thus the product of a personal network that grew organically and in the course of time presented the opportunity of compiling an edited volume. Through it I pay tribute to a group of bright young scholars whose ideas have helped refine my own thinking and whose innovative work is transforming our understanding of the nature and history of coloured identity. For me this book is thus a celebration of academic fellowship that in some cases has matured into highly valued friendships.

A special thank-you to Juliette Milner-Thornton for providing the wonderfully expressive photograph used on the cover of this book. I am indebted to all of the anonymous readers who, no doubt, took time out of busy schedules to evaluate the manuscript and provide constructive commentary. I would also like to acknowledge research funding from the University of Cape Town's University Research Committee.

As usual I salute the close circle of very dear family members who have enriched my life immeasurably over the years. Although the Friday night gym sessions are now a nostalgic memory, the Sunday afternoon shenanigans are still the highlight of my week. And for me, over the last decade, Saturday has not been Saturday without lunch with Nasreen, Riaz and the recently deceased Kader 'smartypants' Adhikari, whose knowledge of the world and hunger for more meat knew no bounds. This intimate clique includes – or included, as some sadly are now departed – Peggy, Ratso, Shadow, Edgar, Lady, Prince, Befok, Oscar and Junior Adhikari. Long may you run Junior, keep on rocking Edgar, and don't you dare start kakling again Mr. Kakles! Finally, the love and warmth of my sons Rafiq and Zaheer make my life a joy.

NOTES ON CONTRIBUTORS

Mohamed Adhikari teaches in the Department of Historical Studies at the University of Cape Town and has published extensively on aspects of coloured identity and politics in South Africa.

Michael Besten is a researcher at the Unit for Khoekhoe and San Studies at the University of the Free State. He recently completed a PhD thesis in history at Leiden University, Netherlands.

Christiaan Beyers is Assistant Professor of International Development Studies at Trent University, Peterborough, Canada. His research on District Six focuses on the politics of community and social citizenship in the ongoing land restitution process, a subject on which he has published a number of journal articles and book chapters.

Christopher Lee is Assistant Professor of History at the University of North Carolina, Chapel Hill. He is currently completing a book on coloured identities in British Central Africa, and has published a number of scholarly articles on the subject.

Juliette Milner-Thornton is a Zambian-born PhD candidate at Griffith University, Brisbane, Australia. Her research focuses on mixed-race history, particularly coloured identity in Zambia. She is a part-time associate lecturer at Griffith University's Centre for Public Culture and Ideas.

James Muzondidya is a Zimbabwean academic and policy analyst currently working at the Human Sciences Research Council. His main area of research interest is in identity politics of the postcolonial African state. He is the author of *Walking a Tightrope: Towards a Social History of the Coloured People of Zimbabwe*.

Michele Ruiters has a PhD from Rutgers University, New Brunswick, United States, and is a senior researcher at the Development Bank of Southern Africa. She has published in the areas of international institutional reform, militarisation in Africa, gender and development, and identity politics.

Helene Strauss is Assistant Professor in the department of English and Cultural Studies, McMaster University, Hamilton, Canada. Her teaching and publishing record reflects a longstanding preoccupation with questions concerning social cohesion, subject formation and ethical interpersonal interaction in South Africa and beyond.

Henry Trotter is a PhD candidate in African History at Yale University. He is researching the history of 20th-century South African port culture, and recently published a book entitled *Sugar Girls & Seamen: A Journey into the World of Dockside Prostitution in South Africa*.

Predicaments of marginality: cultural creativity and political adaptation in southern Africa's coloured communities

In southern Africa, the term 'coloured' has a specialised meaning in that it denotes a person of mixed racial ancestry rather than one who is black, as it does in most other parts of the world. In addition to this racialised attribution which defines 'colouredness' in the popular mind, it was the marginality of coloured communities that was central to the manner in which the identity manifested itself socially and politically across the subcontinent. Other common features that have historically marked coloured communities include a strong association with Western culture and values in opposition to African equivalents, their claim to an intermediate position in the racial hierarchy, and negative racial stereotyping derived mainly from the idea that racial mixture is pejorative, and results in degeneration and weakness. Though much more pronounced under white supremacy, these characteristics are still present, though usually in modified, veiled or symbolic forms, in the postcolonial environment, as several of the studies in this collection demonstrate.[1]

This book is not an attempt to cover its subject in any systematic or comprehensive way but rather to showcase current innovative work on coloured identity in southern Africa. It is eclectic in that contributions draw on a wide range of disciplines and are written from a variety of theoretical positions.[2] There are nevertheless a number of intertwining themes running through the volume that bind it together. They, among other things, highlight common elements in the origin of coloured identities in the region as well as the shaping influence of that familiar historical trajectory of colonial conquest, segregation and resistance, and the reconfiguration of identities in the wake of the overthrow of white rule. These interlinking themes also accentuate common concerns among researchers in the field derived from recent historiographical developments, the application of new theoretical insights and the changing political environment.

In one sense, coloured identity is a product of European racist ideology which, through its binary logic, cast people deemed to be of mixed racial origin as a distinct, stigmatised social stratum between the dominant white minority and the African majority. In colonial society, effect was given to this ideology through both official and customary discrimination. The colonial state, in its drive to classify and control people, played an important role in demarcating social identities by imposing racially based legal categories and segregatory policies on the population. Colouredness was also partly shaped by colonial social relations in that both settler and indigenous communities helped determine how people of mixed racial heritage were accommodated in these societies. However, in another sense, coloured identity is also very much the product of its bearers who, I would argue, were in the first instance primarily responsible for articulating the identity and subsequently determining its form and content. It is thus not surprising that the most important and most insistent of the themes that unify the contributions to this collection is the agency of coloured and proto-coloured people in the making of their own identities.

All of the contributors argue for a nuanced understanding of coloured and 'mixed-race' identities. Their analyses are highly sensitive to changes in the way it has found expression and of the impact of variables such as class, locality, context and ideology on senses of colouredness. They all recognise that an integral part of human social existence is that people self-reflexively create, maintain and revise their perceptions of who they are, and how and why they espouse the values and identities they do, and that social identities are by their very nature contested and unstable. While there is no gainsaying there being a substantive commonality to the concept of colouredness across all of its varied forms in southern Africa,

Christopher Lee's injunction that local understandings of colouredness be acknowledged and understood is broadly observed by contributors. There is clear consensus in this book that states and ruling groups do not create identities among subject peoples. While they may reinforce, constrain or manipulate such identities with varying degrees of success, bearers in the first instance create and negotiate their own social identities. As James Muzondidya so eloquently summarises this standpoint, 'coloured people themselves were the primary authors of their identity text'. The challenge is to explain how and why identities come into existence and evolve over time. The contributors to this book approach the problem from many different angles and collectively advance our understanding of this process for coloured identity well beyond the limits achieved by the extant literature.

The significance of colonialism in the making of coloured identities in southern Africa comes through most clearly in the non-South African case studies because colonialism in its formal sense lasted into the mid-1960s in these societies. The Zimbabwean and Malawian examples illustrate very clearly the ways in which colonial social relations and the policies of the colonial state placed limitations on the ways in which coloured identities were able to find expression, yet at the same time presented opportunities for coloured leaders and organisations to take the initiative in advancing identity claims. The Zambian example, because of its focus on a family history, provides insight into how the vagaries of colonial policy and customary discrimination played out in individual lives and across generations in particular families. Colonialism is not synonymous with white domination in this set of case studies because settler, as opposed to metropolitan, control of the state was significant in two of them. In Zimbabwe, white rule was prolonged by a decade and a half as a result of the Rhodesian Front's Unilateral Declaration of Independence in November 1965.[3] In the case of South Africa, colonial rule was of limited significance because it had given way to a settler-dominated, white supremacist state in the early part of the 20th century as a result of the political settlement following the South African War (1899–1902). In both cases, the ending of metropolitan control exacerbated racial tensions and sharpened the predicaments facing their respective coloured communities.

Despite its relatively early termination in South Africa, colonialism was nevertheless critical to the genesis of coloured identity because it had emerged under the aegis of British rule at the Cape Colony in the late 19th century. Although the process of social amalgamation that was to give rise to coloured identity dates back to the period of Dutch colonialism, it was in the decades after the emancipation of the Khoisan in 1828 and slaves in 1834 that various components of the heterogeneous black labouring class at the Cape started integrating more rapidly and developing an incipient collective identity based on a common socio-economic status and a shared culture derived from their incorporation into the lower ranks of Cape colonial society. This emergent community of assimilated colonial blacks consisted overwhelmingly of a downtrodden labouring class of African and Asian origin variously referred to as half-castes, bastards, Cape Boys, off-whites or coloureds, until the last-mentioned became the standard appellation from the latter half of the 1880s onwards. This category was usually taken to include sub-groups such as Malays, Griquas and 'Hottentots'. It was the transformative impact of the mineral revolution with the discovery of diamonds in 1867 and gold in 1886 in the southern African interior that helped crystallise the identity in the late 19th century. The rapid incorporation of significant numbers of Bantu-speaking Africans into the burgeoning capitalist economy served as the catalyst for assimilated colonial blacks to assert a separate identity and organise politically under the banner of colouredness. With their appeals for acceptance into the dominant society firmly rebuffed, and locked in intensifying competition with culturally distinct Bantu-speaking Africans for social resources, assimilated colonial blacks asserted a separate identity in order to claim a position of relative privilege to Africans on the basis that they were 'civilised' and partly descended from European colonists.[4]

This historical background is crucial to an understanding of coloured identity free of the essentialist notion that colouredness is an automatic product of miscegenation. There is an abiding popular perception that colouredness is an inherent, biologically determined condition that originated almost immediately with the onset of Dutch colonisation of the Cape – 'nine months after Van Riebeeck landed', as a popular joke would have it.[5] It is also important to an understanding of the making of the identity in the region as a whole because British colonialism expanded from its Cape colonial base into the subcontinent in the late 19th century under the twin influences of the 'scramble for Africa' and the development of large-scale mining in southern Africa. Not only did these factors precipitate the South African War, but the hope of discovering a second Witwatersrand motivated Cecil John Rhodes's drive into south central Africa. Hand in hand with the spread of British colonial rule in southern Africa went a particular set of attitudes and practices towards people of mixed racial origin encapsulated in the particular meaning of the term 'coloured' as it had developed in the Cape Colony.

A point made in all three of the chapters on societies north of the Limpopo is that South African notions of colouredness influenced local conceptions of the identity. This was most patently the case during the earlier years of British rule when colonial administrations first sought to racially classify and regulate the population using received notions of racial difference, and when ideas, experience and immigrants from the Cape were at their most influential. Later, these governments also looked to neighbouring states for suitable models on which to base policies toward people of mixed racial origin. South African influence is clearest in the case of Zimbabwe. James Muzondidya on several occasions demonstrates how ideas and circumstances in South Africa, often through the influence of South African-born immigrants, impacted the life of the Zimbabwean coloured community. Both Juliette Milner-Thornton and Christopher Lee allude to the significance of South African assumptions about racial mixture for their case studies. Not surprisingly, being more remote, South African perceptions and developments had less of an impact on Zambian and Malawian senses of colouredness than they did in Zimbabwe. The relatively small sizes of their settler populations were also significant because this affected both the size of the 'mixed race' populations as well as the tenor of colonial policy towards this group.

The pronounced role of segregation and apartheid in the moulding of coloured identity is a common theme that shines through in this collection of essays. Being racially classified by the white supremacist state and pushed together into racially defined residential areas, with many, especially among the small elite, spending their formative years in educational institutions reserved for coloured students, were all significant factors in creating a sense of separateness and community among people of 'mixed-race' parentage. There is no shortage of examples in this book that illustrate this, whether it be Helene Strauss's subtle analysis of what Chris van Wyk's reminiscences of life in the coloured township of Riverlea during the 1960s reveal about the making of his personal sense of colouredness, or James Muzondidya's discussion of the significance of the cadastral development of Zimbabwe's two main cities for reinforcing coloured identity in the first half of the 20th century. In this regard, one can also point to Juliette Milner-Thornton's reflections on how the colonial administration's collusion in the omission of white fathers' names from the official records in Northern Rhodesia affected their 'mixed-race' progeny's 'bonding in their abandonment'. Christopher Lee details the interesting example of Nyasaland, where the possibility of privileged treatment, though never realised, had an important and lasting imprint on expressions of coloured identity in Malawi.

The considerable effect of forced removals in consolidating communal consciousness among coloured people features prominently in this anthology, with two chapters devoted to the issue. These studies give substance to the familiar observation that being compelled to live in racially homogeneous residential areas under apartheid reified coloured identity as never before. Henry Trotter explains how evictions under the Group Areas Act helped to bond removees and their social networks into a more intimate sense of what it meant to be coloured, while Christiaan Beyers shows how symbolic meanings attached to District Six after forced removals helped produce a more exclusionary sense of colouredness in contemporary Cape Town.[6] What both Trotter and Beyers very effectively demonstrate is that while it might have been the apartheid state that enforced residential segregation and other draconian forms of social engineering on the coloured community, it was the victims of these injustices themselves who gave content and meaning to the identity reconfigurations that ensued. Both emphasise the significance of a common experience of trauma and a deep sense of social injustice in cementing solidarity within the coloured community in the second half of the 20th century.

As important as such measures imposed from above were, one cannot ignore the complicity of coloured people, both individually and collectively, in the implementation of segregation. They often exploited, supported and sometimes even demanded segregatory measures where these were seen to be to their advantage. As John Cell observed in his study comparing segregation in South Africa and the American South, even though 'force lay behind segregation … most of the time segregation was self-enforcing'.[7]

The fundamental reason for this acquiescence in their own oppression among coloured communities is patently clear. The original motivation behind the expression of a separate coloured identity, and the most consistent dynamic behind its subsequent assertion under white supremacist rule, was to claim and protect a status of privilege relative to Africans. First prize for the coloured elites of southern Africa would have been acceptance into the dominant society, even if only on the basis of individual merit. Since white racism ruled out any such accommodation, the coloured communal and political leadership successfully claimed second prize, an intermediate standing in the society that privileged coloured people over Africans. The greatest threat they perceived to their communities' well-being and future was for coloureds to be relegated to the status of Africans in the eyes of the white supremacist state. Despite the history of coloured politics in the region under white domination being a sorry tale of compromise, retreat and failure – essentially because of their marginality – the strategy of claiming a position of relative privilege was nevertheless highly successful. This approach paid off because it resonated so strongly with the ruling establishment's perception of humanity as consisting of a racialised hierarchy ranked in terms of the degree to which people conformed to the somatic and cultural norms of western Europe and its diaspora. Coloured communities and identity entrepreneurs were able to capitalise on the dominant societies' perception of them as 'different' because of their racial hybridity, and as 'superior' to Africans because of their European parentage, and use these to claim an intercalary ranking in the racial order.

Under white rule, the instrumental and material motivations for associating with whiteness and distancing themselves from Africanness through the espousal of coloured identity were considerable for people who were able to claim mixed racial ancestry. Africans were subject to pass laws, and often to curfews, and were restricted in their ability to do things such as buy liquor or own firearms. Also, coloureds were accorded better political representation, had access to superior housing and social services, and generally earned higher salaries. It is thus not surprising that just as there were some coloureds who managed to pass for white, there were also Africans who succeeded in passing for coloured. It was in particular the growing coloured petty bourgeoisie that benefited from this status of relative privilege and that spearheaded the drive for coloured exclusivism. Each and every one of the contributors to this volume acknowledges the considerable extent to which coloured individuals and communities benefited from, and defended, their intermediate position in the racial hierarchy. Of all the cases considered in this collection, only in Malawi did this strategy not lead to the institutionalisation of coloured privilege vis-à-vis Africans despite a fair degree of official sympathy for coloured lobbying in this regard. Besides the miniscule size of its coloured community, the exigencies of indirect rule in Nyasaland pushed the colonial state into playing down racial distinctions among subject peoples in the colony.

All of the studies in this book to varying degrees engage with the ways in which the transition to majority rule affected coloured identities. In all four of the societies under scrutiny, the new political paradigms and the social changes that came in their wake undermined, and even invalidated, the most basic assumptions and practices that framed the expression of coloured identity under white supremacy. Very importantly, that central pillar in the affirmation of a separate coloured identity – the protection of a status of relative privilege on the basis of its proximity to whiteness – was no longer legitimate. Also, Africanist and nationalist values and identities were now emphasised in contrast to the racial solidarities and Western mores that prevailed under white domination. In all of the societies surveyed, there is clear evidence of a hasty re-alignment of political priorities within coloured communities with the approach of majority rule. Most striking, however, has been a newfound creativity in the manifestation of coloured identities in the postcolonial and post-apartheid milieus.

Although the newly democratic environments brought a measure of freedom of association and possibilities for ethnic mobilisation not possible under white domination, they also presented obstacles to the pursuit of coloured communal interests, and posed dilemmas for the political leadership and identity entrepreneurs who sought to mobilise coloured ethnic sentiment. The continued salience of race in the postcolonial situation has left coloured communities in a most uncomfortable position. In addition to still having to shoulder the racial baggage and stigmas historically attached to colouredness, in the new dispensation coloured communities have had to face up to accusations of having benefited unfairly under white rule and of having been complicit in African oppression. Coloured leaders and organisations have also had to tread warily for fear of being accused that they were subverting the state's nationalist project, be it the rainbowism of the new South Africa or the more Africanist conceptions of the nation north of its borders.

If anything, the postcolonial situation seems to have intensified coloured perceptions of their marginality. Many coloured people, especially among the poorer and less-skilled sectors, have felt more vulnerable to unfair discrimination than under white supremacy. Some even argue that they were better off under white authority. Whereas under white rule they enjoyed a degree of privilege, albeit that their second-class citizenship was inscribed in law, they now see themselves as occupying the lowest rung in the social pecking order and as defenceless victims of unscrupulous governments that favour their own racial and ethnic constituencies. Ongoing African racial chauvinism towards coloured people only serves to deepen coloured disaffection and feelings of insecurity under the new order. Thus despite the coming of independence and democratic government having endowed coloured people in these societies with full citizenship rights, many would argue that they are still being marginalised. This sentiment of being trapped in a perpetual state of marginality is captured in the refrain common within South Africa's coloured community that 'first we were not white enough and now we are not black enough'.

Coloured communities in the region have accommodated themselves to majority rule in a variety of ways. In Zambia, a dominant trend has been for the coloured community to develop a diasporic outlook that sees Great Britain, and to a lesser extent other parts of the English-speaking First World, as places of possible refuge from a hostile homeland. The Zambian nationalist movement, understandably, had no sympathy for coloured exclusivism and, as Milner-Thornton reports, expected coloured people to renounce their European ancestry. Economic decline from the early 1970s onwards accelerated the exodus. By now over half the Zambian coloured population has left the country. Those who have remained, especially the generation born after independence, have generally come to accept majoritarian norms and values to the point where intermarriage with Africans has become common.[8] In Malawi the coloured community by and large resigned itself to suppressing separatist tendencies and embracing, as best it could, state-sponsored visions of an inclusive Malawian nationalism under the autocratic regime of Hastings Banda, who followed a policy of 'non-tribalism' for the three decades he was at the helm. Today the term 'Anglo-African' is regarded as anachronistic and most people of 'mixed-race' descent identify primarily as Malawian although there were attempts at rallying separatist coloured sentiment after the dissolution of the Banda dictatorship in 1994.[9] In Zimbabwe, while some coloured people sought to reinvent themselves as African with the advent of independence, the majority had little option but to acclimatise to living in a society politically dominated by an African exclusivism that envisions the nation in terms of race and indigeneity, and that shows scant regard for coloured communal interests. Like other non-autochthonous minorities, coloured people suffer discrimination in the economic arena and are effectively excluded from political power. The remnant that has not fled deteriorating conditions during the latter part of Mugabe's rule remains unorganised and completely marginalised.[10]

In South Africa there has been a resurgence of colouredism from the early 1990s onwards in stark contrast to the growing and vocal coloured rejectionism fostered by the non-racial democratic movement of the 1980s. Aided by ever more strident appeals to coloured identity from across the ideological spectrum for political support, including from the ANC that sidelined its anti-racist lobby soon after its unbanning, it once again became acceptable to espouse a coloured identity. Fear of African majority rule, the exploitation of these anxieties by political parties and leaders in pursuit of factional agendas, perceptions that coloureds were being marginalised, a desire to project a positive self-image in the face of pervasive negative racial stereotyping and attempts at capitalising on the newly democratic environment to mobilise coloured communal resources have all played a part in fuelling coloured assertiveness in the new South Africa.[11] The most dramatic and forthright manifestation of this trend came with the majority of coloured voters rallying behind the National Party in the 1994 elections. It is ironic that with the abolition of legally binding race classification as enshrined in apartheid legislation, coloured identity has gained renewed salience in South African public life under democracy. South Africa's contrasting experience to the rest of the subcontinent in this regard is mainly due to the relatively large size of its coloured population and its regional concentration, giving coloured people considerable political clout in the Western and Northern Cape provinces, where they form a majority of the population.

Attempts at re-conceptualising coloured identity have thus been particularly conspicuous in the case of post-apartheid South Africa. Not only is South Africa's transition to democracy the most recent, but it also exhibits a much broader range of responses to the postcolonial situation. The precipitate change in the political and moral climate in which the identity has had to operate has faced the political and intellectual leadership within the coloured community with the unenviable task of reorienting a profoundly racialised identity in an environment in which racial ideology has been thoroughly discredited. This quest has been complicated by the widely held perception of coloured complicity in maintaining white supremacy.[12] The transition to democracy has, on the other hand, opened new ways of perceiving and articulating colouredness. It has brought forth creative responses to questions around the nature of colouredness, and stimulated innovative ways of marshalling coloured ethnic resources. After nearly a century of remarkably stable existence under white supremacy, coloured identity has been in flux since the early 1990s and there have been unprecedented changes in the ways the identity has found expression. This fluidity has resulted in a degree of uncertainty, even confusion, around colouredness and the extent to which it is appropriate to espouse or invoke it. Within South Africa's coloured community there is a tentativeness about whether members should express their identity as black, as African, as South African, as coloured, as Khoisan or as descendants of slaves, or whether they should make a stand on the principle of non-racism – or what combination of these forms of self-understanding are pertinent in what contexts. There have been various attempts at reconfiguring the identity by small groups of intellectuals and community activists, none of which has yet found general acceptance within the broader community.[13]

Two chapters in this compilation focus squarely on the attempts by political elites within the South African coloured community to realign the identity in ways that are commensurate with the values of the new order. Michele Ruiters unpacks some of the key challenges of being coloured in the post-apartheid environment in her broad survey of endeavours to refashion coloured identity. Ruiters points out that the political leaders and organic intellectuals involved in this formidable enterprise need to make meaning out of the identities and histories of a disparate group in a situation of radically changed power relations and rapid social transformation. In addition to overcoming a historical legacy of oppression and racial stigma, this reformulation needs effectively to happen within a framework acceptable to the ruling party's nation-building project. Michael Besten narrows his focus to the ways in which the Khoisan revivalist movement and claims to indigeneity by various interest groups within the broader coloured community have been used to distance themselves from what they see as a humiliating form of self-identification. To them, colouredness represents the coloniser's perverted caricature of the colonised. Their Khoisan heritage is being creatively exploited to affirm a new identity in which they feel they can take pride and assert legitimate claims to national resources. Besten identifies some of the tensions between competing interests within this movement, and spotlights the tendency for what are essentially coloured concerns and interests to be clothed in Khoisan garb. It seems clear that elements within this movement are trying to use their claims to indigeneity as a way of legitimising a new form of relative privilege, that of being the true indigenes or 'first nation' of South Africa. Helene Strauss's chapter is also fundamentally about the adaptation of coloured identity to the new South Africa because it examines how intercultural interactions under apartheid are being interpreted from a post-apartheid perspective by a coloured author. She explores some of the new ways of thinking about colouredness that have emerged in contemporary South Africa, and some of the revisions to apartheid-era notions of the identity that are being made in recent 'stagings' of the identity.

A consistent thread that runs through this collection of essays is the extent to which the marginality of coloured communities has governed their social and political lives. In the context of inter-group relations, marginality implies a predicament, that of overcoming the disabilities of being marginal or, worse, of being marginalised.[14] All marginalised groups, whatever the basis of their marginalisation, confront the challenge of countering their exclusion from the mainstream of society. The marginalised – those who are deliberately singled out for collective discrimination – of necessity face severe disabilities, especially if they form a small minority and lack political clout.[15] Being marginalised entails suffering varying degrees of political repression, economic exploitation and social stigma, and the erection of barriers, whether legal or customary, to specific forms of social interaction between dominant and marginalised groups. By these measures, all the coloured communities of southern Africa were marginalised under white dominion even though they may have enjoyed a status of relative privilege.

The coloured communities of southern Africa have been marginal both in terms of their small proportions of national populations and also their lack of political or economic power. In South Africa the coloured population as enumerated in censuses has remained stable at between eight and nine per cent of the national total over the last century. The Zimbabwean, Zambian and Malawian coloured communities have been much smaller, all below one third of one percent of their respective domestic populations at any time during their existence.[16] During the 1930s, the period on which Christopher Lee focuses his analysis, the Malawian community formed a miniscule 0.07 per cent of the territory's inhabitants. Their lack of political and economic power is clearly also the product of a history that included slavery, dispossession, enserfment and institutionalised racial discrimination. The coloured communities of southern Africa are also marginal in other senses in which the concept has been used within the scholarly literature, ranging from Robert Park's initial idea of applying it to those who live in two social spheres but feel accepted and comfortable in neither,[17] to the more conventional conception that it refers to social groups who have been alienated from the mainstream of society through a stigmatised identity linked to otherness, and inferiority.[18]

Their marginality has been of fundamental significance to the social experience of the coloured communities of southern Africa, as these contributions collectively demonstrate. Most obviously, their options for social and political action have been severely constrained. A lack of political power meant that coloured people have had little influence on national politics and at times have effectively had no say on issues of vital importance to their communal lives or status as citizens. This largely accounts for the pragmatism and opportunistic nature of coloured politics, which in turn fed ambiguities and contradictions in the identity.[19] Under white supremacy, coloured communities often found themselves isolated and powerless because their assimilationist overtures were bluntly rejected by the dominant societies, and association with Africans was usually not seen as a viable or attractive option. Trapped by their condition of marginality, the political strategy that seemed most viable to coloured leaders was to bow to white power, work towards the incremental upliftment of their communities and to protect their position of relative privilege.[20]

Marginality should not, however, be conflated with inertia or impotence in people's abilities to shape their social identities – of who they are, how they have come to be what they are, and how they relate to others. While their marginality as well as the racist dictates of the dominant society may have placed acute restrictions on their freedom to act, it did not curb their ability to give meaning to their lives and creatively interpret their role and place in society. Christopher Lee makes the important point that it is often in marginal social situations and among marginal groups that cultural innovation flourishes, 'precisely because they are beyond the hegemony of mainstream patterns and practices'. This book contains abundant evidence of such creativity by coloured people, both individually and collectively, in the making and remaking of their social identities and in their engagement with the state and broader society in the pursuit of coloured communal interests.

As indicated earlier, the overthrow of white rule did not put an end to the predicament of marginality faced by coloured communities. Their predicament was simply cast in different terms dictated by the realities of the postcolonial situation. Needing to adapt to changed power relations and a radically different moral code, coloured identity became more fluid under conditions of majority rule, a point made repeatedly in this volume. One thing that did not change under the new dispensation, however, was the continued existence of a brand of racial thinking that delineated coloured people as a distinct group and that continued to inform all aspects of social life despite a veneer of political correctness and nation-building rhetoric that avoided overt reference to race. The prevalence of a race-based world view that constructs people of mixed racial origin as anomalous, even aberrant, has thus continued to reinforce coloured feelings of vulnerability and marginality in the postcolonial and post-apartheid situations. It is thus apparent that coloured racial hostility towards Africans is defensive in nature, and arises from their position of weakness.

The postcolonial coloured experience in southern Africa demonstrates Bettina von Lieres's observation that the mere extension of political and civil rights to small minorities in liberal democracies usually does little to mitigate the marginality of such groups and may exacerbate feelings of political impotence especially in societies that are racially and culturally cleavaged. There is clearly a tension between coloureds being part of the body politic and participating in the liberal democracy as equal citizens on the one hand, and a desire among many to secure group recognition and access to national resources on the other, in an environment of distrust of central government and the continued salience of race in the political sphere.[21] Under white supremacy, exclusion from power was a major factor in coloured marginality. In the post-apartheid era, their marginality stems more from their minority status and being part of a political system that reproduces their marginality by accommodating them fully as individuals but not allowing an opportunity for the expression of group aims and interests.

The collection begins with my own essay on the historiography of coloured identity in South Africa because it provides useful context for the chapters that follow. While most obviously pertinent to the South African chapters, it is also of relevance to the other case studies. This is most patently the case with Zimbabwe. In both societies, one witnesses similar patterns in both popular thinking and historiographical trends relating to the identity. Muzondidya himself draws on South African scholarly analyses to take the lead in developing a social constructionist interpretation of coloured identity in Zimbabwe. The most striking parallel between the histories of coloured identity in the two societies is that colouredness was almost without exception accepted as a product of racial mixture until the latter part of the 1970s when coloured intellectuals and political activists in both societies, for different reasons and under different circumstances, started espousing an instrumentalist view of the identity in terms of which it was seen as an invention of the white establishment to divide and rule the black oppressed. Black Consciousness ideology with its emphasis on an inclusive sense of blackness was the common catalyst.

The first chapter traces changing interpretations of the nature of coloured identity and the history of the coloured community in South Africa in both popular thinking as well as the academy. It explores some of the main contestations that have arisen between rival schools of thought, particularly their stance on the popular perception that colouredness is an inherent racial condition derived from miscegenation. The nature of coloured identity has from its inception in the late 19th century been an emotive issue, and the politics around it acutely contested. Also, controversy around coloured identity has tended to escalate through the 20th century, especially from the late 1970s onwards, because new understandings of the identity were not compatible with more conservative and accommodationist political and ideological agendas within the community. Colouredness thus became a site of struggle, and interpretations of the identity and its history a weapon in the battle for people's hearts and minds in the fight against apartheid. After the transition to democracy it became a focal point of debate and dissension over the nature of South African society, and strategies necessary for reconciliation and nation-building.

Because conflicting perceptions of colouredness imply different interpretations of the past, there has been a wide range of approaches to the history of the coloured grouping. This essay identifies four distinct paradigms in historical writing on the coloured people. Firstly, there is the essentialist school, which regards colouredness as a product of miscegenation and represents the conventional understanding of the identity. Because essentialism covers such a broad spectrum of approaches, this category is subdivided into three ideological genres, which I refer to as the traditional, liberal and progressionist interpretations. Secondly, instrumentalists view coloured identity as an artificial creation of the white ruling class who used it as a ploy to divide and rule the black majority. This explanation, which first emerged in academic writing in the early 1980s, held sway in anti-apartheid circles. Opposing these interpretations are what may be termed social constructionists who, from the early 1990s, stressed the complexities of identity formation and the agency of coloured people in the making of their own identities. Most recently the rudiments of a fourth approach, of applying postmodern theory, especially the concept of creolisation, to the making of coloured identity have appeared. In this collection, Helene Strauss and Christopher Lee use creolisation theory to cast new light on processes of coloured identity formation.

In the next chapter, Helene Strauss starts by presenting an authoritative exposition of the impact of creolisation theory on the South African critical landscape and then applies it to coloured identity through a reading of coloured writer Chris van Wyk's childhood memoir, *Shirley, Goodness and Mercy*.[22] Characterising creolisation as consisting of 'complex, and often violent processes of cultural exchange that take place between various, already creolized identities in the aftermath of colonization and slavery', Strauss in some detail considers the relevance of this import from the Caribbean to the making of coloured identity, especially in literary expressions of the identity. *Shirley, Goodness and Mercy* is particularly suited to her purposes, not only because of the nuanced insights it offers into 'performances' of colouredness but also because it allows a comparison between the ways in which creolisation operated in both the apartheid and post-apartheid environments. In a masterly analysis of the conflicts and subtle changes in behaviour that occur in situations of intercultural contact and how these play out against the backdrop of larger social and political developments, Strauss delves into the minutiae of daily life as depicted in Van Wyk's memoir to reveal how creolisation may be theorised as being at work in the making of coloured identity.

Chapter three provides a stimulating analysis of the way in which forced removals under the Group Areas Act influenced expressions of coloured identity in Cape Town. Henry Trotter notes that, unlike most communities that consolidate around remote historic injustices, coloured Capetonians have instead drawn on this traumatic experience within living memory to help provide a sense of self and an understanding of what it means to be coloured in contemporary South Africa, and to cope with their feelings of marginality. Trotter quarries an extensive empirical base that includes over 100 life-history interviews, several hundred land-claim submissions as well as the growing literature on apartheid-era forced removals, and combines this with an impressive range of theoretical insights to argue that coloured removees coped with the trauma of their eviction by developing an idealised vision of life in their destroyed communities through which they mourned their loss and consoled one another. Because apartheid social engineering herded removees together into racially defined residential areas, they were able to swap stories and to reminisce with one another about their former lives, creating what Trotter calls a 'narrative community'. Through 'a reflexive, mutually reinforcing pattern of narrative traffic' they over the decades created a 'commemoration narrative', a stylised way of honouring a treasured past and coming to terms with a trying present. Trotter persuasively argues that the senses of intimacy and self-understanding promoted through this shared narrative of trauma are integral to contemporary manifestations of coloured identity in Cape Town. His sympathetic, evocative account goes further and demonstrates how the commemoration narrative of forced removees has become a dominant strain in popular perceptions of the city's history itself.

Chapter four also deals with the ways in which historical memory and the tendency to sentimentalise life in communities destroyed by apartheid-era forced removals has impacted on contemporary expressions of coloured identity. In his contribution, Christiaan Beyers focuses on District Six and the significance of its symbolic status as a pre-eminently coloured space in crafting senses of belonging and community, as well as claims to a special ethos of racial tolerance in contemporary perceptions of the place. Using interviews with former residents as well as fictional and autobiographical literature on District Six, Beyers with consummate skill analyses the construction of a coloured-centric discourse around the District in the context of its history of racially differentiated identities. He demonstrates how the relatively privileged status of coloured residents, their numerical preponderance as well as the more intense oppression and earlier expulsions of Africans allowed discourses about the area to be dominated by coloured voices to the virtual exclusion of Africans. Beyers reveals the operation of this exclusionary perception of community in District Six through analyses of Richard Rive's *Buckingham Palace* and the autobiographical writing of former residents, and engages with Crain Soudien's theorising around the production of identity and notions of hybridity in the District. He then uses the counter-perspective of Nomvuyo Ngcelwane's *Sala Kahle District Six* with its tacit critique of coloured-centric perceptions of the place and its past to question current constructions of District Six as a community.

The next two chapters deal with the refashioning and re-alignment of coloured identities in post-apartheid South Africa. Michele Ruiters's accomplished study opens by observing that coloured identity, like all South African social identities, is in the process of being reconstructed in response to the fundamental changes brought about by the transition to democracy. She notes that the distinctive political pattern within the coloured community prior to the 1990s of protecting a position of relative privilege was invalidated with the ending of apartheid. Enforced change has left this group, which had previously been defined through legislation and had been constructed as homogeneous by the apartheid system, grappling to come to terms with the reality of its diversity. Ruiters concentrates mainly on elite identity claims that draw on Khoisan, slave and creolised pasts in their attempts to forge new understandings of their identities and position in South African society. In a nuanced analysis that makes extensive use of interviews with coloured community leaders and identity entrepreneurs, and draws on the wealth of documentation generated by the government's various nation-building initiatives, she explores the broad spectrum of new identity claims that have been made within the coloured community since 1994. Ruiters concludes by considering the implications the reconstruction of coloured identities have for the nation-building project and for the future of democracy in South Africa.

Michael Besten's chapter breaks new ground as the first substantive, published analysis of Khoisan revivalism in post-apartheid South Africa. Besten begins by providing historical background and showing how people of Khoisan descent tended to be reclassified as 'coloured', 'Native' or 'Bantu' under white domination. This happened not only because of unilateral action on the part of the white-supremacist state that used racial classification as a means of social control but also as a result of the agency of Khoisan people and their descendants in response to the uneven power relations they needed to negotiate. He argues that because colouredness, with the advent of democracy, lost much of its attraction as a category that conferred a status of relative privilege on its bearers within the South African racial system, a growing number of people turned to some form of indigenous Khoisan identity as an alternative. They did so partly as a means of bolstering claims to social and economic resources under the new dispensation and partly because it gave them a sense of geographic rootedness, ethnic integrity, cultural unity and an enhanced sense of self-esteem during a time of rapid social change and uncertainty about the future. Besten surveys a wide range of attempts to capitalise on claims to Khoisan indigeneity. He shows how coloured concerns have in many instances surreptitiously been re-articulated in neo-Khoisan terms, and how reciprocity and melding between coloured and Khoisan subjectivities are influencing identities and political agendas in the coloured community.

In a forcefully argued contribution, James Muzondidya analyses the growth of coloured group consciousness in colonial Zimbabwe over nearly a century using an impressive array of primary and secondary sources. His subtle, systematic exposition of the intricacies of identity politics in this coloured community from the time of the founding of Southern Rhodesia to the eve of independence is a model of compression. Unpacking both popular misconceptions as well as fallacies about coloured identity propagated in the academic literature, Muzondidya insists that an understanding of identity formation within Zimbabwe's coloured community needs to transcend both essentialist notions of colouredness as the biologically determined result of miscegenation as well as the idea that it was an invention of the colonial state. His analysis not only follows the contours of academic debate around coloured identity in South Africa but also demonstrates striking resonances between the development of the identity in the two societies. Muzondidya argues that the construction of coloured identity in Zimbabwe was a dialectic process negotiated both within the culturally diverse coloured community as well as with external agencies that included the colonial state, and the settler and indigenous communities. By focusing on debates and conflicts over the nature of coloured identity, Muzondidya emphasises the contestedness and fluidity of the identity. These characteristics were nowhere more clearly demonstrated than in the decades-long tussle between 'Cape coloureds' and 'locally born coloureds' over group boundaries and what it meant to be coloured. They also came to the fore when some coloured people were able to use African family connections to re-invent themselves as African with the approach of independence.

In the penultimate chapter, Juliette Milner-Thornton investigates the dynamic behind the expression of coloured identity in 20th-century Zambia through the case study of her own family history. Hers is a poignant and compelling story of rejection, loss and displacement, but ultimately also one of resilience in the face of adversity. Milner-Thornton's great-grandfather, Dr Sidney Spencer Broomfield, was born in July 1847 in the south of England and came to Northern Rhodesia in the late 1890s, where he made a name for himself as a hunter, adventurer and gold prospector. Here he married several African women in traditional ceremonies. While his wives continued to live in the African community, Broomfield raised the children born of these unions separately at his homestead on the Jessie Gold Mine near Mkushi, central Zambia. In 1928 he abandoned his African family in Northern Rhodesia. Broomfield's Zambian family

knew nothing about his whereabouts or fate until Milner-Thornton in
1999 discovered his grave in Brisbane, Australia, where he had died in
1933. She soon thereafter came across his autobiography *Kachalola or the
Mighty Hunter*.[23] Her study compares Broomfield's autobiography to his
Zambian family's oral history as a means of exploring the central significance
of absentee white fathers to the coloured community of Zambia. This
analysis is largely written in the first person as Milner-Thornton uses auto-
ethnography which she characterises as 'the autobiographical response
of the subjugated to European or metropolitan representations'. In a
sensitive, evocative exploration of her family history, Milner-Thornton
deconstructs the legacy of alienation, cultural displacement, social stigma
and diaspora that resulted from the refusal of white fathers, with the
collusion of the Northern Rhodesian state, to acknowledge their African
families. She explains how the Broomfield case history reflects the social
experience of a large proportion of the Zambian coloured community,
which consists in large part of the unacknowledged descendants of British
colonial men.

The final chapter in this collection returns to the theme of
creolisation in the making of coloured identity in southern Africa
by showing how Anglo-African identity entrepreneurs in Nyasaland
creatively drew on both European and African cultural domains to forge
a new social consciousness and a niche in that society for people of mixed
racial origin. In this essay, Christopher Lee examines the formation of
the Anglo-African Association and its role in shaping coloured identity
in Nyasaland during the 1930s. Through an incisive reading of archival
material and astute argumentation, Lee demonstrates that Anglo-African
identity was a product of initiatives on the part of a small group of
identity brokers who seized on an opportune court ruling to form the
Anglo-African Association which they then used to try to secure a status
of relative privilege for people of mixed racial descent in Nyasaland.
Besides agitating for a favoured legal status, the Association also pushed
hard for separate, superior educational facilities for Anglo-Africans on
the grounds that their partial descent from European colonists entitled
them to preferment over indigenes. The chapter stresses the importance
of the inventive use of kinship norms by members of the Association in
justifying privileged treatment. The Association's efforts were thwarted by
the colonial state which, because of its system of ethnicity-based indirect
rule, resisted the creation of racially defined administrative categories.
Also, the colonial government sought to play down appearances of racial

domination or favouritism for fear of provoking African resistance. Their marginality and the dictates of Malawian nationalist politics have resulted in coloured identity having had a rather tenuous existence in that society after independence.

The contributions to this volume are innovative in a variety of respects besides presenting the findings of original research on diverse aspects of coloured identity in southern Africa. Several, most notably the analyses of Henry Trotter, Helene Strauss, Christopher Lee and Christiaan Beyers, apply fresh theoretical insights drawn mainly from the fields of postmodern, postcolonial and cultural studies to bring new levels of understanding to processes of coloured self-identification. These contributions significantly extend the as yet embryonic literature examining the more subjective and 'interior' aspects of coloured identity.[24] They go beyond the more explicit political, economic and social motives and behaviours on which analyses have hitherto tended to focus, to examine what Trotter summarises as the 'tacit, dispositional, emotional and non-instrumental aspects of coloured identity'. The issue of self-understanding is, in addition, foregrounded in Juliette Milner-Thornton's essay on her family history. Cultural creativity is given prominence, most overtly, in those chapters that draw on creolisation theory. This book also introduces new methodologies to the study of coloured identity. The auto-ethnography of Milner-Thornton, Strauss's close literary analysis of subjective transformations in situations of intercultural contact and Trotter's deconstruction of narrative and memory production among Group Area removees are examples that most readily spring to mind. These contributions, furthermore, theorise the making of coloured identity in ways that have broadened the field of enquiry substantially, bringing new sensitivities to a range of issues, whether it be the symbolic construction of self and community, the impact of state policy-making decisions on processes of coloured self-identification, the social significance of the stories that coloured people tell of themselves or the creative use of kinship norms to justify identity claims.

Another novel aspect of this collection of essays is that several probe current developments in coloured-identity politics in southern Africa. The contributions of Michele Ruiters and Michael Besten, in particular, concentrate on contemporary coloured political organisation in South Africa, an area where little writing besides journalistic and fragmentary accounts exists. While contemporary history has its own challenges, these studies help to bring order and meaning to the tumult of conflicting impressions left by erratic reporting in the mass media and ongoing controversy around issues of colouredness in post-apartheid South Africa. An area in which this volume breaks new ground is that it provides fresh, well-researched studies of coloured identities in southern African societies beyond South Africa's borders. James Muzondidya, Juliette Milner-Thornton and Christopher Lee pioneer scholarly enquiries into coloured identity in societies where none previously existed except for essentialist popular accounts or scant and dated academic tracts.

A natural question that arises is in what directions research into coloured identity in southern Africa might develop in future. While there are hazards to making predictions of this sort, it is worth noting that this book is able to suggest fruitful avenues for further enquiry. There are two ways in which it may do so. The first is through inviting amplification of novel and less-developed themes, methodologies and lines of enquiry presented in its pages. A path that seems to hold much promise is the application of creolisation theory to the making of coloured identity. A second, and less direct, way would be through a recognition of some of the lacunae and silences in this volume. Being, until recently, a neglected area of research, there are a number of conspicuous gaps in the literature on coloured identity. And although this collection breaks important new ground, it nevertheless shares in some of these omissions. The most obvious gap in the history of the coloured community is that there is no comprehensive account of the 19th-century genesis of coloured identity.[25] A second area of neglect is that, except for Elaine Salo's writing, there is very little by way of work that in any systematic way genders the production of coloured identities.[26] Also, studies have hitherto tended to focus on elite, urban and, in South Africa, Western Cape expressions of the identity. More thorough investigation of senses of colouredness in other segments of this diverse grouping will complement our understanding of the identity. Comparative studies between coloured identities in the region or with other marginal minorities are bound to yield useful insights. Possible comparisons in the latter category that spring to mind are with Indian or Jewish identities in South Africa, or with ethno-racial identities further afield such as with Berber communities in north Africa,[27] Anglo-Indians or one of the many communities around the globe to which the term 'creole' has been applied, be they in the Caribbean, southeast Asia or the Indian Ocean islands. A change in perspective is likely to be productive as well. For example, a switch from the usual standpoint of minority–majority relations to one that draws on 'the literature on minority rights, multiculturalism or the relationship between citizenship and diversity' may be a way of advancing discussion around coloured identity. Likewise, locating such studies within 'debates on the relationship between law and identity [or] theories of subjection and agency' might prove rewarding.[28]

Until fairly recently, academic analyses of coloured identity in southern Africa were few and far between, itself a reflection of coloured marginality. Indeed, less than two decades ago, treating colouredness as social reality was frowned upon, if not taboo, in 'progressive' circles in South Africa, as the first chapter explains. The tide has turned, and today coloured identity has become a mainstream academic topic, and this book, drawing on recent innovative research on the subject, is evidence of this. Contributors to this volume build on, question, challenge, subvert and rebut aspects of the current state of scholarly knowledge on coloured identity and history in southern Africa. They are all, to varying degrees, conceptually and methodologically innovative, and together they inaugurate a new phase in the historiography of coloured identity, pushing our understanding of the phenomenon to new levels of sophistication.

Endnotes

1   For detailed scholarly studies of the nature of coloured identity in southern African societies, see Adhikari M. 2005. *Not White Enough, Not Black Enough: Racial Identity in the South African Coloured Community*. Athens: Ohio University Press; and Muzondidya J. 2005. *Walking a Tightrope: Towards a Social History of the Coloured People of Zimbabwe*. Trenton: Africa World Press.

2   My stance as editor is one of non-interference in the ideological and intellectual viewpoints of contributors. It thus follows that, except for chapter one, the contributions to this book do not necessarily reflect my point of view. While I fully embrace a great deal of what is said in the book and although I find by far the greater part of it enlightening, there are nonetheless elements I disagree with.

3   For a detailed discussion of the coloured political response to UDI, see Muzondidya, *Walking a Tightrope*, ch 4.

4   See Adhikari M. 1993. *'Let Us Live for Our Children': The Teachers' League of South Africa, 1913–1940*. Cape Town: UCT Press, 11–18; and Adhikari M. 1992. 'The sons of Ham: slavery and the making of coloured identity'. *South African Historical Journal*, 27, for a more detailed discussion of the origins of coloured identity. For case studies of the process in Cape Town and Kimberley respectively, see Bickford-Smith V. 1995. *Ethnic Pride and Racial Prejudice in Victorian Cape Town, 1875–1902*. Cambridge: Cambridge University Press, 186–209; and Lawrence P. 1994. 'Class, colour consciousness and the search for identity at the Kimberley diamond diggings, 1867–1893'. MA thesis, University of Cape Town.

5   See Adhikari, *Not White Enough*, 19–32, for an analysis of this and similar jokes about the origin of coloured people.

6   For other innovative work on the significance of spatial confinement in townships to the making of coloured identity, see Salo E. 2004. 'Respectable mothers, tough men and good daughters: producing persons in Manenberg township South Africa'. PhD dissertation, Emory University.

7   Cell J. 1982. *The Highest Stage of White Supremacy: The Origin of Segregation in South Africa and the American South*. Cambridge: Cambridge University Press, 19.

8   E-mail communication from Juliette Milner-Thornton, 22 January 2008.

9   E-mail communication from Christopher Lee, 11 February 2008.

10 E-mail communication from James Muzondidya, 12 February 2008. The initiative of establishing the National Association for the Advancement of Mixed Race Coloureds in Harare in June 2002 was effectively stillborn.

11 For a more detailed discussion of the issue, see Adhikari M. 2004. 'Not black enough: reflections on changing expressions of coloured identity in post-apartheid South Africa'. *South African Historical Journal*, 51, 167–178.

12 For the argument that coloured identity was relatively stable under white supremacy, see Adhikari M. 2006. 'Hope, fear, shame, frustration: continuity and change in the expression of coloured identity in white supremacist South Africa, 1910–1994'. *Journal of Southern African Studies*, 32, no. 3, 467–488.

13 See Adhikari, *Not White Enough*, 175–187 for a discussion of coloured identity in post-apartheid South Africa.

14 Some social groups may be marginal largely through circumstance, such as forming a small percentage of the population, while being marginalised implies deliberate action on the part of the dominant society, or part of it, to ostracise or oppress a target population.

15 Although it is usually minorities that are marginalised, as many colonial situations and apartheid South Africa demonstrate, majorities can also suffer this fate.

16 For South Africa, compare statistics in Census of the Union of South Africa, 1911 (U.G.32-1912), Annexure 1, 7–11, with The People of South Africa Population Census, 1996: Primary Tables – The Country as a Whole (Report no. 03-01-19), 6; *Statistics South Africa, 2000*. 2001. Pretoria: Government Publications Department, 1.1, 6. For estimates of the size of coloured communities in various southern African countries, see Muzondidya, *Walking a Tightrope*, 15.

17 This applies more to the non-South African cases.

18 For further discussion of the concept, see Dennis R (ed). 2005. *Marginality, Power and Social Structure*. London: Elsevier. See also Park R. 1928. 'Human migration and the marginal man'. *American Journal of Sociology*, 33, 881–893.

19 See Adhikari, *Not White Enough*, especially 12, 72–74, 86–89, 123–126; Adhikari M. 1997. '"The product of civilization in its most repellent manifestation": ambiguities in the racial perceptions of the APO, 1909–1923'. *Journal of African History*, 38, no. 2.

20 One needs to take account of the exception of a handful of South African radicals who from as early as the 1920s advocated an alliance with African nationalism or took what was effectively a non-racial stance. Also, it needs to be noted that in South Africa and Zimbabwe support for this position grew significantly towards the end of white rule.

21 Von Lieres B. 2005. 'Marginalization and citizenship in post-apartheid South Africa', in *Limits to Liberation after Apartheid: Citizenship, Governance and Culture*, ed S Robins. Cape Town: David Philip, 24–25, 30.

22 Van Wyk C. 2004. *Shirley, Goodness and Mercy*. Johannesburg: Picador Africa.

23 Broomfield S. 1931. *Kachalola or the Mighty Hunter: The Early Life and Adventures of Sidney Spencer Broomfield*. New York: William Morrow.

24 See footnote 61 in chapter 3 for a list of such works.

25 The works referred to in endnote 4 are partial accounts that allow for a broad understanding of the historical process.

26 See Salo, 'Respectable mothers'; Salo E. 2005. 'Negotiating gender and personhood in the new South Africa: adolescent women and gangsters in Manenberg township on the Cape Flats', in *Limits to Liberation*, ed S Robins; Salo E. 2007. '"Mans is ma soe": ganging practices in Manenberg, South Africa, and the ideologies of masculinity, gender, and generational relations', in *States of Violence: Politics, Youth, and Memory in Contemporary Africa*, eds E Bay & D Donham. Charlottesville: University of Virginia Press.

27 This inspired idea comes from James Muzondidya.

28 I am indebted to an anonymous reviewer of this manuscript for these suggestions.

CHAPTER 1

From narratives of miscegenation to post-modernist re-imagining: towards a historiography of coloured identity in South Africa

BY

MOHAMED ADHIKARI

UNIVERSITY OF CAPE TOWN

The marginality of the coloured community under white supremacy is reflected in South African historiography in that relatively little was written on the history of this social group prior to the mid-1990s and much of what was written was journalistic, polemical, speculative, poorly researched or heavily biased. In nearly all general histories of South Africa, coloured people have effectively been written out of the narrative and marginalised to a few throw-away comments scattered through the text. This tendency was noted as early as 1913 by Harold Cressy, a coloured educationist and school principal, when he called on the coloured teaching profession to dispel the myth that coloured people played little or no part in the history of South African society.[1] Les Switzer, professor of media studies at the University of Houston, put it eloquently when in 1995 he wrote that 'South Africa's coloured community has remained a marginalized community – marginalized by history and even historians'.[2]

Ever since its emergence in the late 19th century, coloured identity, its nature and the implications it holds for South African society have nevertheless been the subject of ideological and political contestation.

Because contending and changing perceptions of colouredness imply different interpretations of their past, there has been a wide range of approaches to the history of the coloured people in both popular thinking and the academy. Also, controversy around the nature of coloured identity has tended to intensify in recent decades, especially after the popularisation of coloured rejectionism in the wake of the Soweto uprising of 1976.[3] Disagreements have often become quite heated because political and ideological agendas, as well as matters of high principle, were increasingly seen to be at stake in particular views of the identity. Indeed, by the mid-1980s issues around coloured identity had become acutely politicised. This chapter will outline competing interpretations of the nature of coloured identity and the history of the coloured people, and explore the main contestations that have arisen as a result.

The changing political context

Today there is intense interest in the nature and history of coloured identity, especially among people who identify themselves as coloured, and the idea of anyone questioning the legitimacy of studying the topic would seem odd, even absurd. Yet it was not always so.

Until the late 1970s, there was a high degree of consensus both within the coloured community and among outsiders about who coloured people were and what the concept of colouredness embodied. The conventional wisdom was that coloured people were a distinct racial group that resulted from miscegenation between European settlers and a heterogeneous black labouring class of African and Asian origin. Like whites, Africans and Indians, the coloured grouping was generally seen as having its own historical trajectory even though there tended to be an emphasis on its strong cultural and genetic links with the dominant white minority, especially within the coloured community itself.[4] In the earlier decades of the 20th century, contestations centred mainly around whether the community should align itself with the English- or Afrikaans-speaking sections of the dominant society. These differences usually surfaced at election time, often at the instigation of the Cape National Party opportunistically seeking to attract coloured voters.[5] Prior to the 1980s, this perception of colouredness as a product of racial mixing was reflected in both popular and academic histories and in the ways the community itself viewed its past.[6]

The conventional wisdom was first challenged in the latter part of the 1930s with the emergence of a radical movement in coloured politics, which introduced the idea that black unity or classed-based identity needed to be cultivated among the oppressed.[7] Radical intellectuals within organisations such as the National Liberation League formed in 1935 and the Non-European Unity Movement (NEUM) founded in 1943 rejected coloured separatism as playing into the hands of the ruling classes who sought to divide the black majority and split the proletariat. The emphasis on 'non-European' unity within this earlier generation of coloured radicals was less a repudiation of coloured identity than an assertion that racial differences were not in any way intrinsic and that coloured particularism undermined the freedom struggle. At no point in the extensive body of publications it produced did the NEUM produce a coherent history of the coloured community itself, and a rejectionist viewpoint was usually implicit in its political analyses of South African society.[8] The earliest example of a purist non-racial stance was in evidence during the early 1950s when a handful of ultra-left Trotskyist intellectuals grouped within the Forum Club, a remnant of the Fourth International Organisation of South Africa, criticised the NEUM's 'Non-Europeanism' as a form of 'voluntary segregation' that favoured the interests of capital and the racist state, and advocated a strictly non-racial strategy.[9] From the early 1960s onwards, however, there also developed an explicit rejection of coloured identity within the NEUM itself, which had become politically dormant by that time.[10] For the next two decades the impact of this non-racial outlook was largely restricted to those sectors of the coloured elite sympathetic to the NEUM. It was only towards the latter half of the 1970s, when Black Consciousness ideology took hold in significant parts of the coloured community, that the rejection of coloured identity found a greater degree of popular support, growing to its zenith within the non-racial democratic movement of the late 1980s and the very early part of the 1990s.

Kept alive by a small group of radical intellectuals with influence in a few coloured schools as well as a handful of cultural and civic organisations, and through its organ, the *Educational Journal*, the NEUM's non-racial philosophy nevertheless had a significant impact on the anti-apartheid movement that emerged in the western Cape in the early 1980s. Firstly, many activists, exposed in various ways to its ideas – particularly as students – imbibed its principle of non-racism without necessarily associating with the NEUM. Secondly, prominent leaders within the United Democratic Front (UDF) who had defected from the NEUM – Dullah Omar and Trevor Manuel being the most prominent examples – helped infuse these ideas into the broader democratic struggle.

I first started researching coloured identity as a postgraduate student in the early 1980s, and for one-an-a-half decades it turned out to be somewhat of a solitary undertaking. Not only were there very few people working in this neglected area but this sort of research was also increasingly frowned upon as the non-racial democratic movement started gathering momentum nationally and coloured rejectionism was rapidly becoming an orthodoxy in anti-apartheid circles. This outlook was succinctly expressed in a letter to the editor published in *Grassroots*, a community newspaper published in the western Cape during the 1980s: '... the people only know about the Human race, not about "coloureds, Indians and Blacks" '.[11] The 1980s, one hardly needs reminding, was a time of upheaval and conflict, of passionate commitment to opposing sets of values in the stand-off between the non-racial, democratic movement dominated by the ANC-aligned UDF and the apartheid state. Coloured identity was a particularly emotive issue in the western Cape, the region being both a focal point of anti-apartheid resistance and home to about 70 per cent of the coloured population.[12] By the mid-1980s people started chiding me publicly for pursuing what was perceived as a racially divisive research agenda, and questioned whether an analysis of coloured identity had any value except for exposing how this wicked invention of the white establishment was used to keep the black majority in subjection. One such critic, for example, demanded to know '[w]hy do you always have to bring up the things that divide us?', while another alleged that taking coloured identity seriously was tantamount to endorsing apartheid policies.[13] By the end of the decade, any recognition of coloured identity as social reality, especially if done publicly, was likely to be condemned as a concession to apartheid thinking, if not rejected outright as racist.

Given the inflamed emotions of the time and the passionate idealism of many that a non-racial, egalitarian society was attainable, the line that coloured identity did not really exist except as a fiction created and nurtured by white supremacists was an understandable reaction both to apartheid and to the stigma historically attached to colouredness.[14] It was also a canny political tactic for mobilising people against the apartheid state, resonating as strongly as it did with the ubiquitous 1980s struggle slogan: 'Apartheid divides, the UDF unites'.

It was obvious from my own extensive experience of coloured communal life in Cape Town, as well as from my knowledge of the historical record, that the rejectionist view was at best a gross simplification of the history and nature of the identity. This was also the case for many 'coloured'[15] political activists, who took a rejectionist stance publicly but privately acknowledged the existence of coloured identity. They nevertheless pushed the rejectionist line energetically as part of a pragmatic strategy of promoting non-racial values and breaking down racial barriers.[16] Other more doctrinaire individuals seem actually to have believed the spurious but politically useful rejectionist claim, presumably expecting the 'false consciousness' of coloured identity to be blown away with apartheid. They tended to be much less tolerant of any recognition of coloured identity as social reality. For example, when I presented a paper on coloured identity at the 'Burden of Race' conference at the University of the Witwatersrand in July 2001, a 'coloured' historian had few qualms about declaring to the session that had I presented that paper at Wits a few years previously, he would have been at the forefront of the mob chasing me off campus.

Researching coloured identity in this environment was a tricky business, especially if one went against the 'progressive' grain by assuming or demonstrating the social reality of colouredness. One ran the very real risk of being accused of being racially divisive or, more seriously, of being a racist and perhaps even worse, of being a closet racist. As indicated earlier, my research did draw disapproving comment of this sort from the rejectionist lobby, and on more than one occasion I was accused of fostering racial division when presenting papers at conferences and seminars. An interesting feature of these accusations is that all were made by white academics, none of whom I would describe as activists or having political credibility within the democratic movement. I take their behaviour to be the result of a combination of white guilt about apartheid giving rise to a more-radical-than-thou attitude, and ignorance due to a lack of exposure to the realities of life beyond the fringe of Cape Town's leafy suburbs. Eager to demonstrate their political bona fides, they were more likely to swallow the myth that colouredness was a white-imposed fiction.

'Coloured' academics whose disagreement with my line of analysis went beyond scholarly grounds, however, seemed more concerned with perceived affronts to the dignity of coloured people and, by extension, to themselves. Two examples stand out in my mind. The first is of the 'coloured' editor of an academic journal to which I submitted an article analysing popular stereotyping of coloured people during the apartheid era. The response was a long, indignant, handwritten letter that listed a number of spurious reasons for not accepting the article and ending with the emphatic rejection that the journal concerned 'does not publish gutter journalism'.[17] The second is of a 'coloured' historian confronting me after I had presented a paper on coloured identity at a colloquium demanding to know why I constantly 'pick on the coloured people', by which he meant why I portrayed them as particularly racist. My response that I was not 'picking on the coloured people' but happened to specialise in the area and that I did not regard coloured people as particularly racist but primarily as victims of racism who, to a fair degree, had internalised the values of their oppressors, did not satisfy him.[18] Both were clearly emotional and defensive responses by otherwise level-headed and competent academics who attributed to me the ideas I was analysing. They were also unconscious acknowledgements of the emotive power of the negative racial stereotyping attached to the identity.

The fatuousness of the more extreme forms of coloured rejectionism was largely swept away in the wake of F W de Klerk's reforms announced on 2 February 1990 and the subsequent fierce competition among political parties for support within the coloured community. There was a defining moment in 1992 when Nelson Mandela himself urged ANC supporters to recognise 'coloured ethnicity as a political reality', his comment clearly aimed at that constituency, derived largely from the UDF, that still put the principle of strict non-racism above political savvy.[19] Any doubts about the political salience of coloured identity were dispelled by the majority of coloured voters flocking to the banner of the National Party in the 1994 elections, partly in response to its racist campaign designed to play on minority fears of African majority rule. This more than any other development put paid to the idea that researching coloured identity was somehow unprogressive. Academic enquiry into coloured identity suddenly became respectable and rather popular, if not fashionable. Indeed, for some, understanding the coloured mentality became a civic duty. How else to win the Western Cape from the racist National Party for the party of liberation? Within a relatively short space of time, a slew of studies trying to account for 'the coloured vote' of 1994 appeared[20] and two conferences to consider the implications of coloured attitudes for the nation-building project were organised.[21] Several popular and academic books as well as fictional work relating to coloured identity and social experience started appearing, and in the last few years a significant number of academic theses on coloured identity have also been completed. A notable trend in the last-mentioned category is that of 'coloured' students completing doctoral dissertations on aspects of the identity at foreign universities.[22] So much writing on coloured identity has appeared over the last decade that it is clear that the topic has entered the mainstream of South African intellectual life.

Paradigms in perspective

Because the conventional categories of South African historiography – imperial, settler, Afrikaner nationalist, liberal and revisionist – are of limited value in analysing and comparing interpretations of the history of the coloured people, an alternative set of categories based on various authors' approaches to the nature of coloured identity is suggested here. Within this framework, four distinct and competing approaches to coloured identity and the history of the coloured community are identified.

Firstly, there is what may be termed the essentialist school, which has been by far the most common approach in historical writing about coloured people. This interpretation coincides with the popular view of coloured identity as a product of miscegenation that stretches back to the earliest days of European settlement at the Cape. All these essentialist histories, in one way or another, are predicated on narratives of racial mixture in pre-industrial South Africa giving rise to a distinct racial group, the coloured people. Within this approach, racial hybridity is taken to be the essence of colouredness. For essentialists there is usually no need to explain the nature or making of coloured identity because it is part of an assumed reality that sees South African society as consisting of distinct races of which coloured people are one. The existence of coloured identity poses no analytical problem for essentialists because it is regarded as having developed naturally, and self-evidently to be the result of miscegenation. While it does not locate the origins of coloured identity in the prehistoric mists of time as many racial and ethnic identities do, essentialist writing is primordialist in that it tends to date the origins of coloured identity to the earliest phases of colonial rule. As one version of a popular joke has it, coloured people were born nine months after Van Riebeeck landed at Table Bay. Another more elaborate version has the punch-line that Jan van Riebeeck and not God made the coloured people. A related jibe is that coloured people celebrate with coon carnivals at New Year to mark their birth as a people – nine months after Van Riebeeck's landing on 6 April.[23]

Because essentialist writing covers such a wide range of interpretations, it is possible to identify three well-defined ideological currents within this broad approach. Firstly, there are what might be labelled traditionalists who analyse coloured identity and history in terms of the racist values and assumptions prevalent in white supremacist South Africa. In general the traditionalist point of view sees black people as racially inferior and assumes that congruities of blood and race have automatically been passed down the generations. It has thus supported segregationism and regarded miscegenation as repugnant, even a threat to 'civilisation' in South Africa. It goes without saying that nearly all of the writing in this genre was produced by whites and is fundamentally eurocentric. The isolated examples of coloured people writing in this vein consist of school textbooks where the syllabus dictated their approach.[24]

This attitude towards coloured identity is tacit in the older and more conservative general histories of South Africa. In histories of this sort, not only are coloured people marginalised but their historical agency is also effectively denied. Where they do appear, coloured people are presented as inert, faceless beings who are acted upon by whites and are incidental to the main narrative of settler conquest and their creation of a Christian, civilised society in southern Africa. Coloured people and their ancestors are little more than bystanders to the unfolding drama of South African history, or impediments to the noble struggle of hardy, pioneering colonists to tame the wild landscape and maintain a civilised existence in barbarous surroundings. This is broadly true of works within the imperial, settler and Afrikaner nationalist stables. C F J Muller's *Five Hundred Years* and Floors van Jaarsveld's *From Van Riebeeck to Vorster* are relatively recent examples that apply in this instance.[25] Where explicit consideration is given to the history of coloured people, as in H P Cruse's *Die Opheffing van die Kleurlingbevolking* and D P Botha's *Die Opkoms van Ons Derde Stand*, the focus is very much on colonial institutions and colonisers who, despite onerous circumstances, do their Christian duty of raising slaves, 'Hottentots', 'Bushmen' and their racially hybrid offspring in the 'scale of civilization'.[26] Equally faceless are those whites, usually regarded as debased, who indulge in miscegenation with black people to produce the coloured population. The traditionalist perspective has been thoroughly discredited in the new South Africa and is no longer publicly propagated except within a fringe receptive to white supremacist ideologies.

The second ideological current within this broad school consists of liberal essentialists who dissented from the dominant racist view and sought to ameliorate racial antagonisms and break down racial barriers. To this school the very existence of coloured people is confirmation of the central contention of the liberal interpretation of South African history, namely, that progress and economic modernisation were predicated upon the integration, cooperation and interdependence of its peoples. To them racial segregation was not only abnormal and a relic of an outmoded frontier mentality but also detrimental to the society's economic development. The miscegenation that is supposed to have given rise to the coloured community is held up as living proof that strict segregation had not always been the norm in South African society and that the dominant theme of its history was that of the acculturation of its various peoples to a common nationhood.

Though sympathetic to the assimilationist aspirations of coloured people, the liberal essentialist approach is nevertheless racialised in that it conceptualises colouredness in terms of race and defines it as a product of miscegenation. And while coloured people were not regarded as inherently inferior, they tended to be seen as relatively uncivilised and in need of white tutelage. The liberal interpretation was common within the English-speaking sector of the academy, the minority of whites opposed to the segregatory ethos of the ruling establishment, and some coloured intellectuals of moderate political persuasion. Before the mid-1980s, by far the best-quality and most thoroughly researched writing on the history of the coloured community came from within the liberal school of South African historiography. The best-known works in this genre are W M MacMillan's *The Cape Colour Question* and J S Marais's *The Cape Coloured People* while Richard van der Ross's *Rise and Decline of Apartheid* is the most prominent example of a moderate coloured writer espousing the liberal interpretation.[27] Indeed, Van der Ross went so far as to present his work as a continuation of the narrative where Marais left off in the early 20th century.[28]

The third distinct strand within the essentialist approach is what might be termed the progressionist interpretation of coloured history and which, for the greater part of the 20th century, represented the conventional view within the educated, politically moderate sector of the coloured community of its own history. In common with the traditional interpretation, it accepted that coloured people formed a separate race and were socially and culturally 'backward' compared to whites but did not regard this condition as innate or permanent. The progressionist perspective was in effect a variation on the liberal essentialist theme in that it combined an environmentalist conception of racial difference with liberal values of personal freedom, interracial cooperation and status based on individual merit to argue that the history of coloured people demonstrated that they were well advanced in the process of becoming as fully 'civilised' as whites and thus deserved inclusion in the dominant society. This view was predicated on an assumption that humanity, and with it coloured people, was on an inevitable path of progress and an Elysian future of prosperity and social harmony. Deeply held religious beliefs that posited the equality of all humans in the eyes of God and that anticipated the ultimate redemption of humanity reinforced the progressionist outlook, as did the Whiggish concept of history transmitted to the coloured elite via an education system dominated by church schools.

Educated and politicised coloured people in the earlier decades of the 20th century exhibited a clear sense of the trajectory of their history as a people through their broad adherence to the progressionist interpretation. This vision of their history harked back to the black night of slavery and the dispossession of the Khoisan, heralded the new dawn of their emancipation in the middle decades of the 19th century under a liberal British administration, and laid stress on a subsequent period of steady advancement through to contemporary struggles for full citizenship rights and a better life for the community. The implementation of segregatory measures in the 20th century were rationalised as temporary setbacks that would be overcome in time and through perseverance.[29] Espoused publicly by organic intellectuals and community leaders, often from political platforms, this interpretation was usually coupled with a plea for fair treatment or the preservation of their status of relative privilege within the South African racial hierarchy.[30] This interpretation found its most elaborate expression in Christian Ziervogel's *Brown South Africa*, in essence the first formal history of coloured people written by a coloured person.[31] Tightening segregation through the 20th century, especially the implementation of apartheid policies, progressively stifled, but never completely extinguished, the optimism and assimilationist impulse on which this interpretation was predicated.

While the essentialist approach is inherently racial because it assigns racial origins and characteristics to the concept of colouredness, it has to be recognised that not all writing within this category is racist.[32] Indeed, a good deal and some of the best writing in this genre was intended to help break down racial barriers and expose the injustices suffered by coloured people under South Africa's racial system.[33] This sort of writing might usefully be described as multiracial in that it recognises the existence of diverse races but advocates racial tolerance and cooperation. Because the essentialist approach embodies the conventional wisdom about coloured identity, it is still very common in popular writing, and even some academic work is still cast in this mould.

Until the 1980s, essentialism was in effect the only paradigm in coloured historical writing. The sole exception was the standpoint of a handful of radical intellectuals within the Trotskyist tradition of the South African left whose critique of South African society and whose interpretation of South African history implied an alternative construction of coloured history. While these radicals never wrote explicitly about the history of the coloured people, their analyses of South African society and history implied that racial divisions, and hence also coloured identity, were products of international capitalist and local settler strategies to divide, rule and exploit the South African masses. In these tracts, the specific history of the coloured community was either ignored, subsumed under a broader black rubric or referred to obliquely. Some of these key works, dating from the early 1940s onwards, include Ben Kies's *Background of Segregation*, Isaac Tabata's *The Building of Unity* and *The Awakening of a People*, William van Schoor's *The Origin and Development of Segregation in South Africa* and Hosea Jaffe's *Three Hundred Years*.[34] The impact of these radical analyses was generally confined to a small sector of the coloured elite where the NEUM retained influence, until their ideas and insights were taken up by a series of studies produced in the 1980s.

A new paradigm in historical writing relating to the history of coloured people emerged in the post-Soweto era in reaction to the essentialist mode of analysis and a desire among scholars both within the liberal and revisionist schools of South African history to distance themselves from racialised thinking or any idea that coloured group consciousness was based on biological or primordial ties. This school, which will be referred to as instrumentalist, regarded coloured identity as an artificial concept imposed by the white supremacist state and the ruling establishment upon an oppressed and vulnerable group of people as an instrument of social control. Positions in this respect range from seeing coloured identity simply as a device for excluding people of 'mixed race' from the dominant society to viewing it conspiratorially as a product of deliberate divide-and-rule tactics by the dominant white minority to prevent black people from forming a united front against racism and exploitation.[35] Written from a point of view explicitly opposed to the apartheid system, instrumentalist histories have tended to focus on coloured politics, especially resistance to white domination.

The initial impetus for popularising the instrumentalist approach came from black-consciousness thinking. A growing sense of black solidarity and defiance of apartheid in the post-Soweto era fed coloured rejectionism. Later in the 1980s, the idea of coloured identity as a product of white supremacist social engineering gained added purchase through the non-racial ethos of the anti-apartheid movement and Marxist notions of false consciousness that were supposedly used by ruling groups to manipulate populations under their control. This view was actively propagated at grassroots level by political activists in the anti-apartheid movement. The new trend, as noted earlier, was built on the foundation laid by a small group of NEUM activists and intellectuals who kept a rejectionist spirit alive in the western Cape through the 1960s and 1970s.[36]

Instrumentalism represented the dominant view within the anti-apartheid movement during the turbulent two decades that followed the Soweto uprising. These ideas, in part, stemmed from a refusal to give credence to apartheid thinking or, in the case of the expedient, the fear of being accused of doing so. Although this approach seemed blind to the reality of racial divisions within black South Africa and of coloured exclusivism, it did score significant political successes in that it helped create a united front against apartheid and played a role in undermining white domination. The revisionist school of South African historical writing that emerged in the 1970s, with its emphasis on class analysis and strong identification with non-racist values, also played down the significance of racial and ethnic identities. This genre tended to support the instrumentalist view where it addressed the issue of coloured identity.

The distinction of being the first instrumentalist history lies with Maurice Hommel's *Capricorn Blues*, published in 1981.[37] Hommel took up the ideas and arguments of preceding radical theorists such as Kenneth Jordaan, Isaac Tabata and Ben Kies and together with his own research, fashioned a political history of coloured people. Hommel's key historiographical innovation is that he switched the focus of historical writing on the coloured community from accounts of interracial mixture in pre-industrial South Africa to coloured protest politics in the 20th century.[38]

There was a sudden spurt in historical writing on the coloured community in the latter part of the 1980s with Gavin Lewis's *Between the Wire and the Wall*, Richard van der Ross's *Rise and Decline of Apartheid* and Ian Goldin's *Making Race* appearing within a year of one another. Although the close spacing of these books was coincidental, it is not in the least fortuitous that this period witnessed the publication of several political histories of coloured people written mainly from an instrumentalist perspective. This surge in historical writing was triggered by intensified anti-apartheid resistance in the western Cape during the 1980s as well as the concomitant controversy over the participation of some coloured leaders in P W Botha's tricameral parliament. Both raised the political profile of the community and upped the stakes in the increasingly bitter wrangle over the racial and ethnic distinctiveness of coloured people. This stimulated interest in the coloured past, particularly in the political struggles of the 20th century. Lewis's thorough and extensively researched *Between the Wire and the Wall* represents a liberal, instrumentalist elucidation of coloured political history in the period from the Anglo-Boer War to 1948. Goldin's book, which focuses on the coloured Labour Preference Policy, is written from a revisionist perspective. Roy du Pre's *Separate but Unequal*, another instrumentalist intervention published in 1994, consists mainly of an angry rant against the apartheid system.[39]

The instrumentalist interpretation lost much of its potency when the ANC in the early 1990s sidelined the anti-racist pressure groups within its fold and openly appealed to coloured identity in an attempt to win coloured political support. The attraction of the instrumentalist view has all but evaporated in the post-apartheid era in which inter-black racial tensions could no longer be explained away as the dastardly machinations of the white supremacist establishment, and a strictly non-racial outlook became a political liability. A few die-hard instrumentalists nevertheless remain within the small anti-racist grouping of left-wing intellectuals and activists. The Khoisan revivalist movement is essentially instrumentalist in that its followers reject colouredness as the colonisers' caricature of the colonised.

A third paradigm, referred to here as social constructionism[40] and in which I place myself, emerged from the latter half of the 1980s onwards in response to the inadequacies of both the essentialist and instrumentalist approaches.[41] The basic assumption of this genre is that coloured identity cannot be taken as given but is a product of human agency dependent on a complex interplay of historical, social, cultural, political and other contingencies. It is neither ordained by God nor a product of nature as essentialists imply, nor is it a device conjured up by the machinations of white supremacism as instrumentalists argue. The creation of coloured identity is also taken to be an ongoing, dynamic process in which groups and individuals make and remake their perceived realities and thus also their personal and social identities. The fundamental concerns of social constructionists are thus to explain how and why coloured identity came into existence and to unravel the intricate ways in which it has found expression.

My own work and that of Zimbabwean historian, James Muzondidya, form the principal contributions to this genre. In the early 1990s, I published a study of the Teachers' League of South Africa which elaborated on an embryonic social constructionist approach to coloured identity.[42] This theme was subsequently developed through a series of scholarly publications[43] culminating in my recent book *Not White Enough, Not Black Enough*, which attempts a more systematic history of coloured identity in South Africa under white supremacy. Muzondidya's *Walking a Tightrope* is a comprehensive study of the making of coloured identity in Zimbabwe from the founding of the colony in the 1890s to the coming of independence in 1980. Muzondidya's analysis is pertinent because it draws extensively on, is significantly shaped by, and engages with South African debates on coloured identity.[44] Noteworthy social constructionist interventions have also been made by Vivian Bickford-Smith, whose final chapter in his study of Victorian Cape Town analyses the emergence of coloured identity in the city, and Birgit Pickel who frames her analysis of coloured voting patterns in 1994 within a social constructionist synopsis of coloured history.[45] While Bickford-Smith and Muzondidya portray the making of coloured identity as a dialectic process of imposition by the ruling establishment from above and coloured initiative from below, I stress the primacy of coloured agency in the making of their own identity.[46]

The main criticisms of both the essentialist and instrumentalist approaches from the perspective of social constructionists are that they tend to accept coloured identity as given and portray it as fixed. They generally fail to take cognisance of fluidities and ambiguities inherent in processes of coloured self-definition. In essentialist histories, this is a product of a eurocentric perspective and a reliance on the simplistic formulations of popular racialised conceptions of coloured identity. The problem in instrumentalist writing is that it shifts agency in the making of coloured identity away from coloured people to the ruling establishment. Not only does this interpretation fly in the face of elementary understandings of the nature of social identity, but it is also dependent on an unlikely conspiracy for which there is little evidence. It also suffers from a narrow focus on coloured protest politics and the social injustices endured by the community. This has had the effect of exaggerating the resistance of coloured people to white supremacy and playing down their accommodation of the South African racial system. The overall result has been that both paradigms present an oversimplified image of the phenomenon and are profoundly ahistoric in their perceptions of the origins and workings of the identity.

A cardinal sin of both these schools is that they deny coloured people a significant role in the making of their own social identities. Essentialist interpretations do this by assuming colouredness to be an inbred quality that arises automatically from miscegenation while instrumentalists share the essentialist premise that coloured identity is something negative and undesirable but blame it on the racism and the exploitative practices of the ruling white minority. Though they may have had the laudable intention of countering the racism of essentialist accounts, instrumentalist histories are nevertheless condescending by denying coloured people a role in the basic cognitive function of creating and reproducing their own social identities. Even the best of these histories, Gavin Lewis's *Between the Wire and the Wall*, despite its firm focus on coloured agency in the political arena, nevertheless asserts that 'the solution to this dilemma [of defining colouredness] is to accept coloured identity as a white-imposed categorization'.[47] Both schools of writing treat coloured identity as something exceptional, failing to recognise it for what it is – a historically specific social construction, like any other social identity. In this respect, both schools have betrayed undue concern with contemporary ideological and political considerations.

Social constructionist histories have therefore been at pains to demonstrate the complexity of coloured identity and, most importantly, to stress the agency of coloured people in the making of their identity. In my own work, emphasis has been placed on the ways in which the marginality of coloured people, their intermediate status in the racial hierarchy, negative racial stereotyping and assimilationist aspirations together with a range of other factors have shaped their identity and influenced their social experience and political consciousness. The resultant ambiguities and ideological conflicts have been central to the making of the identity. Far from being the inert anonymous entities of the essentialist school or the righteous resisters of instrumentalist histories, coloured people exhibited a much more complex reaction to white supremacism that encompassed resistance as well as collaboration, protest as well as accommodation.

Social identity is by its very nature mainly the product of its bearers even though it is partly formed through interactions with and against the perceptions of outsiders. It can no more be imposed upon people by the state or ruling groups than it can spring automatically from miscegenation or people's supposed racial constitution. Social identity is cultural in nature in that it is a product of learnt behaviour, and is moulded by social experience and social interaction.[48] Identities can be influenced, even manipulated, by outsiders but then only to the extent that they resonate strongly with people's self-perception. In this regard instrumentalists usually confuse status with identity when arguing that the state, especially during the apartheid period, imposed coloured identity on a particular group of people. A distinction needs to be drawn between the two. It is clear that while a status can be imposed upon people by the state or ruling groups, an identity cannot, though a social identity may well be the basis upon which a particular status is foisted on a group. In the case of the coloured community under white supremacist rule, it was both through customary discrimination and the various ways in which the state was able to assert its power that a particular status was imposed upon coloured people. This was most transparently the case with the legislative and administrative programmes that put the apartheid system in place from the late 1940s onwards. There can be no gainsaying that whites broadly colluded in the oppression of black people through nearly all of South Africa's history and that racial categories were manipulated to the advantage of the ruling classes. Hertzog openly tried to manipulate the coloured community in the 1920s in this way, as did P W Botha in the 1980s. This does not, however, amount to the imposition of their identity on coloured people.

Recently the rudiments of a fourth approach, of conceptualising coloured identity as a product of creolisation, have emerged. This viewpoint, which draws on postmodern and postcolonial theory, shares much of the critical outlook of social constructionists, and may be seen as social constructionism informed by a particular theoretical perspective. It is, as one would expect, nuanced and sensitive to the complexities of identity politics and, by its very nature, critical of the simplistic paradigms of essentialist and instrumentalist writing. Zimitri Erasmus's introduction to her edited volume, *Coloured by History, Shaped by Place*, published in 2001, initiated the application of creolisation theory to coloured identity.[49] It is a pity that Erasmus does little beyond proposing the idea. Erasmus's basic premise is that coloured identity is not a product of racial mixture as popular wisdom and much academic writing would have it, but of cultural creativity shaped by South Africa's history of colonialism and white domination. Using creolisation to explain the making of coloured identity is an innovative line of enquiry that seems to hold much potential. In this volume, Christopher Lee and Helene Strauss take up the challenge of applying creolisation theory to substantive case studies. Elaine Salo's intricate anthropological studies of the roles of gangsterism, global consumer culture and the imagination in the making of racialised and gendered self-perceptions of youth in the working-class Cape Town suburb of Manenberg represent important recent interventions in the understanding of localised coloured identities.[50] As both Salo and several contributions in this volume demonstrate, the use of theoretical perspectives derived from postmodernism, postcolonialism and cultural studies are yielding rich results.

Conclusion

Coloured social experience in South Africa is mirrored in the historiography of coloured identity in a number of ways. Under white domination it was largely a combination of coloured marginality and growing coloured resistance to racial domination that influenced the content and quality of historical writing on the community. Features of the historiography during this period that stand out are its relatively poor quality, its paucity and the degree to which political and ideological considerations overtly influenced positions staked out by contributors. The poor quality and scantness of this historiography under white supremacy were to a considerable extent products of racial oppression and the marginalisation of the coloured community. From the 1980s there was a clear tendency for opinions to be polarised, with coloured identity either being taken for granted or imbued with intense political significance resulting in it often being rejected with vehemence. The rapid retreat of coloured rejectionism and the transition to democracy has resulted in the mid-1990s forming a watershed in both academic and popular writing on coloured identity. With far greater freedom to give expression to their social identities and with the new order being much more conducive to creativity in this arena, it should not be surprising that the new South Africa has witnessed an efflorescence of studies on the subject.

Endnotes

1   *Cape Argus*, 22 March 1913; *Cape Times*, 22 March 1913.
2   Switzer L. 1995. Review of Adhikari M. 1993. *Let Us Live for our Children: The Teachers' League of South Africa, 1913–1940*. Cape Town: University of Cape Town Press, in *Journal of African History*, 36, no. 2, 338.

3   For a detailed discussion of coloured rejectionism, see Adhikari M. 2005. *Not White Enough, Not Black Enough: Racial Identity in the South African Coloured Community*. Athens: Ohio University Press, ch 5.

4   For further details on this assimilationist outlook, see Adhikari, *Not White Enough*, 8–12, 72–78, 92–94.

5   On this, see Shifrin T. 1962. 'New deal for coloured people? A study of National Party policies towards the coloured people'. BA (Hons) thesis, University of Cape Town; Lewis G. 1987. *Between the Wire and the Wall: A History of South African Coloured Politics*. Cape Town: David Philip, 83–84, 119–149; and Giliomee H. 1995. 'The non-racial franchise and Afrikaner and coloured identities, 1910–1994'. *African Affairs*, 94, no. 375.

6   For contending views on coloured identity within the coloured community itself, see Adhikari M. 2002. 'Hope, fear, shame, frustration: continuity and change in the expression of coloured identity in white supremacist South Africa, 1910–1994'. PhD dissertation, University of Cape Town, ch 2.

7   Earlier on, individual activists had touted the idea of black unity. The maverick Francis Peregrino had, for example, done so soon after the turn of the 20th century, and Jimmy la Guma and John Gomas advocated this cause from the mid-1920s onwards.

8   For further details, see Adhikari, *Not White Enough*, 45–49.

9   Alexander N. 1979. *One Azania, One Nation: The National Question in South Africa*. London: Zed Press, 112–113. See also 'Discussion on the role of the non-European teacher in the liberatory movement'. 1952. *Discussion,* 1, no. 5, 12.

10   See Adhikari M. 2005. 'Fiercely non-racial? Discourses and politics of race in the Non-European Unity Movement, 1943–70'. *Journal of Southern African Studies,* 31, no. 2, 403–418, for a detailed analysis of this issue.

11   *Grassroots*, April 1983.

12   'The people of South Africa population census, 1996: primary tables – the country as a whole'. Report no. 03-01-19, 6; *Statistics South Africa, 2000*. 2001. Pretoria: Government Publications Department, 1.1.

13   Both censures occurred at academic conferences in the latter half of the 1980s. To the first I responded that it was not my intention to create divisions but if there were divisions it would be better to face up to them. My response to the second, a noted historian of Cape slavery, was that my analysis of coloured identity was no more an endorsement of apartheid than his work an advocation of slavery.

14   For discussions of shame and coloured identity, see Adhikari, *Not White Enough*, 22–23; and Wicomb Z. 1998. 'Shame and identity: the case of the coloured in South Africa', in *Writing South Africa: Literature, Apartheid and Democracy, 1970–1995*, eds D Attridge & R Jolly. Cambridge: Cambridge University Press, 91–107.

15   The use of quotation marks indicates that the individuals alluded to reject the label 'coloured'.

16   See Adhikari M. 2002. '"You have the right to know": South, 1987–1994', in *South Africa's Resistance Press: Alternative Voices in the Last Generation under Apartheid*, eds L Switzer & M Adhikari. Athens: Ohio University Press, 351–352 for an example of two media activists who privately recognised the existence of coloured identity but publicly tried to use the rejectionist line as a means of fostering a non-racial ethos in the western Cape.

17 This article was first published in attenuated form in 1992 as 'God, Jan van Riebeeck and the coloured people: the anatomy of a South African joke'. *Southern African Discourse*, 4. A later, fully fleshed-out version appeared in 2006 as 'God made the white man, God made the black man …: popular racial stereotyping of coloured people in apartheid South Africa'. *South African Historical Journal*, 55, 142–164.

18 For the record, let me say that although I have described many instances of coloured racism in my writing, I most certainly do not regard coloured people as particularly racist. Whites were after all the ones who constructed the racist system and imposed it on South African society. Also, anyone who has experienced the chauvinism and ethnocentrism typical of Indian middle-class life, as I have, is likely to agree with me that coloured people as a group do not rank second in this league table. Then there is the small matter of African racism towards coloured people, an issue too often ignored, the furore caused by the aptly named Roderick Blackman Ngoro notwithstanding. The reality is that South African social life has always been, and still is, shot through with racist thinking, and even today one seldom has to dig beyond a veneer of political correctness and nation-building rhetoric to expose it.

19 Adhikari M. 1994. 'Coloureds', in *Illustrated Dictionary of South African History*, advisory ed Saunders. Sandton: Ibis Books, 79.

20 See James W, Caliguire D & Cullinan K (eds). 1996. *Now that We Are Free: Coloured Communities in a Democratic South Africa*. Boulder: Lynne Rienner, chs 4–7; Eldridge M & Seekings J. 1996. 'Mandela's lost province: the African National Congress and the Western Cape electorate in the 1994 South African elections'. *Journal of Southern African Studies*, 22, no. 4; Reynolds A. 1994. *Election '94: South Africa*. Cape Town: David Philip, 192–193; Mattes R, Giliomee H & James W. 1996. 'The election in the Western Cape', in *Launching Democracy in South Africa: The First Open Election, April 1994*, eds R W Johnson & L Schlemmer. New Haven: Yale University Press, 108–167. Pickel B. 1997. *Coloured Ethnicity and Identity: A Case Study in the Former Coloured Areas of the Western Cape/South Africa*. Hamburg: Lit Verlag, 84–101.

21 In August 1995, the Institute for Democracy in South Africa organised a conference entitled 'National unity and the politics of diversity: the case of the Western Cape', and in June 1998, University of Cape Town sociologist Zimitri Erasmus organised the conference 'Coloured by history, shaped by place'.

22 These theses include Besten M. 2006. 'Transformation and reconstitution of Khoe-San identities: AAS Le Fleur I, Griqua identities and post-apartheid Khoe-San revivalism, 1894–2004'. PhD dissertation, Leiden University; Ruiters M. 2006. 'Elite (re-)constructions of coloured identities in a post-apartheid South Africa: assimilations and bounded transgressions'. PhD dissertation, Rutgers University; Salo E. 2004. 'Respectable mothers, tough men and good daughters: producing persons in Manenberg township, South Africa'. PhD dissertation, Emory University; and Hendricks C. 2000. 'We knew our place: a study of the constructions of coloured identity in South Africa'. PhD dissertation, University of South Carolina.

23 See Adhikari, 'God made the white man'; and Steinberg J. 2004. *The Number: One Man's Search for Identity in the Cape Underworld and Prison Gangs*. Johannesburg: Jonathan Ball, 264.

24 The earliest example is Hendricks D & Viljoen C. 1936. *Student Teacher's History Course: For the Use in Coloured Training Colleges*. Paarl: Huguenot Drukkery. See also Viljoen C & Hartzenberg P. 1933. *History: Summary and Notes*. Paarl: Private publication.

25 Muller C. 1969. *Five Hundred Years: A History of South Africa*. Pretoria: Academica; Van Jaarsveld F. 1975. *From Van Riebeeck to Vorster: An Introduction to the History of the Republic of South Africa*. Johannesburg: Perskor.

26 Cruse H P. 1947. *Die Opheffing van die Kleurlingbevolking: Deel I: Aanvangsjare, 1652–1795*. Stellenbosch: Christen Studentevereniging; Botha D P. 1960. *Die Opkoms van Ons Derde Stand*. Cape Town: Human & Rousseau. While the former is openly racist, the latter displays a good deal of sympathy for coloured people.

27 MacMillan W M. 1968. *The Cape Colour Question: A Historical Survey*. Cape Town: Balkema, first published in London by Faber & Gwyer, 1927; Marais J S. 1968. *The Cape Coloured People, 1652–1937*. Johannesburg: Witwatersrand University Press, first published in London, by Longmans, Green, 1939; Van der Ross R. 1986. *The Rise and Decline of Apartheid: A Study of Political Movements among the Coloured People of South Africa, 1880–1985*. Cape Town: Tafelberg.

28 Van der Ross, *The Rise and Decline of Apartheid*, xi.

29 For further detail, see Adhikari, *Not White Enough*, 8–10, 36–45.

30 The address by John Tobin, a prominent coloured politician, to a Stone meeting as reported in the *South African News*, 28 November 1903, and some speeches made by Dr Abdullah Abdurahman, the most eminent coloured political leader of the first half of the 20th century, provide good examples of this interpretation. Refer in particular to Abdurahman's presidential addresses to the African Political Organisation of 1909, 1923 and 1939. See APO, 24 May 1909; 21 April 1923; and Van der Ross R. 1990. '*Say It Out Loud*': *The APO Presidential Addresses and Other Major Political Speeches, 1906–1940, of Dr. Abdullah Abdurahman*. Bellville: University of the Western Cape Institute for Historical Research, 106–117.

31 Ziervogel C. 1938. *Brown South Africa*. Cape Town: Maskew Miller.

32 A distinction needs to be drawn between the terms 'racist' and 'racial' as used here. Whereas the former always involves a judgement about the supposed inferiority or superiority of one or other racial group, the latter refers to distinctions made between groups of people on the basis of racial characteristics but does not necessarily contain inferences of superiority or inferiority. Such recognition of racial differences are, indeed, often accompanied by explicit assertions of racial equality.

33 Marais and Van der Ross's books are leading examples, and although MacMillan's writing at times descends into a patronising racist tone – see MacMillan, *Cape Colour Question* 13 and 289 for examples – he strongly opposed the government's segregationist policies.

34 Kies B. 1943. *Background of Segregation*. Cape Town: Anti-CAD; Tabata I. 1945. *The Building of Unity*. Cape Town: Non-European Unity Committee; Tabata I. 1950. *The Awakening of a People*. Johannesburg: People's Press; Van Schoor W. 1951. *The Origin and Development of Segregation in South Africa*. Cape Town: Teachers' League of South Africa; Mnguni (H Jaffe). 1952. *Three Hundred Years*. Cape Town: New Era Fellowship. See also the journal *Discussion* put out by the Forum Club in the early 1950s.

35 These two variations on the instrumentalist theme are respectively represented by Du Pre R H. 1994. *Separate but Unequal: The 'Coloured' People of South Africa – A*

Political History. Johannesburg: Jonathan Ball; and Goldin I. 1987. *Making Race: The Politics and Economics of Coloured Identity in South Africa.* Cape Town: Maskew Miller Longman.

36 For further discussion on this point, see Adhikari, *Not White Enough*, 134–135.

37 Hommel M. 1981. *Capricorn Blues: The Struggle for Human Rights in South Africa.* Toronto: Culturama.

38 For an evaluation of Hommel's book, see Adhikari, *Not White Enough*, 49–53.

39 For detailed evaluations of these works, see Adhikari M. 1988. 'Responses to marginality: twentieth century coloured politics'. *South African Historical Journal* 20, 115–126; Adhikari M. 1996. 'Blinded by anger: coloured experience under apartheid'. *South African Historical Journal*, 35, 169–182.

40 The first known usage of this term in relation to coloured historiography occurs in Trotter H. 2000. '"What is a coloured?": definitions of coloured South African identity in the academy' (unpublished paper in possession of the author, Yale University), 11–12, 21. Trotter distinguishes between positive social constructionists (myself and Bickford-Smith) and negative social constructionists (what I call instrumentalists).

41 The first tentative ventures in this direction are to be found in Adhikari M. 1986. 'The Teachers' League' of South Africa, 1913–402. MA thesis, University of Cape Town; Bickford-Smith J V. 1989. 'Commerce, class and ethnicity in Cape Town, 1875–1902'. PhD dissertation, Cambridge University.

42 Adhikari, *Let Us Live for Our Children*; Adhikari M. 1992. 'The sons of Ham: slavery and the making of coloured identity'. *South African Historical Journal*, 27.

43 The main publications include Adhikari M. 1994. 'Coloured identity and the politics of coloured education: the origin of the Teachers' League of South Africa, 1880–1913'. *International Journal of African Historical Studies* 27, no. 1, 101–126; "The product of civilization in its most repellent manifestation": ambiguities in the racial perceptions of the *APO (African Political Organisation)*, 1909–1923'. *Journal of African History*, 38, no. 2 (1997), 283–300; Adhikari, You have the right to know' See also Adhikari, *Not White Enough*.

44 Muzondidya J. 2005. *Walking a Tightrope: Towards a Social History of the Coloured People of Zimbabwe.* Trenton: Africa World Press.

45 Bickford-Smith V. 1995. *Ethnic Pride and Racial Prejudice in Victorian Cape Town, 1875–1902.* Cambridge: Cambridge University Press, 186–209; Pickel, *Coloured Ethnicity*, 13–38.

46 Muzondidya's suggestion that the social constructionist approach is a product of rational choice theory is misguided in that writers in this genre have not explicitly used any such theory to analyse or explain coloured identity, and there is no evidence to suggest that they believe that social change or identity can be explained simply as a matter of rational choice. If anything, social constructionist analyses are marked by an emphasis on non-rational elements such as the ambiguities and contradictions within coloured identity. Muzondidya J. 2001 'Sitting on the fence or walking a tightrope? A political history of the coloured community of Zimbabwe, 1945–1980'. PhD dissertation, University of Cape Town, 13.

47 Lewis, *Between Wire and Wall*, 4.

48 This much can be established from introductory social psychology texts. See, for example, Abrams D. 2001. 'Social identity, psychology of', in *International Encyclopedia of the Social and Behavioural Sciences*, eds N Smelser & B Baltes, vol 21. Oxford: Elsevier, 14306–14309.

49 Erasmus Z. 2001. *Coloured by History, Shaped by Place: New Perspectives on Coloured Identities in Cape Town*. Cape Town: Kwela Books, 13–28. While others have referred to Cape colonial society, and therefore the origins of coloured identity, as creolised, Erasmus is the first to have applied creolisation theory to coloured identity per se. See Shell R. 1994. *Children of Bondage: A Social History of the Slave Society at the Cape of Good Hope, 1652–1838*. Johannesburg: Witwatersrand University Press, 415; Martin D. 1999. *Coon Carnival: New Year in Cape Town, Past and Present*. Cape Town: David Philip, 53–57, 94–95.

50 Salo E, 'Respectable mothers'; Salo E. 2005 'Negotiating gender and personhood in the new South Africa: adolescent women and gangsters in Manenberg township on the Cape Flats' in *Limits to Liberation*, ed S. Robins; Salo E. 2007. '"Mans is ma soe": ganging practices in Manenberg, South Africa, and the ideologies of masculinity, gender, and generational relations', in *States of Violence: Politics, Youth, and Memory in Contemporary Africa*, eds E Bay & D Donham. Charlottesville: University of Virginia Press.

CHAPTER 2

'… [C]onfused about being coloured'[1]: creolisation and coloured identity in Chris van Wyk's *Shirley, Goodness and Mercy*

BY

HELENE STRAUSS

MCMASTER UNIVERSITY

E ven though the term 'creolisation' is used primarily to describe Caribbean and 'new world' processes of cultural cross-fertilisation, theories of creolisation have travelled far and wide, especially since the early 1990s, when postcolonial studies came to be institutionalised in universities across the globe. The term, which broadly signals complex and often violent processes of cultural exchange that take place between various, already creolised identities in the aftermath of colonisation and slavery, has featured prominently in post-apartheid South African critical debates. This chapter considers the significance of this critical import in relation to post-apartheid literary articulations of colouredness.[2] After contextualising the terms 'creole' and 'creolisation' in the Caribbean and South African contexts, an assessment is made of both the drawbacks and the critical potential of this transplanted concept when used to theorise coloured identities in South Africa. Does creolisation help clarify processes of coloured identity formation, or does it reinforce apartheid-era essentialisms and undermine the very transgressive potential that has made it so attractive for revising cultural exclusivity? To what extent do received cultural and racial categories continue to inflect the ways in which processes of creolisation take place?

These questions are specifically considered through a reading of Chris van Wyk's *Shirley, Goodness and Mercy*, published in 2004. This post-apartheid text is useful for the new perspectives it offers on the tensions and contradictions that plagued performances of colouredness[3] during the apartheid years, as well as for what it says about the difficulties of deciphering what colouredness as a cultural identity might mean in the post-apartheid era. The stories that Van Wyk shares in this memoir are important conveyors of the identities and experiences of a range of coloured South Africans during the apartheid and post-apartheid eras and as such enable a consideration of the extent to which the production of coloured subjectivity[4] during this period might be analysed as examples of creolisation.

When working with a term such as creolisation, which has taken on a considerable number of meanings and has generated an enormous amount of scholarship internationally, one necessarily has to be selective. This study favours work that offers insight into the minutiae of subject formation and racialisation, and that theorises some of the social meanings that are assigned to people's bodies as a result of popular assumptions about race. This chapter privileges theories of cultural creolisation that shed light on the manner in which people who are labelled, who self-identify, or who resist identification as 'coloured' accommodate at times conflicting ideologies in their day-to-day lives. The small-scale identity alterations that people have to make in moments of intercultural contact, and the psychological divisions that people have to negotiate in contexts of conflict and domination, are necessarily staged against the backdrop of larger political and social developments. Van Wyk's *Shirley, Goodness and Mercy* proves particularly instructive in this regard, since it situates the production of 'coloured' subjectivity firmly within historical moments of social and political change.

Situating creolisation in the post-apartheid imagination

Since the disintegration of apartheid in the late 1980s, South Africans have been searching for new ways in which to relate to one another. The search for a vocabulary that might offer alternatives to the limiting and racially hierarchised identity categories of apartheid has, since 1994, yielded a wealth of terms, tropes and critical frameworks. At the forefront of these has been the terminology that has come to mark nation-building projects of the post-1994 era, such as the Rainbow Nation trope,[5] former president Thabo Mbeki's notion of the African Renaissance[6] and the rhetoric of reconciliation central to the Truth and Reconciliation Commission (TRC). The language generated by these initiatives reflects the ANC government's attempts at reshaping social relations and promoting national symbols that might foster reconciliation. While the extent of South Africa's reconciliation remains a topic of considerable debate,[7] and while many of the social inequalities of the past remain firmly in place, there can be little doubt that the transition from apartheid to democracy has created an opportunity for people to articulate a range of hitherto suppressed identity narratives. As a result of greater personal freedom underwritten by their progressive constitution, South Africans are now at liberty to explore alternative forms of self-imagining.

While these freedoms have offered exciting possibilities for all South Africans to find more equitable and ethical ways in which to stage their identities to one another, many are uncertain about the extent to which inherited performances of identity require revision to fit the ideological projects of the new order. These uncertainties are reflected, for instance, in the recent proliferation of writings on what it means to be an 'African' in South Africa – on who has the right to lay claim to this label and who has the necessary credentials to police access to this category.[8] The identity shifts that have been taking place in relation to the category 'African' speak to larger insecurities about cultural belonging that can be seen also to inform the different ways in which the category 'coloured' has been revised and/or rejected in post-transition South Africa. Academic attempts at accounting for this fluidity have culminated in an outpouring of texts that analyse the social construction of identity through the critical lenses of postcolonial cultural studies. In this area of study, terms such as 'diaspora', 'hybridity', 'cultural translation' and 'creolisation' have been invoked with varying degrees of enthusiasm over the past few decades to address processes of cultural exchange that have taken place under the circumstances specific to slavery, colonisation and globalisation. In South Africa, the term 'creolisation' in particular seems to have captured the interest of academics who are trying to find new terms with which to articulate the uncertainties of the new order.

The terms 'creole' and 'creolisation', as demonstrated elsewhere, have taken on a wide array of meanings in the relatively short time since they first entered South African academic debates.[9] Elleke Boehmer uses the term 'creoleness', for instance, to signal the hidden difference of her own white identity as a Dutch immigrant in South Africa during the apartheid years;[10] Robert Shell describes the cultures that developed at the Cape between 1652 and 1838 as a result of slavery as 'creolised';[11] while Ulf Hannerz suggests that the global, cosmopolitan cultural connections that were formed in erstwhile Sophiatown might be read as a process of creolisation that served local resistance politics.[12] The most hotly debated of recent usages of the term 'creolisation' has arguably been that of Sarah Nuttall and Cheryl-Ann Michael in their editorial introduction to *Senses of Culture*,[13] a collection of essays that offer novel interpretations of South African popular and youth cultures.[14] In this introduction, they argue that readings of the contemporary South African cultural landscape should move away from the apartheid fixation on race, separation and resistance. Reading South Africa as a site marked by myriad previously unexplored local and transnational intercultural connections, they offer the term 'creolisation' as a possible frame for rethinking the ways in which cultural identities are formed in contemporary South Africa. This term, they argue, brings into focus the ongoing processes of cultural transformation that everyday living in a country of such cultural complexity and heterogeneity has necessarily produced – efforts at limiting these exchanges notwithstanding. Since the publication of this collection of essays, their theoretical frameworks have been the subject of considerable discussion, with critics suggesting that this kind of theoretical framing is incapable of addressing the contemporary dynamics of class, race and power that still shape identity formation in present-day South Africa.[15]

The reluctant initial reception of their choice of creolisation as a conceptual frame was partly the result of its timing. Undertaken when discourses of cultural interchange abounded in both popular and scholarly debates, it is not surprising that they have subsequently been read as having downplayed race, domination and resistance. The Mbeki presidency was characterised by a 'return to race' in public discourse, as Veerle Dieltens terms it.[16] Recent scholarship has been paying closer attention to entrenched racialised, heterosexist and culturally essentialist thinking and to the segregationist legacies of apartheid that continue to shape the South African cultural landscape. A resurgence of interest in the social effects of essentialist discourses of racialisation can partly be blamed on the emphasis placed on unity and reconciliation by the South African media and the ANC government in the years immediately following the transition to democracy. The TRC's ironic silence on the issue of race[17] can be read as both symptomatic and constitutive of this drive for unity. Yet, as many scholars of the post-Mandela era have pointed out, in light of South Africa's singular history of racial engineering, it is indeed surprising that so little work has been done to lay bare the cultural processes whereby racial identities are produced and performed.[18]

To Nuttall and Michael's credit, it must be acknowledged that debates about racial essentialism and about creolisation are not mutually exclusive. To describe coloured identities as creolised is not to deny the ongoing salience of essentialist racial categories in coloured self-imagining. Creolised identities cannot be read as socially progressive per se. It should be noted, furthermore, that even though processes of creolisation necessarily produce new cultural and identity formations, the speed at which these processes take place varies depending on the social factors at play in the cultural exchange. In contexts of extreme inequality and poverty, for instance, where people from divergent cultures are thrown together and the stakes of claiming cultural allegiances are high, processes of creolisation tend to take place more rapidly than in contexts where people enjoy the relative cultural stabilities that economic privilege can offer. Not all coloured identities are therefore creolised in the same way, since the pressures faced by people to adjust their self-definitions in the face of cultural difference tend to depend on a range of social and economic factors.

It is also important not to confuse the process of creolisation with what in apartheid and eugenicist discourse has come to be known as 'race mixture'. Zimitri Erasmus has done important work in this regard by offering creolisation as a term that might move discussions of coloured identity away from racist assumptions about supposedly natural links between racial identity, read in essentialist biological terms, and cultural expression.[19] Instead, Erasmus uses the term to refer to the ways in which colouredness has historically come into being as a *cultural* identity in South Africa. By conceptualising coloured identity as the product of 'cultural creativity, creolized formations shaped by South Africa's history of colonialism, slavery, segregation and apartheid', Erasmus seeks to undermine the widely held notion that colouredness is 'something produced by the mixture of other "purer" cultures'.[20]

Erasmus's account of processes of coloured creolisation is heavily indebted to Caribbean theorisations of the term. Heuristically, the importation of Caribbean theories of creolisation into South Africa for illuminating colouredness as a social identity makes sense for reasons that a brief consideration of Caribbean thinking on the term will clarify. The term 'creole' came into being in both the French Antilles and in the Anglophone Caribbean within vernaculars of race thinking developed in contexts of slavery and colonisation. Yet despite the term's frequent historical inscription in essentialist racial theory, and as a sign of racial miscegenation in particular, Caribbean theories of the *process* of creolisation, as Stuart Hall points out, have 'in fact emphasized the hybridity of cultures rather than the impurity of breeding and miscegenation'.[21] In this context, creolisation – as a process of cultural exchange and transformation – has been theorised, furthermore, as encompassing two interrelated tendencies. On the one hand, the collision of cultures in the Caribbean has been credited with enabling possibilities for cultural and literary creativity – what Hall calls the 'good' side of creolisation.[22] This approach is generally associated with the work of the French Caribbean *créolité* theorists Jean Bernabé, Patrick Chamoiseau, and Raphäel Confiant.[23] On the other hand, the process has been shown to be embedded in extreme forms of violence, inequality, domination and resistance as, for instance, exemplified in the writings of Wilson Harris and Antonio Benítez-Rojo.[24] Hall defines this as the 'bad side' of creolisation entailing 'questions of cultural domination and hegemony, of appropriation and expropriation, conditions of subalterneity and enforced obligation, the sense of a brutal rupture with the past, of 'the world which has been lost,' and a regime founded on racism and institutionalized violence'.[25]

In her reading of South African coloured identities as culturally creative responses to the violent legacies of slavery, colonialism and apartheid, Erasmus is in fact mobilising both the celebratory and the more pessimistic readings of the process that emerge in these Caribbean conversations. Yet the crucial difference between the Caribbean and South African (post)colonial contexts is that colouredness in South Africa designates a minority identity, even if one relatively privileged as a result of apartheid classification. Even though all Caribbean islands still bear the psychological and institutional markings of hierarchical race thinking, the category 'coloured' as a cultural identity is arguably more mainstream in this context than in South Africa, where eugenicist assumptions about race succeeded in the creation of particularly rigid divisions between differently racialised South Africans. This was especially the case in apartheid South Africa where constructions of cultural and racial superiority – and the economic privileges secured by these constructions – were threatened by a blurring of social boundaries. As a result, South Africans who identify as, or are identified as, coloured have had to negotiate a historically distinctive set of social pressures related to the formation of group consciousness and to the realisation of substantive citizenship in the context of marginality.[26]

Yet this distinctiveness does not invalidate the lessons to be learned from the Caribbean – it simply means that the experience of creolisation in the South African context will have to be read with an eye that is attentive to historical and cultural specificity.

My own interest in processes of cultural creolisation in South Africa has been driven by questions about the kinds of identities created when conflicting cultural codes converge in individual bodies, as well as about the manner in which these bodies are subjected to and resist oppressive social norms. In this regard, Caribbean articulations of creolisation have also proven instructive. Drawing on novelist and social theorist Erna Brodber's exploration of some of the ways in which contemporary Jamaican subjects positioned at the crossroads of culture are fashioning creolised identities,[27] I have argued elsewhere that the term 'creolisation' can be useful for elucidating some of the specific meanings that processes of cross-cultural exchange have for differentially racialised[28] South Africans. This is the case especially if creolisation is read as a difficult and at times violent process whereby differing cultural codes are crafted into identity performances that may or may not be socially credible and sustainable.[29] Creolisation is here understood, in other words, also as a process of subjection to social norms that nonetheless leaves room for agency. I see this process as producing shifting performances of identity relative to the specific demands that unfamiliar or oppressive cultural categories make on a person's sense of self. The extent to which a person will feel constrained to adjust his or her identity to changing social pressures usually depends on that person's location on socially constructed racial, class and gender hierarchies. As such, the discursive and economic legacies of slavery, colonialism and apartheid necessarily inform contemporary cultural exchanges in South Africa, yet the repercussions of these historical realities are not felt exclusively by those who cohere around the identity label 'coloured'.

Creolisation, in other words, is a complex process that affects all of South Africa's diverse social groupings, though the extent to which the process is experienced as violent and coercive varies according to a person's social positioning. Chris van Wyk's *Shirley, Goodness and Mercy* offers an opportunity for one to consider how such an understanding of creolisation might illuminate some of the ways in which coloured identities are imagined and staged in contemporary South Africa, as well as how past performances of colouredness are re-imagined from a post-apartheid perspective. This text provides a useful platform from which to consider small-scale subjective, as well as larger socio-political, processes of cultural creolisation.

Remembering, resisting and re-imagining colouredness in *Shirley, Goodness and Mercy*

A number of scholars of coloured identity in South Africa have suggested that the onset of democracy has permitted the creative and affirmative re-articulation of colouredness as a social identity in ways that were impossible under white supremacist rule.[30] The creative energy brought by the transition has been harnessed in particular by literary and cultural workers, who have produced a wealth of texts in recent years to validate some of the previously suppressed identity narratives surrounding colouredness in South Africa. This process of re-articulation is intimately tied to the construction of cultural memory, since group consciousness is reliant on the production of a shared historical narrative within which individuals with divergent personal backgrounds can imagine the interconnectedness of their past, present and future with others.

Cultural workers such as Zoë Wicomb, Rayda Jacobs, Achmat Dangor, Yvette Christiänse and Chris van Wyk have done a lot of work since the end of apartheid to revise the historical script handed to coloured South Africans by showing the historical strands that are woven into contemporary performances of colouredness to be fraught with contradictions, silences and ambiguities. Wicomb's novel *David's Story*,[31] for instance, offers fresh perspectives on the difficulties of creating an accurate historical account of the processes whereby Griqua, Khoi and coloured identities were formed from the late 17th century through to the early 1990s, whereas Jacobs's *The Slave Book*, and Christiänse's *Unconfessed*[32] form part of an emergent post-apartheid body of literature that offers creative and critical revisions of South Africa's legacy of slavery at the Cape from 1652 to 1838.[33] Achmat Dangor's *Bitter Fruit*,[34] in turn, exposes some of the silences related to apartheid era gross human rights violations that were left unaddressed by the South African TRC, especially for those inhabiting colouredness as a social identity.

Whereas each of these texts can be read as taking part in an ideological project prioritised by the Black Consciousness Movement (BCM) already in the early 1970s – namely to challenge dominant colonial and apartheid versions of history through the dissemination of suppressed local histories – they do so from a post-apartheid perspective. Academic, political and popular interest recently expressed in indigenous Khoi histories, as well as in South Africa's slave past, has been facilitated by the freedoms brought by the onset of democracy, yet the explosion of writing on these topics also speaks to some of the anxieties about identity and belonging tabled for coloured South Africans by this transition.[35] Chris van Wyk's *Shirley, Goodness and Mercy* – another text that revises apartheid versions of history from a post-apartheid perspective – reveals some of the causes of these anxieties, since it exposes many of the ideological pressures of apartheid that continue to reverberate through contemporary performances of colouredness. The text also enables a rethinking of creolisation as a process of identity formation that takes place in contexts where the cultural codes governing behaviour are difficult to decipher.

Van Wyk's delightful autobiographical collection of stories centres on the gradual process of maturation whereby he learns to map out the boundaries of identity and difference in Riverlea, a township to the southwest of Johannesburg for people designated 'coloured' by the apartheid state. The text charts both the personal and political coming of age of an inquisitive young boy who struggles to sift through all the unwritten rules that regulate behaviour in apartheid South Africa. The retrospective narrative voice makes it clear from the outset that this is a story in which the personal and political are intimately intertwined. The narrative opens with an account of the political dramas unfolding in South Africa in 1961, when Van Wyk is four years old: the Sharpeville massacre, the banning of the ANC and PAC, and the incarceration of many political activists.[36] Even though the young Chris, for the moment, is unaware of this, the narrator makes it clear that even at this stage in the child's life, the social and political realities of apartheid inevitably press in on the private delights and disappointments that shape his burgeoning sense of self.

The interrelatedness of the personal and the political in the domestic spaces of apartheid is captured in a poem entitled 'The Road', introduced in the first chapter. The poem recounts the death of Van Wyk's younger sister Allister, who lives for only a few hours after she is born. The news of her death comes to him as it:

> does to all four-year-olds
> from the overhanging vines
> of the adults, through the eaves
> of the wise who suddenly
> are not so wise.

Upon receiving the news, his *ouma* (grandmother) wraps him in a blanket:

> as cold as the flag
> of a sad country,

and sets out on the road to his grieving mother. For his *ouma*, the poetic voice explains, this road, which is:

> cobbled with the dirges of beer cans
> tremulous with stones
> and filled with more people than children
> born to the world that day

grows gradually shorter, but for Van Wyk:

> staring over her shoulder,
> it grew longer and longer.[37]

As a prelude to the autobiographical journey that follows, the poem forcefully draws the reader into Van Wyk's travels through the social and political absurdities of apartheid South Africa. The moment of his sister's death marks the beginnings of his growing awareness of the difficulties that attach to discussions of national and cultural belonging for those relegated to the margins of this 'sad country'. Van Wyk's use of the term 'eaves' in the first stanza is particularly significant, since it anchors the trope of eavesdropping that runs through the rest of the text. The term 'eaves' denotes the lower edges of an overhang or roof that peers over the side of a wall, or, more broadly, an overhanging edge or a border of some sort. Since the young Chris is not made privy to the talk of grownups, he positions himself at the edges of their exchanges, where he snatches titbits of conversation and pieces them together into what he hopes are reliable versions of events. Throughout the narrative, Van Wyk's eavesdropping on people's conversations serves as a metaphor for the process whereby racial and cultural identities might be forged through the assemblage of snippets of information and stories from the radio, from school, from family and friends – from a person's cultural and social worlds. By devising a set of rules to facilitate successful eavesdropping on grownup conversation, the narrator–protagonist manages not only to accumulate the juiciest gossip on offer in his community, but also to decipher, and later to challenge, the myths whereby white identities are constructed as more worthy than any of South Africa's other racialised identities. These rules are:

1. Don't sit quiet as a mouse. If you can hear them out there in the lounge, they can hear you here in the kitchen. And if you're quiet they know you're listening. Make busy noises like drinking a glass of water, singing bits of pop songs, calling the dog outside. But don't overdo it.

2. Do something while you're listening. Read a book or do some homework. If they come into the kitchen to switch on the kettle or something, they see a boy struggling with maths and not just staring at a wall.

3. Be wary of jokes coming from the lounge. If someone in the lounge tells a joke, try not to laugh. They'll know you've been listening all along.

4. If Ma calls you, don't answer immediately. If you do it's a dead giveaway and means that you've had your ears tuned on them all the time.[38]

The art of eavesdropping, which serves as a trope for the process whereby South Africa's absurd rules for the performance of racial identities might be accessed, is clearly something to which the young Chris has devoted much thought and time. His success at eavesdropping in Riverlea also speaks to the realities of cramped township living – '[i]t's hard to keep secrets in a Riverlea sub-economic matchbox'. For the young Chris, listening in on the conversations of others functions as the only way in which to decode his political positioning in South Africa, since there are two things the Van Wyks never talk about in their home; 'sex and where babies come from, and why white people and Coloured people and African people and Indian people live in different places'. Chris frequently laments his parents' failure to educate him on the political realities of the day: his dad, he suggests, sends him and his five siblings 'out into a racist world without any preparation. But [his] family is not unique in this regard. The whole of Riverlea goes about in this happy or unhappy state of amnesia'.[39]

In the absence of any active political engagement and instruction beyond the 'odd, bitter remark about white bosses and white people in general' in the coloured community of Riverlea, Van Wyk learns by 'picking up all kinds of information in the streets' and on the radio, from which he 'begin[s] to understand that, according to the law, [he is] not as good as a white person'. Discourses that construct white privilege as both normative and deserved permeate the programmes on Springbok Radio that people in Riverlea listen to. 'Radio,' the narrator explains, 'is definitely a white-people-only thing. White people have phones and so they can phone in and win prizes. We listen to the radio, but like eavesdroppers, listening to white people talk and laugh and cry and win prizes and stuff like that.' Van Wyk's location within South African discourses of racialisation is clearly reliant on narratives of white superiority in relation to which he internalises feelings of coloured self-doubt and resentment. The eavesdropper always has to hide in the wings, and is continually at risk of being exposed and shamed.[40]

Zoë Wicomb accurately identifies the feelings of shame that haunt coloured identity as tied to the historical mythologising of racial mixture as a product of degeneracy and coloured female concupiscence,[41] yet Van Wyk's embarrassment about his family can be tied to much more immediate, practical concerns related to white privilege in apartheid South Africa. When offered the opportunity to be tutored by a white female student from the University of the Witwatersrand, for instance, he declines because of his feelings of inadequacy about his family's poverty. The Van Wyk household, he explains, usually runs out of toilet paper by the middle of the week, when sheets cut up from used copies of *The Star* have to serve as a substitute. Van Wyk cannot bear letting a white woman witness this: 'There's no way I'm going to let a pretty white lady from some larney suburb, used to a lifestyle of two-ply Kleenex, come and use our loo'. Whereas his friend Keith, whose family is no more well-off than the Van Wyks, seems not to labour under such apprehensions, Chris's thoughts are consumed with what he calls 'stupid things': 'I'm scared of this, worried about that, embarrassed about most things, especially white people.'[42]

In the socially hierarchical contexts in which creolisation takes place, as Erna Brodber reminds us, 'it is important for social and psychological peace that one know one's place'.[43] Yet it is precisely because it is so difficult to figure out what exactly this 'place' might be that creolisation is such a psychologically unsettling process, she suggests. In the South African context, the social and psychological peace of which Brodber writes is elusive especially for those, like Chris, who try to make sense of South Africa's absurd racial hierarchies and are left feeling 'confused about being Coloured'.[44] Van Wyk attempts to allay these feelings of discomfort and confusion, motivated by considerations of both class and race, in the only way he knows how – by keeping his eyes and ears open: '... when my granny talks to a white man in the bookshop, I check him out from top to bottom to see what it is that makes him better than me. I listen to [white people] carefully on the radio, taking note of what makes them laugh or sing out loud'. He notices that his granny 'put[s] on her musical voice' when addressing the white shopkeeper, and the young Chris mimics her by bidding the white man 'good afternoon' instead of 'goodbye' because 'it sounds posh'.[45] The subjective alterations that Chris and his *ouma* make for the benefit of the white man draw attention to identity as performance, and to the extent to which South Africa's racial hierarchies require subjective shifts relative to the power dynamics at play in the intercultural encounter. The subjectivities that are staged in *Shirley, Goodness and Mercy* are shown to be incomplete and to require adjustment according to context. Yet do these shifts necessarily produce creolised formations of identity? Creolisation, writes Françoise Vergès:

> ... is not about harmony and conformity but about adjustment, accommodation, arrangements, recognition of differences. Creole cultures are not about the mechanics of mixing – the literal analogy of 2 + 2 is not useful. Creolisation is about a *bricolage* drawing freely [sic] upon what is available, recreating with new content and in new forms a distinctive culture, a creation in a situation of *domination and conflict*.[46]

Creolisation, in other words, can be understood both in terms of transformations of group identity and in terms of the small-scale everyday decisions that people have to make to accommodate the demands of cultural difference, power imbalances and inequalities. The act of eavesdropping serves as a fitting metaphor for the creolisation process, for it requires a person to listen attentively, to learn, unlearn, resist and negotiate the information gleaned from overheard exchanges, and to shape this knowledge into performances of identity that range from being self-directed to being coerced. The eavesdropper is necessarily subjected to a set of social norms that constrain his or her agency. Yet the creolisation process, as defined by Vergès, also entails an interruption of these social norms; as Judith Butler puts it in a different context, such norms 'cannot continue to enforce themselves without a continual action. It is in the thinking through of this action that change can happen, since we are acting all the time in the ways that we enact, repeat, appropriate and refuse the norms that decide our social ontology'.[47] For the growing Van Wyk, the *bricolage* of which Vergès writes involves both the processes whereby his own identity is moulded in the context of racial and cultural domination and conflict, and the manner in which he manages to creatively resist such subjective constraints.

It is worth noting, furthermore, that the subjective shifts that Chris makes through the course of the text play out on the larger stage of coloured group self-imaging, which the autobiographical narrative voice chronicles through the early apartheid years to the present. The pressures that shape racial and cultural identification for Van Wyk interestingly shift in accordance with the changes that national and struggle politics undergo throughout the 1970s, 1980s and 1990s. These shifts can be recognised in the different ways in which he tries to make sense of coloured identity as positioned midway between white and black in the racial hierarchy. The manner in which he negotiates this positioning works to a number of ends in the text. As a child, he on occasion finds himself unable to resist drawing on the racist ideology that circulates freely in Riverlea. He even admits to participating in racist name-calling as a young boy, when, for instance, he attempts to deflect taunts from a friend about his squint by calling the boy a 'kaffir'.[48] Van Wyk is clearly at pains to acknowledge coloured complicity in the racist othering of black South Africans. Yet he also demonstrates that the coloured community of Riverlea is anything but uniform in their support for discourses of intra-black racism. Van Wyk's friend Alan Walburgh and his family, for instance, have a take on intra-black distinctions and apartheid politics that differs markedly from the views espoused by Chris's parents. For example, Alan scoffs at the Van Wyk siblings for calling their African domestic worker 'Auntie', and preaches to Van Wyk about how much prime minister Verwoerd 'has done for Coloured people'. Chris's dad, in contrast, in his characteristically brusque manner, calls Verwoerd 'an idiot'. His mother, in turn, is incensed when hearing about the Walburghs's attitude to Verwoerd, saying: 'Look here. Those white hoboes that you see in the streets, they can vote but we can't. So fuck the Walburghs and fuck Verwoerd.'[49]

Through a series of similar encounters, Van Wyk cultivates a growing irritation with the indignities that the apartheid system imposes on people racialised as coloured and African. He begins to recognise that expressions of intra-black racism among his peers are closely tied to the psychological divisions that pervade coloured self-imagining. These divisions are spawned in large measure by discourses of racialisation within which human worth is measured in terms of arbitrary somatic markers, and people are judged according to their perceived physical and, by implication, moral proximity to whiteness. These judgements find expression in overheard statements cited by the narrator as examples of the absurdity of racist constructions of coloured embodiment: 'He's dark-skinned but quite handsome'; 'She hasn't got straight hair but she's quite pretty. Actually her hair isn't that bad, it's sort of on the straight side'; 'They're getting married, but he's dark and she's dark so imagine what their children are going to look like'.[50] The pervasiveness of such views within coloured communities during the apartheid era demonstrate that processes of cultural creolisation rarely produce progressive readings of cultural and racial positioning. The cultural inequalities that permeate colonial and apartheid discourse instead tend to filter into day-to-day interpersonal interactions, where processes of creolisation produce interpretations of identity and of bodily markers along hierarchical lines.

Van Wyk registers his growing alienation from such expressions of racial self-loathing and finds himself drawn to the BCM which he accesses through an interest in poetry and writing. His discovery of Oswald Mtshali's poetry in the mid-1970s, for instance, serves as a watershed in his political awakening. Listening to his teacher read from *Sounds of a Cowhide Drum*, he realises that until that moment he had not 'even know[n] one could write a poem about being black'. From this moment on, he takes an active role in the struggle against the knowledge systems of apartheid, and swiftly internalises Black Consciousness ideology in his poetry. As a self-proclaimed member of the '1976 generation of poets', Van Wyk composes poems that are 'filled with, if not a hatred, then at least a sharp loathing for white people'. His writing 'is brash and full of black consciousness pride'.[51]

During his late teens and early twenties, Van Wyk finds in Black Consciousness ideology a refuge from the alienating contradictions and confusions that plague common-sense assumptions about race in Riverlea. In 1980 Van Wyk is appointed as the editor of *Staffrider*, the Black Consciousness-inspired South African literary journal first published in 1978. It functioned, at the time, as an important platform from which Black Consciousness writers such as Mtutuzeli Matshoba, Miriam Tlali, Njabulo Ndebele and Joël Matlou could voice resistance to white dominance. By refusing to acknowledge the terms within which apartheid attempted to fix race, the BCM of the 1970s and 1980s did important work to expose the slipperiness and arbitrariness of racial signification. For Van Wyk, the Movement opened up avenues of interracial identification within which performances of colouredness – subsumed under the heading 'blackness' – could be staged as resistance to apartheid. The oppositional vocabularies forged by the BCM during these years broadened the identity narratives available to coloured South Africans by foregrounding intra-black connections. Yet despite its crucial revision of interpersonal relations, Black Consciousness ideology did not always accommodate all oppressed groups equally. Heribert Adam and Kogila Moodley point out that the BCM secured a greater following from coloured than from Indian activists, in part because many of the Indian supporters of the movement felt 'rejected as insufficiently black enough'[52] and resisted pressures to cast aside their cultural heritage and replace it with African symbols.[53] Even coloured activists did not always find easy access into the BCM since, as Zimitri Erasmus argues, it 'tended towards a universal and single notion of being black which privileged black African experiences (narrowly defined) and papered over racial hierarchies and differential racialisation among racially oppressed South Africans'.[54] The BCM's emphasis on black unity failed to account for the psychological effects of the apartheid state's construction of an intra-black hierarchy. A similar argument could be made in relation to the production of discourses of non-racialism by the United Democratic Front (UDF) in the 1980s.

That the search for a workable identity continues to be a troubled one in the post-apartheid era is evident in Van Wyk's refusal to present a vision of coloured identity as unified, clearly demarcated and complete. Van Wyk's account of the centrality of Black Consciousness ideology to the production of coloured subjectivity during the 1970s and 1980s offers important insights into the social and political conditions that yielded the view, to quote Richard Rive, that '"Coloured" is offensive in the South African context because it has hierarchic implications – inferior to Whites and superior to Blacks'.[55] Van Wyk explains the position he and fellow activists adopted during these years: 'We are black, not carbon copies of white people. We reject the term "non-white"; when we are forced, for whatever reason, to use the term "Coloured" we make two little double quotes in the air.'[56] Yet his autobiographical reflection on these ideological imperatives is situated firmly in the post-apartheid moment, when many of the certainties of the anti-apartheid struggle have given way to more nuanced and open articulations of racial and cultural identification. Van Wyk's memoir indicates that neither dominant nor resistant identity narratives offer lasting certainties about the ideological and cultural allegiances that might produce convincing performances of colouredness in the post-apartheid era.

That these certainties have shifted is evident, for instance, in the story that Van Wyk tells of his encounters with Mr Lawrence, the principal of the primary school he attended. Van Wyk's animosity towards Mr Lawrence, who is described in the most unflattering of terms, stems in part from the man's refusal to take a stand against Mr Kelly, an uncommonly sadistic teacher who gave the 12-year-old Chris 100 lashes on the buttocks for some minor infringement. Instead of dismissing the teacher on grounds of child abuse, a disinterested Mr Lawrence left it up to the boy's father to talk to the teacher. Years later, after Van Wyk has confronted an unrepentant Mr Kelly about his abusive behaviour, he runs into Mr Lawrence again. To his surprise, Mr Lawrence, who 'is still distant, aloof, like the white person he wishes he was', is aware that Van Wyk has become a writer. Lawrence comments disparagingly: 'I see you're concentrating on the blacks in your writing. Why don't you write about your own people, the Coloured people?'. The narrator addresses Mr Lawrence's question with words which serve as a defiant conclusion to the harrowing tale of Mr Kelly's cruelty: 'Well, here it is, Mr Lawrence, and I hope you like it.'[57]

The representational complexities signalled by this statement are indicative of the difficulties inherent in an autobiographical memory project that tries to reconstruct, from a post-apartheid perspective, a collective identity labelled 'coloured'. Van Wyk occupies the position of story collector in his community, since to tell his own story he has had to tell the reader 'about [his] family, friends, the people of Riverlea'. After the onset of democracy, Van Wyk decides to stay in the township of Riverlea, unlike many of his friends for whom the 'leafy, formerly white suburbs beckon with undue haste'. He decides to stay because there remain many stories in Riverlea that need to be told, 'stories that are part of our history and which apartheid had made us believe should never be told.... But now these people are telling these stories. And they're telling them to me'. No longer the apprenticing eavesdropper, Van Wyk now legitimately listens in on and records the life stories of his community. But this is no uncomplicated, romanticised act of representation. As with the story of Mr Kelly and Mr Lawrence, Van Wyk does not shy away from foregrounding the contradictions and confusions that continue to plague attempts at articulating coloured identities in Riverlea. In this context, political apathy and various acts of racial othering still seem to be the most fashionable approach to handling the crushing realities of poverty, unemployment and crime endemic to township living.[58]

Van Wyk's identity is no longer demarcated in the clear activist terms that informed claims to blackness during the years in which Black Consciousness ideology, and later UDF-inspired non-racialism, dominated self-representation among coloured activists and intellectuals. Nor is the autobiographical voice now claiming a position uncomplicatedly marked 'coloured'. The transition to democracy, as Pumla Gqola states, 'has allowed for a revisiting of identities, or has enabled more sublimated tendencies to surface. For Black people this has meant the opening up of Coloured subjectivity to a new kind of questioning, and the reviewing of what identifying as coloured can mean'.[59] For Van Wyk, this process of revision enables a newly honest reflection on the racism coloured activists encountered among black comrades during the apartheid years. At an informal gathering of activists in the late 1970s, for instance, Fikile, a black acquaintance, rejects Van Wyk and his Indian friend, Benjy, because they are 'not black enough. Coloureds and Indians, he says, are not black'.[60] These post-apartheid recollections also facilitate a rethinking of the difficult questions around the excavation of racial and cultural roots in a country in which claims to historically indigenous identities are made for reasons that are not always progressive.

The project of excavation that Van Wyk undertakes is openly reflexive about the difficulties of accessing a past obscured by colonial and apartheid historiography. In line with the overall tone of the memoir, Van Wyk tackles this problem through humour, as when he juxtaposes historical records on the Khoikhoi with a description of a personality trait of his cantankerous grandfather Frank: 'One day I open up a book and I read about the Khoikhoi. These ancestors of ours spoke a clicking language. Well Grandpa Frank clicked his tongue at me often enough, I'll tell you that'.[61] Far from romanticising these roots, Van Wyk points to the losses, uncertainties and silences that have to be navigated by those who, in post-apartheid South Africa, are at liberty to push against the historically and socially policed boundaries of colouredness. That the identities and histories that Van Wyk attempts to reconstruct and remember are troubled centrally by loss reinforces Françoise Vergès's point that creolisation 'is not about retentions but about reinterpretations. It is not about roots but about loss'.[62]

Van Wyk further complicates the process of historical revision by questioning the assumption that claims to white ancestry necessarily work to reactionary ends. Upon seeing a picture of his white great-grandfather in his *ouma's* photo album, Van Wyk was aggravated:

> This is not good news. I am black. I write black poetry. I am a follower of the black consciousness philosophy of Steve Biko. And here's a white guy in the family messing up my past and

my future. For God's sake, white people are the enemy, I don't want the enemy in my family. Shit![63]

Of significance here is not so much the Black Consciousness position that the young Van Wyk articulates, but that the story is told from the post-apartheid perspective of the autobiographer amused by the inexperience of a younger self. This ironic passage indicates that the complicated cultural and racial disavowals spawned by the ideological absolutes of apartheid are now open to reflection, and that the uncertainties that produced these disavowals might now be openly discussed.

Conclusion

Van Wyk's memoir, while attentive to the violent inequalities produced by the apartheid state, and to the ongoing repercussions of this history for people trying to shape their identities in a post-apartheid South Africa, can nonetheless be read as a celebration of life and laughter amidst these troubling realities. There are, however, many contemporary processes of creolisation in South Africa that entail the production of subjectivity in contexts of much more extreme violence and inequality than those of which the relatively privileged Van Wyk writes. These processes are reflected in many of the cultural texts that explore the subjective transformations that people have to make in contexts of violent inequality. These texts include the writings of K Sello Duiker, Phaswane Mpe and Zakes Mda.[64] Each of these writers explores in detail the demands for continual self-invention that poverty and cultural exchanges make on those who occupy the edges of the contemporary South African city, where, to quote AbdouMaliq Simone, '[m]aking lives from the provisional is an essentially unstable process, and such instability can produce enormous creative change, but also devolve into spreading violence'.[65]

Nonetheless, the preceding analysis of Van Wyk's *Shirley, Goodness and Mercy* does reveal some of the ways in which the identities of those who either self-identify or resist being labelled as 'coloured' might be theorised as undergoing creolisation. The feelings of embarrassment, uncertainty and confusion that trouble the young Chris as he tries to map out the parameters of 'colouredness' in Riverlea are indicative of a process of creolisation that necessarily 'entails inequality [and] hierarchization' for those situated at the crossroads of different cultural and racial formations.[66] While creolisation is usually theorised in generalising terms as a process of cultural intermixture that produces new cultural identities on a grand scale,[67] it is important not to lose sight of the small-scale psychological struggles that people face as they try to construct socially accepted identities for themselves. This is a struggle that the young Chris faces daily as he attempts to negotiate the confusions that South African constructions of racial inbetweenness bring. His feelings of discomfort and cultural alienation can be read as partly informing his decision to embrace Black Consciousness ideology in the 1970s and 1980s. Yet the retrospective autobiographical narrator strains to find a comfortable fit for his younger self even in this site of identification. Also, that Van Wyk offers no clear guidelines on how colouredness might be inhabited in post-apartheid South Africa speaks to its ongoing open-endedness and mutability. The post-apartheid perspective that the text offers on the historical identity alterations that someone like Chris has had to make reinforces Zimitri Erasmus's point that 'what is distinctive about Coloured identity is the condition of its making and re-making'[68] – something that she reads as central to the creolisation process.

Why then, to sum up, do the vocabularies of creolisation theory lend themselves so readily to analyses of coloured identity formation in South Africa? What is it about South African expressions of colouredness that inspire academics to gravitate towards theories of cultural creolisation such as those developed in the Caribbean by writers such as Wilson Harris, Stuart Hall, Erna Brodber, Edouard Glissant, Jean Bernabé, Patrick Chamoiseau, and Raphäel Confiant?

These are questions that can be fruitfully addressed in the contemporary political and cultural climate in South Africa, where scholars are beginning to recognise the importance of trying to understand why essentialist racial categories continue to circulate in the ways that they do. Sarah Nuttall's warning about the pitfalls of conceptualising coloured identity in terms of creolisation if this process is read in biological terms is an important one. She suggests that one of the reasons why some critics have been hesitant to enter into debates about South African processes of creolisation is that they have assumed that '"creolisation" is tantamount to "Colouredness" as a biological and cultural construct'. Contributing to this assumption, presumably, has been 'the apartheid state's construction of Colouredness as a political buffer between blacks and whites, and the interpellation of "Colouredness" as neither black nor white (according to an ideology of racial purity)'.[69] This warning does nonetheless not negate the fact that many who either self-identify as coloured, or who are trying to resist such racial or cultural labelling, continue to struggle with anxieties about racial inbetweenness which are often articulated in the popular imagination in essentialist terms. While it is necessary to challenge conceptualisations of race as biologically determined, and while creolisation theories have been relatively successfully re-articulated in counter-essentialist terms, it is nonetheless crucial to pay attention to the continued cultural and affective currency of the racial markers inherited from colonial and apartheid South Africa in people's day-to-day lives. The feelings of cultural confusion that the young Chris learns to navigate, and the difficulties that the older Chris faces when trying to find a stable 'coloured' identity to inhabit in post-apartheid South Africa, can be read in part as a corollary of the continued cultural circulation of deeply problematic discourses of racial inbetweenness in South Africa. The impact that these ideas have on people's sense of self is perhaps no less forceful in post-apartheid South Africa than during the apartheid era, particularly in the context of political discourses that construct coloured South Africans as 'not black enough' in the new dispensation.[70] While it is important to recognise that creolisation is a cultural process that 'no people has been spared',[71] the particular salience that South Africa's racial vocabularies have in everyday understandings of colouredness centrally inflect how processes of creolisation unfold in this context. And while, as Zimitri Erasmus argues, the term 'creolisation' is useful for enabling a re-articulation of coloured identity in cultural as opposed to racial terms, it must be remembered that processes of cultural formation in South Africa continue to be informed by reactionary assumptions about race.

Caribbean theories of creolisation can shed light on processes of coloured identity formation in South Africa, one might argue, precisely because the terms 'creole' and 'creolisation' have historically functioned as markers of cultural as well as racial identities. The complex imbrication of these two theories of identity – the one progressive, the other reactionary – has been central to the ways in which processes of creolisation have been theorised in the Caribbean, which explains in part why these theories fit so well in the South African context.

Endnotes

1 Van Wyk C. 2004. *Shirley, Goodness and Mercy*. Johannesburg: Picador Africa, 324.

2 Throughout this chapter, I use the term 'coloured' to refer to either self-identified members of, or ones previously legislated as belonging to, this group. It is used with full awareness that many who were classified as 'coloured' under apartheid actively resisted this racial nomenclature, and refused to self-identify as such. The term 'coloured' is acknowledged, in other words, as insufficient as a referent for the

myriad and complexly articulated identities that were both impacted by, and resistant to, its legislative and discursive reach. This chapter reads Van Wyk's novel *Shirley, Goodness and Mercy* with the aim precisely of understanding some of the multifaceted ways in which the marker 'coloured' invites both identification and dis-identification. Terms such as 'colouredness', 'coloured identity' or 'coloured community' should thus be read throughout this chapter as contested and provisional.

3   The term 'performance' is used in this chapter in an effort to contest the idea that a person's identity is shaped first and foremost by a fixed stable 'essence' from which the world is experienced. Identity is read, instead, as socially and historically constituted, and as something that comes into being in and through performance – that is, through the ways in which people live out or enact social norms. Identities, in other words, are assumed to be formed through the various ways in which people, through their daily choices, either affirm or challenge the socially and historically circumscribed cultural codes that regulate behaviour in society. The idea that identity comes into being through performative acts was first formulated by Butler J. 1990. *Gender Trouble: Feminism and the Subversion of Identity*. New York & London: Routledge. For an analysis of racial identities in South Africa as 'performed,' see Distiller N & Steyn M. 2004. 'Introduction', in *Under Construction: 'Race' and Identity in South Africa Today*, eds N Distiller & M Steyn. Sandton: Heinemann, 1–11. Coloured identities are read as performatively enacted in an attempt to undermine apartheid constructions of racial identity as unchanging and biologically determined.

4   The term 'subjectivity', which often functions as a synonym for the term 'identity', is used in this chapter because it signals the myriad ways in which identities are socially embedded and constructed. As Donald Hall puts it, the term 'subjectivity', which is 'often used interchangeably with the term "identity", […] more accurately denotes our social constructs and consciousness of identity. We commonly speak of identity as a flat, one-dimensional concept, but subjectivity is much broader and more multifaceted' (134). See Hall D. 2004. *Subjectivity*. New York: Routledge.

5   For an analysis of some of the pitfalls of the post-apartheid rhetoric of 'rainbowism,' see, for instance, Gqola P. 2001. 'Defining people: analysing power, language and representation in metaphors of the new South Africa'. *Transformation* 47, 94–106.

6   Since former president Thabo Mbeki introduced it in a speech in 1997, the phrase 'African Renaissance' has spawned a considerable number of analyses and debates that consider its critical potential and drawbacks. See, for instance, Distiller N. 2004. 'English and the African Renaissance'. *English Studies in Africa,* 47, no. 2, 109–124; Lodge T. 2003. *Politics in South Africa from Mandela to Mbeki.* Bloomington & Indianapolis: Indiana University Press, 227–240; Ahluwalia P. 2003. 'The struggle for African identity: Thabo Mbeki's African Renaissance', in *Media, Identity and the Public Sphere in Post-Apartheid South Africa*, eds A Zegeye & R Harris. Leiden & Boston: Brill, 27–39; and Strauss H. 2006. 'Hesitating at the intersection: trans-cultural encounters in the post-1994 South African literary and cultural imagination'. PhD dissertation, University of Western Ontario, 39–51.

7   This debate continues in scholarly publications and fora. The most accessible is the *SA Reconciliation Barometer*, published by the Institute for Justice and Reconciliation at <http://www.ijr.org.za/publications/publ/index_html>.

8   Refer to Strauss, 'Hesitating at the intersection', 58–66 for further details.

9   See Strauss H. 2004. 'Living the pain of creolisation: shifting context of subject formation in K. Sello Duiker's *Thirteen Cents* and Lueen Conning's *A Coloured Place*', in Distiller & Steyn, *Under Construction*, 26–37.

10 Boehmer E. 2003. 'Off-white: creolite and hidden "difference" under apartheid'. *Kunapipi*, 25, no. 1, 54–64.

11 Shell R C H. 1994. *Children of Bondage: A Social History of the Slave Society at the Cape of Good Hope, 1652–1838*. Hanover & London: University Press of New England, 40–65.

12 Hannerz U. 1996. *Transnational Connections: Culture, People, Places*. London & New York: Routledge, 160–171.

13 Nuttall S & Michael C. 2000. 'Introduction', in *Senses of Culture*, eds S Nuttall & C Michael. Oxford: Oxford University Press, 1–23.

14 See Strauss, 'Living the pain' for an analysis of the questions raised by some South African cultural critics after Nuttall and Michael introduced the term 'creolisation' into discussions of new cultural formations in South Africa.

15 See, for instance, Wasserman H & Jacobs S. 2003. 'Introduction', in *Shifting Selves: Post-Apartheid Essays on Mass Media, Culture and Identity*, eds H Wasserman & S Jacobs. Cape Town: Kwela, 15–28; and Hlongwane G. 2002. 'What has modernity to do with it?: camouflaging race in the "new" South Africa'. *Journal of Literary Studies*, 18, no. 1/2, 111–131.

16 Dieltens V. 2005. 'Learning anew: truth and reconciliation in education'. *Race and Citizenship Series: 2005*. Centre for the Study of Violence and Reconciliation, 27 August, <http://www.csvr.org.za/papers/paprctp6.htm>.

17 See, for instance, Valji N. 2004. 'Race and reconciliation in a post-TRC South Africa'. Ten Years of Democracy in Southern Africa Conference, Queen's University, Kingston. 2–5 May.

18 This surprising gap in research is pointed to, for instance, by Taylor R & Foster D. 1999. 'Advancing non-racialism in post-apartheid South Africa', in *National Identity and Democracy in Africa*, ed M Palmberg. Pretoria: Human Sciences Research Council of South Africa, Mayibuye Centre at the University of the Western Cape & Nordic Africa Institute, 328–341; Posel D, Hyslop J & Nieftagodien N. 2001. 'Debating "race" in South African scholarship'. *Transformation*, 47, i–xviii; and Distiller & Steyn, 'Introduction'.

19 Erasmus Z. 2001. 'Introduction', in *Coloured by History, Shaped by Place: New Perspectives on Coloured Identities in Cape Town*, ed Z Erasmus. Cape Town: Kwela, 13–28.

20 Erasmus, 'Introduction', 14.

21 Hall S. 2003. 'Créolité and the process of creolisation', in *Créolité and Creolisation: Documenta11_Platform3*, eds O Enwezor, C Basualdo, U Bauer, S Ghez, S Maharaj, M Nash & O Zaya. Ostfildern-Ruit: Hantje Cantz, 30.

22 Hall, 'Créolité', 31.

23 Bernabé J, Chamoiseau P & Confiant R. 1990. 'In praise of creoleness'. Trans. Mohamed B Taleb Khyar, *Callaloo*, 13, 886–909.

24 See, for instance, Harris W. 1999. 'Creoleness: the crossroads of civilization?' in *Selected Essays of Wilson Harris: The Unfinished Genesis of the Imagination*, ed A J M Bundy. London & New York: Routledge, 237–247; and Benítez-Rojo A. 1992. *The Repeating Island: The Caribbean and the Postmodern Perspective*. Durham: Duke

University Press.

25 Hall, 'Créolité', 31.

26 Citizenship is understood here as referring to more than simply a set of legal rights and responsibilities, including the right to vote and the right to call on the state to provide certain services. In the words of Cheryl McEwan, citizenship also 'confers belonging and embeds the notion of recognizing individuals' social standing and historical agency'. See McEwan C. 2003. 'Building a postcolonial archive? Gender, collective memory and citizenship in post-apartheid South Africa'. *Journal of Southern African Studies*, 29, no. 3, 739–775, 741.

27 Brodber E. 1998. 'Where are all the others?', in *Caribbean Creolisation: Reflections on the Cultural Dynamics of Language, Literature, and Identity*, eds K M Balutansky & M A Sourieau. Gainesville: University Press of Florida, 53–61.

28 I borrow this phrase from Zimitri Erasmus, who uses it to refer to 'the various ways in which different black people have been and continue to be racialised. This conceptualisation is based on an understanding of racisms and racialisation as processes which are not uniform and immutable. Racisms and racialised identities are formed in the context of, and so shaped by, very specific relations of social power'. Erasmus, 'Introduction', 27.

29 See Strauss 'Living the pain' and 'Hesitating at the intersection', 85.

30 See, for instance, Adhikari M. 2005. *Not White Enough, Not Black Enough: Racial Identity in the South African Coloured Community*. Athens: Ohio University Press, 162–187; Gqola P. 2003. 'Shackled memories and elusive discourses? Colonial slavery and the contemporary cultural and artistic imagination in South Africa'. PhD dissertation, Ludwig-Maximilians-Universität München, 205.

31 Wicomb Z. 2000. *David's Story*. Roggebaai: Kwela.

32 Jacobs R. 1998. *The Slave Book*. Cape Town: Kwela; Christiansë Y. 2006. *Unconfessed*. New York: Other Press.

33 For more detail on slavery at the Cape during these years, see, for instance, Shell R. 1994. *Children of Bondage*; Ross R. 1983. *Cape of Torments: Slavery and Resistance in South Africa*. London: Kegan Paul; Loos J. 2004. *Echoes of Slavery: Voices from South Africa's Past*. Cape Town: David Philip; and Gqola, 'Shackled memories'.

34 Dangor A. 2001. *Bitter Fruit*. Cape Town: Kwela.

35 In his analysis of the ways in which coloured self-definition has been shifting since the onset of democracy, Mohamed Adhikari lists a number of newfound sites of identification around which politicians, intellectuals and activists have been trying to organise coloured opinion since 1994. These processes of identification, which work to a diversity of ends, include the privileging of a shared slave past, the re-invigoration of indigenous Khoisan identities, as well as an identification with continental Africa and all that it stands for. Adhikari, *Not White Enough*, 178. Scholars such as Gabeba Baderoon, Shamil Jeppie and Pumla Gqola have identified similar shifts in identification related to slave memory and to renewed articulations of diasporic Malay identity at the Cape. See, for instance, Jeppie S. 2001. 'Re-classifications: coloured, Malay, Muslim', in Erasmus, *Coloured by History* 80–96; Baderoon G. 2002. 'Everybody's mother was a good cook: meanings of food in Muslim cooking', *Agenda*, 51, 4–15; and Gqola, 'Shackled memories'.

36 Van Wyk, *Shirley*, 1.

37 Van Wyk, *Shirley*, 10.

38 Van Wyk, *Shirley*, 160.
39 Van Wyk, *Shirley*, 112, 156, 197.
40 Van Wyk, *Shirley*, 22, 111, 197.
41 Wicomb Z. 1998. 'Shame and identity: the case of the coloured in South Africa', in *Writing South Africa: Literature, Apartheid, and Democracy 1970–1995*, eds D. Attridge & R. Jolly. New York: Cambridge University Press, 91–107.
42 Van Wyk, *Shirley*, 110, 111.
43 Brodber, 'Where are all the others?', 73.
44 Van Wyk, *Shirley*, 110, 111, 324.
45 Van Wyk, *Shirley*, 111, 72.
46 Vergès F. 2003. 'Kiltir kreol: processes and practices of créolité and creolisation', in Enwezor et al, *Créolité* 184. Emphasis in original. As indicated elsewhere in this chapter, processes of creolisation do not draw 'freely' on available cultural resources, but are always in some way constrained.
47 Reddy V. 2004. 'Troubling genders, subverting identities: interview with Judith Butler'. *Agenda*, 6, 115–123, 117. For more on the process of subjection whereby identities are constrained into iterating social norms, as well as on the possibilities for a kind of constrained agency that opens up within this process of iteration, see Butler J. 1997. *The Psychic Life of Power: Theories in Subjection*. Stanford: Stanford University Press.
48 Van Wyk, *Shirley*, 183.
49 Van Wyk, *Shirley*, 90–92.
50 Van Wyk, *Shirley*, 249.
51 Van Wyk, *Shirley*, 230, 239, 254. 1976 was the year of the student-led Soweto uprising.
52 Adam H & Moodley K. 1993. *The Opening of the Apartheid Mind: Options for the New South Africa*. Berkeley, Los Angeles & London: University of California Press, 107.
53 See also Desai A & Maharaj B. 1996. 'Minorities in the Rainbow Nation: the Indian vote in 1994'. *South African Journal of Sociology*, 27, no. 2, 118–125, on the formative role played by the anti-Indian sentiments of Inkatha, along with the hostility of the white minority, in strengthening a collective, resistant Indian identity during apartheid.
54 Erasmus, 'Introduction', 19.
55 Rive R. 1981. *Writing Black*. Cape Town: David Philip, 2. For an analysis of the shifting claims made on coloured subjectivity by, on the one hand, Black Consciousness (BC) ideology and on the other, the non-racial ethos that predominated after the formation of the United Democratic Front in 1983, see Adhikari's discussion of coloured rejectionism during these years, *Not White Enough*, 131–161. See also Zegeye A. 2001. 'General introduction: imposed ethnicity', in *Social Identities in the New South Africa – Volume One*, ed A Zegeye. Cape Town: Kwela, 10–11, for an analysis of the general shift in struggle politics away from BC ideology towards a greater focus on non-racial unity in opposition during the early 1980s.
56 Van Wyk, *Shirley*, 281.
57 Van Wyk, *Shirley*, 217.
58 Van Wyk, *Shirley*, 329.

59 Gqola, 'Shackled memories', 205. Gqola uses the term 'black' inclusively.

60 Van Wyk, *Shirley*, 266.

61 Van Wyk, *Shirley*, 278.

62 Vergès, 'Kiltir', 184.

63 Van Wyk, *Shirley*, 280.

64 See, for instance, Duiker K S. 2000. *Thirteen Cents*. Claremont: David Philip; and Duiker K S. 2001. *The Quiet Violence of Dreams*. Cape Town: Kwela; Mpe P. 2001. *Welcome to Our Hillbrow*. Pietermaritzburg: University of Natal Press; and Mda Z. 1997. *Ways of Dying*. Cape Town: Oxford University Press.

65 Simone A. 2005. 'Introduction: urban processes and change', in *Urban Africa: Changing Countours of Survival in the City*, eds A Simone & A Abouhani. Dakar: Codesria Books, 24.

66 Hall, 'Créolité', 31.

67 See, for instance, Ashcroft B, Griffith G & Tiffin H. 1998. *Key Concepts in Post-Colonial Studies*. London & New York: Routledge, 58–59.

68 Erasmus, 'Introduction', 22.

69 Nuttall S. 2004. 'City forms and writing the "now" in South Africa'. *Journal of Southern African Studies* 30, no. 4, 731–748.

70 See Adhikari, *Not White Enough*, 175–187.

71 Glissant E. 1999. *Caribbean Discourse: Selected Essays*, ed and trans. J M Dash. Charlottesville: University Press of Virginia, 140.

CHAPTER 3

Trauma and memory: the impact of apartheid-era forced removals on coloured identity in Cape Town

BY

HENRY TROTTER

YALE UNIVERSITY

Communities often cohere around memories of historical suffering. Black Americans look back to the atrocities of enslavement, Hutus to the injustices of pre-colonial Tutsi domination, and Afrikaners to the abuses of British imperialism. For coloured[1] South Africans, a people whose diverse ancestry experienced enslavement, dispossession, genocidal extermination and apartheid degradation the question of historical memory is fraught with difficulty. A striking aspect of coloured people's memory today is that, for the most part, they do not invest in a remote past. Some scholars have even implied that they suffer from historical amnesia.[2] Most coloured Capetonians instead focus upon a painful experience within living memory: the forced eviction of 150 000 coloured people from their natal homes and communities in the Cape Peninsula between 1957 and 1985 under the Group Areas Act.

Based on over 100 life history interviews with coloured forced removees, this chapter examines the impact of Group Areas evictions on contemporary coloured identity.[3] It suggests that, in the wake of mass social trauma, coloured removees coped with their pain by reminiscing with one another about the 'good old days' in their destroyed communities.

Their removal to racially defined townships ensured that they shared their memories almost exclusively with other coloured people, and only infrequently with Africans, Indians or whites. Apartheid social engineering determined the spatial limits within which coloured memories circulated, creating a reflexive, mutually reinforcing pattern of narrative traffic. Over the past four decades, the constant circulation of these nostalgic stories has developed a narrative community among coloured removees in the townships. This experience of popular sharing and support in the context of loss gives coloured identity in Cape Town a salience today that would be lacking if it were based solely on political or economic interests.

Measuring the 'resonance' of identity – its depth, power and relevance – involves understanding it beyond its explicit manifestations. Most studies of coloured identity deal with its overt characteristics, such as the apartheid state's categorisation of people as coloured, or of white society's external identification of people perceived as being of mixed racial descent as coloured, or of assimilated colonial blacks' self-identification as a middle-tier coloured group situated between 'Europeans' and 'Natives' after the mineral revolution.[4] These analyses are crucial for our understanding of coloured identity in its more explicit forms, but their focus on categorisation and identification do not cover the interior dimensions of the concept. They reveal little about the significance of coloured identity for the people who have identified or have been identified as such. They do not ascertain what commonalities they share, by what means they are connected, and what level of boundedness they feel as a racial community. Essentially, they do not probe coloured self-understanding. This chapter thus seeks out the tacit, dispositional, emotional and non-instrumental aspects of coloured identity that are negotiated and reinforced implicitly through the circulation of narratives. It also attempts to understand the relationship between these tacit understandings of self with more explicit and political identity claims.[5]

Group Areas

After coming to power in 1948, the National Party moved quickly to implement its vision of a segregated racial utopia. After passing the Population Registration Act of 1950, it sought to segregate the officially identified races. Because the status of the coloured category was ambiguous in terms of the binary racial logic of the time, the mechanics of their separation was up for debate.[6] According to Ian Goldin, after the Transvaal and Cape branches of the National Party argued the issue at length, officials decided that the western Cape would become a coloured labour preference area. The policy was designed to remove Africans from the region and to promote a stronger sense of colouredness by privileging coloureds economically, relative to Africans. And within urban areas, coloureds were to be relocated to racially homogeneous townships.[7]

Although the Group Areas Act was passed in 1950, forced removals did not begin in earnest in Cape Town until the late 1950s. Some of the smaller coloured neighbourhoods were summarily evacuated, as was generally the case with Africans, but the fate of most people was decided by the Group Areas Board (GAB), which claimed that it would determine the racial character of an area only after public consultation. Thus, before classifying an area 'white', 'coloured' or 'Indian', the Board held public hearings allowing people to voice their opinions. Though some whites supported Group Areas evictions, many people of all racial groups opposed the proposed removals at these hearings. Even the Cape Town City Council challenged them, stalling implementation when possible. Most residents argued that their neighbourhoods should stay just as they were. They rejected the government's rationales for removals, claiming that such extreme intervention was unnecessary. Their protests seem to have had no effect on the outcome of the hearings, though, as racial zoning followed a predictable pattern in which whites obtained the prime real estate near Table Mountain and the coasts, while coloureds, Africans and Indians were banished to racially homogeneous group areas on the periphery of the city.[8]

Before the implementation of the Group Areas Act, Cape Town was arguably the most racially integrated city in South Africa. People from different racial and ethnic backgrounds lived interspersed, shaping one another's lives.[9] This is not to say that they were haphazardly spread across the peninsula, or that residential areas did not have distinct racial characters. As Vivian Bickford-Smith shows, racialised space has been a normal part of Cape Town's life since at least the late 19th century.[10] The drastic measures taken to segregate the city illustrates how racially entangled its residential areas had been and how diverse the living conditions of its coloured community was before it was homogenised by racial zoning.

Coloureds responded in various ways to their eviction. In Sea Point and Rondebosch respectively, two coloured men committed suicide, preferring death to dispossession.[11] According to virtually every removee, many older people died just before or just after moving. Survivors blame this on the trauma of eviction. Leonard Levendal of Red Hill provides a typical example: 'You know, my father, he was blind, so when they moved him, chucked him out of Simonstown, they put him in the flats down here [in Ocean View]. It was about a year, he got a stroke, he died! Heartbroken!'[12] Most residents, especially homeowners, tried to find some means of staying in the area a bit longer, petitioning for an extension. Others left as soon as possible, hoping this would ensure a better choice of accommodation in the townships. A few fought their fate. Norma Solomons refused to move out of District Six, even after her home was bulldozed. She and her children moved from one 'broken palace' (evacuated house) to another as the bulldozers slowly ate away at the District. For years, they managed to stay in the area until there were no more broken palaces in which to squat.[13] Some were caught by surprise. Cecil McLean remembers returning from work one day in 1969 only to find that his family had been relocated to Manenberg, a distant township he had never heard of before.[14] Sadness pervaded these communities when they were notified that they would have to leave their homes. Everyone faced their hardship with great bitterness and resentment. Hopelessness and resignation overtook some, impotent rage others.[15]

Official and counter transcripts

The apartheid government justified Group Areas removals in a range of ways. Most importantly, it claimed that racial mixing bred conflict. Introducing the Group Areas Bill into parliament, the Minister of the Interior, T E Donges, confirmed that the policy was 'designed to eliminate friction between the races'.[16] Also, officials believed that most coloured people lived in overcrowded, unhygienic conditions that needed to be eliminated in accordance with the dictates of public health policy and principles of modern urban planning. Removals were seen as necessary for halting urban decay and were construed as philanthropic. Thus the chairman of the Group Areas Board enthused that, 'Truly, for the majority of people the advantage would be that they will be provided with better housing and living under much better hygienic circumstances.'[17] It was argued that this exercise in slum clearance would provide the coloured under-classes with a new start.[18] A consistent theme in government rationalisations was that criminal activity, which was seen as especially prevalent in coloured areas, would be curbed. Segregation rather than better policing was touted as the solution to crime. These justifications constitute the core of the official transcript for Group Areas evictions in the Cape Peninsula.

James Scott claims that elites generate a public transcript to justify their acts of domination. This transcript is composed of a series of rationalisations which explain how and why one social group deserves the power it exercises or desires.[19] While elites hope that subordinates will accept these rationalisations, the oppressed usually respond by developing a 'hidden transcript'. Instead of passively accepting the word of the elites, subordinates construct narratives that embody their real hopes and longings as well as a different understanding of their subjugated status. They question the foundations on which their domination is based and fantasise about a reversal of roles. Because they are in relationships of inequality with elites, who often hold a monopoly of coercive force, they face constraints on their capacity to reveal their opinions publicly. Thus the development of this vision from below takes place away from the surveillance of elite power in the relative safety of peer groups and like-minded discontents. Among themselves, subordinates construct and circulate oral transcripts that reject the degrading terms of their subjugation and attempt to salvage a sense of pride, dignity and self-worth despite their condition. In the company of their superiors, they may abide by the ritual conduct demanded by the public transcript and may even go so far as endorsing the virtues of the official transcript in the presence of elites. Scott argues that 'the public transcript of domination [is] ontologically prior to the hidden, backstage transcript'.[20] Elites create narratives while attempting to enforce their will, after which subordinates react by conjuring their own hidden transcript, which comprises 'the offstage responses and rejoinders to that public transcript'.[21] The public transcript has a structuring effect on the hidden transcript.

In Cape Town, coloured rejoinders to the public transcript were not completely hidden. Throughout the city they responded to the government's rationalisations for Group Areas removals with a counter transcript. They stated their arguments against segregation at Group Areas Board meetings, in newspaper articles, and when interviewed. They also developed these arguments away from the ear of power, in a hidden fashion, when commiserating with one another or discussing their plight. But, as Scott's theory suggests, coloureds responded on a one-for-one basis to the government's justifications with counterarguments of their own.

For example, many challenged the main justification of Group Areas removals by detailing how friendly their relations with people of other races were. One removee was reported in the *Cape Argus* as insisting that '[w]e have been very happy and secure living here among the Whites'[22] while another claimed that 'here we find the people who have learnt to live in peace and harmony as good neighbours. Racial and religious friction is virtually unknown'.[23] Coloured people often made the counterclaim that 'the application of the Group Areas Act over the years has created, rather than averted friction and resentment.'[24] Mrs Brown summed up the feelings of the District Six community when she told a reporter, 'We were like one family with no divisions between whites, Coloured people, Indians or African. But then the Group divided us all.'[25] Many individuals and groups presented their opinions to the Group Areas Board on the excellent race relations that existed in their communities.[26] In some instances they were supported by their white neighbours. In Lansdowne, whites and coloureds formed the Lansdowne Ratepayers' and Tenants' Society to protest the removal of coloureds. They petitioned the GAB, claiming, 'The application of the Group Areas Act in Lansdowne is seriously threatening to disrupt a stable, law-abiding community where white and Coloured families have lived in friendship and trust.'[27]

Many coloured people, particularly within the petty bourgeoisie, justifiably rejected the notion that they were living in slums. While they did not challenge the idea of urban renewal, they denied that their particular neighbourhoods were in need of such intervention. The Black River Ratepayers' and Residents' Association's submission to the GAB provides a good example:

> The residents in the area include people who … cleared the bush, drained the swamps, and eradicated the snakes, lizards and harmful insects, and have converted the area into a decent habitable one. The residents have invested their life savings in the construction of houses that met with the most stringent building regulations of the council of the City of Cape Town … [and] measure up to the most modern standards.[28]

Newspapers and GAB hearings show that residents also repudiated the notion that crime and gangsterism were significant problems in their neighbourhoods. The Black River Ratepayers' and Residents' Association asserted 'that the area has been singularly free of serious crime'.[29] Others stressed that crime was not a problem but that it would become one if the government went ahead with its removal plan.[30] Nasima Ebrahim, who was forced out of District Six, claimed in a newspaper article that '[t]here were no knife-wielding or undesirable elements to take the joy out of our evening stroll'.[31] One District Six woman, interviewed about gang fights in her neighbourhood before Group Areas evictions, refused to describe the fighters as gangsters, saying rather that they 'were not gangs at all but just rival groups out to have some fun'.[32] Suffusing their defence was the premise that their lifestyles, including racial mixing, were morally wholesome and that there was no justification for their eviction.

Circulating narratives in the townships

Despite their rejection of the official transcript, people classified 'coloured' were taken from all over the Cape Peninsula and lumped together in racially homogeneous townships on the Cape Flats. Residents who had identified with particular neighbourhoods were dispossessed of them, deprived of their patrimony, sundered from their social networks, and forced to accommodate themselves to a new existence with strangers from other communities. In many ways, they had to recreate their sense of self and their social lives as their old networks were torn apart.

When they first arrived in the townships, removees felt only a tenuous connection to the people around them, unless they were fellow removees from the same area. Many say that they just 'couldn't get used to it'.[33] They were mixed in with all sorts – removees from their own neighbourhoods, removees from other areas, migrants who had voluntarily moved to the townships for the opportunity of having their own home, and former shanty-dwellers who were given formal accommodation by the City Council. In this diasporic context, removees tried to rebuild their lives, seeking one another out for support. Their shared experience of dispossession bonded them as they struggled to make sense of their altered situation. They grieved and gossiped together, commiserated and consoled one another, railed against apartheid and complained about the shabby housing. They also commemorated their destroyed communities, sharing with one another beautiful memories of their cherished pasts. Across the Cape Flats, forced removees mixed socially, creating interlocking webs of connection, circulating their stories within the boundaries of the legislated coloured areas. They also shared this discourse with empathetic non-removee neighbours who validated their pain through emotional support. No doubt they also disagreed with one another about many things, but this did not cloud their desire to honour their lost communities in appropriate ways. Cut off from meaningful interaction with Africans, whites and, to a lesser extent, Indians, apartheid social engineering determined the geographical limits within which coloured memories spread, creating a reflexive loop of narrative circulation.

Over the past four decades, the constant exchange of nostalgic stories about the 'good old days' has developed a narrative community among coloured removees. Through interaction with one another, they developed a shared set of narrative conventions for remembering a past characterised by traumatic loss. Through sharing they came to agree on what was appropriate to remember about this past and their relationships to their destroyed homes and communities. This helps explain the uncanny resemblance that removee life histories bear to one another. Their stories were forged in the same cauldron of traumatic loss and were animated by the same moral and emotional purposes.

Coloured removee life histories and the stories that they share with one another in everyday conversation can be termed a commemoration narrative.[34] Their memory production is driven by three moral intentions: to counter the government's rationale for Group Areas (counter memory); to compare the difficult present to an idealised past (comparative memory); and to commemorate their former communities with highly selective stories which honour their former homes, communities and identities (commemorative memory). These three agendas come through in virtually every coloured removee life history. An analysis of these narrative components helps explain the conventions shaping life history production among removees as well as subjective aspects of coloured identity.

Counter memory

Though the counter transcript was developed in reaction to the official transcript, the ideological commitments of that effort continue to find expression in removee memory to this day, despite the ending of apartheid. Not surprisingly, a key feature of their life histories today is the reproduction of the counter transcript – now a counter memory – point by point. The counter memory essentially restates the values of the counter transcript in nostalgic terms, thus stories of interracial harmony abound. The Cape Town they remember before Group Areas removals was a place without racial conflict. Removees remember their former homes as fully meeting their aspirations and almost always being better than the ones they were forced into in the townships. Many of the conditions Group Areas officers regarded as deleterious were interpreted as qualities that gave their communities wholeness. What the government saw as overcrowding, residents saw as 'closeness'; what officials feared was interracial friction was interpreted as racial tolerance by locals. Though some gained access to modern conveniences such as electricity, water-borne sewerage and running water in their township homes, they are quick to stress that the government could have upgraded their old homes instead of forcing them into the townships. Criminality in the old neighbourhoods is denied or qualified, as when District Sixers conjure the image of the gentlemen gangster to challenge the area's reputation for violence. Removees also remember their communities as suffused with positive values, especially regarding respect for elders and tolerance of social difference. Though apartheid is over and its transcripts discredited, removees continue to advance arguments of the counter transcript in their memories lest anyone think that there might have been some truth to National Party justifications for evictions.

Comparative memory

The commemoration narrative also posits an explicit comparison between two distinct moral eras separated by the rupture of eviction. This radical divide is a classic feature of nostalgia. It declares that life was better in the past than it is in the present. But unlike general nostalgia in which a vaguely constituted past is compared to an equally vague present, removee nostalgia posits eviction as the critical divide. Removees often characterise their eviction in terms of a fall from a state of grace, though through no fault of their own. Their former communities were Edens compared to the postlapsarian townships. Following contours reminiscent of the story of Adam and Eve, removees plot their lives according to a narrative of descent. As so many removees declare: '[E]ver since we were moved out from there, everything went wrong. Everything.'[35] Their stories chart the fall from a plane of moral perfection in their old communities to one of moral degradation in the townships.[36]

Comparative memory operates by treating current concerns through the lens of nostalgia. Many of these concerns are shared by other Capetonians, regardless of race or whether they were victims of Group Areas. Coloured removees, however, tend to use them to compare the pre-removals era to the post-removals one. They use these concerns to highlight the particular role of evictions in bringing about current hardships. The main themes that occur in comparative memory are crime, gangsterism, fear, respect for elders, the value of money, entertainment and community spirit. Other themes such as unemployment, social opportunities and government service delivery are also pronounced in life histories, but these only became concerns after 1994 when the ANC took power.[37]

The attention that crime receives in public discourse, newspapers and over-the-fence conversation – not to mention its effects on people's lives and psyches – highlights the extent to which vice and violence are critical issues for people living on the Cape Flats. Murder, rape, assault, robbery, car hijacking, domestic abuse and kidnapping are constant features of their lives. And for forced removees, whose own past must seem like a 'foreign country', the crime and violence permeating their lives is an indication of just how much better the old days in the former communities were.[38] As Zulfa Wagner claims, in Goodwood '[w]e didn't live in violence, man. Only here in Lavis [township], then we used to get violence'.[39]

Whether removees have personally experienced crime or violence, or whether they have had to sacrifice dearly held freedoms such as taking evening strolls, their present-day concerns have a major impact on their memories of their former lives. Virginia Elissac, who grew up in Rondebosch, illustrates this: 'I prefer those days: they were peaceful and quiet and everybody was loving. Yes, oh God, my father warned us about so-called *skollies* [thugs] at that time. "Ooh, they would stab you with a knife" or "they would do all of these horrible things". But basically, when one looks at today, it's violent and a violent way of life; then what happened in those days was nothing, totally nothing.'[40] For her father, the *skollies* may have been truly worrisome characters and may have merited concern but present dangers make a mockery of this concern. The past seems safe and innocent in comparison.

While crime and gangsterism seem to go hand in hand today, it was not always so for many interviewees. For them gangsters fulfilled a variety of roles in the past, such as communal protection, neighbourhood entertainment and even assisting the elderly. Some communities, especially those with a rural character, had little exposure to gangsterism. The move to the townships and the introduction to the world of gangsterism was a rude shock that symbolised the shift between 'then' and 'now'. For Elizabeth Williams, gangs belong to the post-eviction era. Before that, in Louw's Cottages (Kirstenhof), 'we didn't have guns, we didn't have gangs'.[41] The very idea of gangs could only belong to the world of the townships.[42]

Crime and gangsterism has bred feelings of fear that most say they never knew before Group Areas evictions. Township life introduced a level of insecurity that never existed in their old communities. They claim that they used to be able to do whatever they wanted without concern for their safety or the threat of violence. Many interviewees lovingly reminisce about how they could walk anywhere at any time back in the old days. When asked if she feared gangsters in her old community, Ruth Petersen of Diep River responded:

> Never, never. We used to go to midnight bioscope ... we used to walk to Wynberg, midnight. The whole crew of us. And as we walked, the others joined. And we sit in midnight bioscope and we all go singing home along the road.[43]

In Claremont, Sarah September shared that same feeling of freedom:

> And what was so easy, you could be out late at night, you could still go down and do window shopping ... We used to go down on Friday evening and we go down, buy fish 'n chips. Shops closed late at night. But here [in Manenberg] you're even too scared to put your head out during the day. You can't go to the store as we stayed before.[44]

Removees feel bitter and betrayed, for it did not have to be so. Present-day fears prompt stark comparisons between a safe and carefree past with current threats of crime and violence.

A common lament among removees is that the destruction of their communities brought about the demise of certain wholesome values in their lives. Their way of life together with its finely tuned social mores were seen to have been ruptured by evictions, making it nearly impossible for them to reproduce those cultural ideals in the alien environment of the townships. Here they met 'people from different ways of living, so you had to accustom yourself with them'.[45] Along with scholars who have analysed the disruptive legacy of the Group Areas Act, removees highlight the rift that evictions created in reproducing their social values in the townships.[46] They claim that respect was the cornerstone of their former communal lives. For most removees, respect is couched in terms of reverence for older people. Mymoena Emjedi stressed the importance of respect in her childhood:

> When we grew up, our parents used to teach us to have respect for the older. We used to go around and knock on elderly people's doors and then go ask them if they don't want anything from the shop because they don't walk. The children

today, they don't do things like that anymore. We used to sit in the bus and when we'd see an elder person getting in the bus, we stand up. We stand up from that chair for that elder person to come sit down. And if we go past an elderly person, we got to greet ... That is why that time, there was no such crimes they got here now, because there's no more respect.[47]

This ethos of respect was lost with their forced removal. As one said: 'The respect we had, we left behind.'[48]

Removees often perceive the value of money as constantly having eroded. Even though some families have more now than ever before, they still present the past as an epoch of abundance compared to today's scarcity. The value of money is used to symbolise that distinction. Sarah September speaks the words of so many removees:

My father earned little, but we had all the comforts. We never struggled. But struggling was when we came down to live here [Manenberg]. That time the earning was very little, but you could buy ... tickey's butter or tuppence jam or so ... But now it's worse than what it was before.[49]

A compelling, but ironic, allegory is usually at play in these memories – back then we earned little money, but it went a long way; today we get much more money, but it does not buy anything. This perception is clearly aided by South Africa having suffered more than two decades of high inflation from the mid-1970s onwards. The cherished 'tuppence jam', 'penny polony' and 'tickey's butter' are quaint images of a time when people say they had all that they needed. Not luxury, but comfort. Not excess, but satisfaction. Group Areas ended an age remembered for its pecuniary innocence.

Coloured removees often reminisce about recreation and entertainment in their old communities, claiming that they were more satisfying than present diversions. Minstrel carnivals, Malay choirs and Christmas bands were annual events that helped make the old times memorable for they were of their own creation.[50] There were bioscopes to attend, dances to frequent, concerts to go to, and beaches to show off at. Those in peri-urban settings entertained themselves through storytelling, kite flying, sewing, window-shopping excursions, and a wide variety of sports and popular games. And for the middle classes, couples would 'relax with their sherry and they'd make some snacks and they'd sit around the piano and they'd sing. They'd sing all the opera arias, so we grew up with opera and music'.[51] Whether a pastoral idyll or an image of urbane sophistication, past forms of entertainment are remembered as salubrious, satisfying, culturally expansive and family oriented. They were also innocent, in that the joy they engendered was genuine and safe. Everyone could participate, and the cultural values of families and communities were reinforced through hearty social interaction. In virtually every way, that entertainment is considered superior to today's pirated DVDs, electronic games, drug-infested nightclubs and garish malls.

Coloured removees make a point of comparing the community spirit of former times to the alienation of today. In the old days, 'everybody knew everybody else' and people treated one another like family. In areas where Muslims and Christians lived intermixed, residents tell stories of deep and meaningful interaction. One Muslim woman from District Six reminisced with tears in her eyes:

> You know, *labarang* is our Christmas, ne? Well, we would go to wish everybody and the Christian people go with us, go wish. And when it's Christmas, then we go with them … And [when] I was small, then I ran away from home and I'd go sit in the mission with the Christian children, then we go sing gospel songs and then sometimes, they'd sit in the mission, then we sing together. Sometimes we go in the evening, we walk from one street to the other street with a piano accordion and then we'd sing …The children don't get that anymore.[52]

The spirit that is said to have once suffused the old communities is now gone. That spirit, of which removees speak so nostalgically, is a quality they were not able to reproduce in the townships, try as they might. New communities have been born, it is true, but they are not seen as worthy successors to the old ones. The spirit lives on only in their stories and memories.

Commemorative memory

Besides countering the rationales for Group Areas and comparing the past to the present, removee life histories commemorate their lost homes and communities. This is the overriding sentiment that animates their production of memory. Through countering government justifications, removees show what wonderful places their communities were. In critiquing the present by comparing it to the past, they show how fantastic that time was. These lesser agendas serve the larger commemorative purpose of honouring their destroyed communities. The idealised recollections of removees help answer the deep emotional need of people who have suffered the trauma of evictions to grieve and come to terms with their loss. They demonstrate their connection to those communities by telling romanticised tales about the old times, when life was innocent and carefree. They honour the passing of their communities by recounting tender memories about them. And they make emotional, social, political and identity claims based on their attachments to those communities.[53]

Svetlana Boym tells us that:

'[n]ostalgia (from *nostos* – return home, and *algia* – longing) is a longing for a home that no longer exists or has never existed. Nostalgia is a sentiment of loss and displacement, but it is also a romance with one's own fantasy. Nostalgic love can only survive in a long-distance relationship.[54]

Thus idealisation and massive omission of negative memories are key ingredients of nostalgic commemoration narratives. As Barry Schwartz explains, '[c]ommemoration lifts from an ordinary historical sequence those extraordinary events which embody our deepest and most fundamental values'.[55] Like grieving parents who honour a dead child with beautiful stories rather than memories of arguments, failures and betrayals, the commemoration narrative focuses on what is good and represses negative memories that might compromise the project. Those are overwritten by successive versions of the narrative which is scripted, rehearsed and refined. Memory is palimpsestual, subject to revision. Through the commemoration narrative, removees express grief, assign blame, treasure good times, value lost relationships and identify with other removees and their old communities.

The narrative also serves as a resource for satisfying a number of crucial needs. First, it has emotional utility. For victims of traumatic loss, narrative development offers a road to psychological recovery and the prospect for healing. It allows victims to keep a sense of connection to the people and places from which they were severed by evoking them verbally. Psychoanalytic theory has long recognised the therapeutic role that narrative construction plays in the lives of trauma victims. By integrating their experiences into their life histories, survivors are able to move on with their lives, no matter how painful that memory may remain.[56]

Secondly, it has archival utility. That is, even though narrative tends to reduce the chaotic mass of impressions that a person has of the past to a more manageable and meaningful set of memories, it enhances their resolution by promoting those memories that fit the narrative's conventions. The commemoration narrative vigilantly guards against the infiltration of the official transcript by carving out a space of 'truth' against the 'lies' of the government and against the risk of forgetting. Like so many post-traumatic commemorative projects – Holocaust museums, war memorials and genocide documentation centres – removee memory fights against both forgetting and mis-remembering an 'authentic' past. In the context of the apartheid townships, in which removee memory remained in oral form without the support of museums, archives, the press or publications until the end of apartheid, the commemoration narrative provided the means through which removees' pasts were kept alive through the years.

Thirdly, it has aesthetic utility in that removees derive immense pleasure both from the recitation and reception of stories that conform to the commemoration narrative's conventions. Similar to singing or listening to a beloved song – where much of the joy is experienced in anticipating and then arriving at critical moments of the composition – the recollection of and response to commemorative stories promise gratification because this elicits aesthetic expectations from removees. Understanding the rules of their collectively constructed genre, they can anticipate and then relish the consummation of crucial moments of the story. By moulding their stories according to this narrative format, removees are assured of, at minimum, communicating meaning successfully. And if they are practised storytellers, with a flair for language or embellishment, then they are able to generate artistic delights by adding personal touches to an otherwise well-known storyline. Those familiar with the rules of the commemoration narrative also appreciate stories that offer unique images or creative use of the genre.

Fourthly, it has social utility, in that narrative sharing allows victims to rebuild new lives together in challenging circumstances. It helps them make sense of a world that has been fundamentally altered. All previous expectations of their life trajectories having been destroyed, narrative development allows for tentative attempts at making meaning of their new state. Through narrative interaction and making sense of the world together, they ended up building new communities in the townships.

Lastly, it has political utility. For people of marginalised oppressed communities, narrative is a crucial 'weapon of the weak'.[57] As we have seen, narrative is a flexible, durable and universal oral resource easily hidden from the ears of power. It can be subtle and non-confrontational, a whisper of protest. A political strength of narrative is its relative illegibility to power as the oppressed group controls the timing of the narrative's broadcast to elites. At the time of removal, most victims believed that they were too weak to challenge the government openly. They could not afford more muscular forms of protest such as strikes, boycotts and riots – the tactics of the next generation. Removee resistance took the form of underground narrative production against the government's justifications for removals.

In the post-apartheid era, the commemoration narrative has taken on a surprising new relevance. With the decline and demise of apartheid, coloured cultural entrepreneurs have been publicising the commemoration narrative beyond the borders of the townships. The publication of Richard Rive's novel, *Buckingham Palace: District Six,*[58] which later became a standard textbook for high school students in the Western Cape, represents a crucial breakthrough in this regard. Then followed musicals by David Kramer and Taliep Petersen, and dramaturgical performances such as *District Six* and *Onse Boet* that embodied the sentiments of the narrative on stage. Very importantly, the District Six Museum was formed to give concrete expression to the memories of the bulldozed community. Today it also acts as a repository for the memories of other Cape Town communities destroyed by apartheid-era forced removals. In this respect, District Six has become symbolic of Group Areas trauma generally, and community members have taken the lead in promoting the commemoration narrative as an alternative to the discredited apartheid transcript. Because of its popular resonance with removees – and its widespread acceptance, or tolerance, by other Capetonians – the narrative has been taken up as the official transcript by the post-apartheid regime.

Moreover, when the ANC came to power, it allowed Group Areas victims to claim some form of restitution, such as their actual land if available, an alternative parcel of land or financial compensation. The process initiated by the Land Claims Commission relied heavily on removees' narratives to substantiate their claims. Besides factual data elicited by the application form – duration of residence, date of expulsion, level of compensation awarded upon their removal, number of rooms in house, whether it was rented or owned – it also asked people to justify their claims by relating their experience of forced removal. In the 550 land claim applications personally analysed, almost all coloured claimants utilise, in some fashion, the template of the commemoration narrative to make their cases.[59] Given the scripted, rehearsed quality of the narrative in their memories, as well as its current ascendancy as the new official transcript, coloured claimants leveraged its legitimacy and simply wrote down what they had been saying for decades in the townships. Their memory has, literally, paid off.

Collective, communal and individual identities

In a recent article provocatively entitled 'Coloureds don't *toyi-toyi*', Shannon Jackson argues that most theorists of coloured identity 'rely on data sources such as voting practices, voluntary behaviour and verbally expressed political positions, particularly amongst elites… [which] valorises the relevance of consciousness and consciously volunteered information at the expense of more tacit and diffuse domains of meaning'. The problem with this is that it 'overlooks some of the contradictory behaviour of coloureds who … voice conscious rejection of a separate Coloured identity in one context and then unreflexively channel their energies into separate Coloured cultural affiliations in another.'[60] She then examines coloured people's relationships to different bodily movements and gestures, such as *toyi-toying* (protest dancing), to see how these implicit indices bear on the question of identity. Other writers have also recognised this bias towards conscious declarations and have turned their attention to more tacit expressions of identity found in annual rituals such as Coon Carnivals and Malay Choirs; linguistic practices such as code-switching; the expression of emotions of shame, longing, denial or desire; the personal politics relating to hair texture and skin pigmentation; consumer behaviour; and humour.[61]

This analysis of the commemoration narrative provides clues for analysing colouredness beyond explicit statements of identity contained within them. The very structure of their narratives tells us something about the way that removees understand themselves, what Margaret Somers calls narrative identity.[62] This section argues that the structure of the commemoration narrative and its meaning-making devices – plots, themes, tropes, and anecdotes – are means through which coloured removees make multiple identity claims.

Essentially, narratives create meaning out of otherwise chaotic memories and impressions through devices such as plots, themes, tropes and anecdotes. These devices work together to help speakers construct intelligible stories structured to convey specific messages. The commemoration narrative exemplifies these qualities, with its pre-removals beginning, its forced removal middle, and its post-removals ending. And their narratives are structured to make three crucial points: that the government's rationales for evictions were illegitimate, that their lives were far better before their removal than after, and that removees honour the memories of their lost homes, communities and identities.

But these devices each serve different functions in narrative production and allow speakers to do more than just create meaning through them. They also allow them to make highly specific identity claims without necessarily doing so overtly. These devices allow for subtle cues of differentiation, tacit expressions of inner disposition and latent manifestations of subjectivity. Margaret Somers argues that 'it is through narrativity that we come to know, understand, and make sense of the social world, and it is through narratives and narrativity that we constitute our social identities'.[63] Coloured removees use these narrative devices in consistent patterned ways which speak to their sense of identity and belonging.

Firstly, plot structures are broad organising devices that determine a story's direction, but not its details. They provide the evaluative framework for making sense of independent events, putting them in relationship to one another. Plot structures also identify a speaker's disposition towards the direction of their own or community's lives. The commemoration narrative locates memories and events along a downward sloping moral trajectory, showing that their lives were made worse by the experience of forced removals. However, coloured removees are not the only group to use this narrative structure. Most working-class coloured people and many whites, Indians and Africans also structure their life histories in this way. Indeed, this shared plot structure promotes a common tenor to many of the minority communities in South Africa, forming the basis for most opposition party claims, especially at election time. For these other groups, the narrative of descent is usually tied to the historical changes inaugurated in 1994 when the ANC came to power. For many who had been privileged or enjoyed privilege relative to the African majority, this is when their fortunes deteriorated. While most coloured removees agree that their lives have taken a turn for the worse since 1994, that historical moment is not pivotal to their life histories. For them, the descent began with forced removals and merely accelerated with the change in regime.

While the narrative of descent gives a similar pitch to pessimistic minority critiques of the post-apartheid order, allowing them to identify with one another politically, coloured removees are distinguished from the rest by positing Group Areas evictions as the moment of historical rupture for them. Coloured removees use their nostalgia for a different moral purpose. Theirs is a specific response to the injustices of removals, thus the narrative of descent both ties and distinguishes them from disaffected minority groups. It, however, mostly serves to identify them as survivors of a historical injustice.

Secondly, themes give flesh to the overarching plot structure. As meaning-making devices, themes remain broad, allowing for any number of tropes or anecdotes to be marshalled under their banners. In the commemoration narrative, the major themes fall under the categories of counter and comparative memory. The main counter memory themes are interracial relations, material conditions, crime, gangsterism and morality. These were arrived at in dialogue with the official transcript. Comparative memory themes include crime, gangsterism, fear, respect, community spirit, the value of money and entertainment. These were arrived at through negotiating the challenges of the townships. These shared themes illustrate the commonalities that removees perceive as having shaped their lives.

When tens of thousands of people living in a confined geographical area utilise the same themes for organising their memories into meaningful life histories, it is clear that those narrative choices are not random. There are countless themes that removees could choose to structure their memories but not all would be socially relevant. In the wake of this mass social trauma, three crucial elements came to define their social context: their audience was now exclusively coloured, most were also fellow removees, and victims sought to heal their emotional and psychological wounds through narrative sharing. This reduced the number of relevant themes to an identifiable core.

Coloured removees established what might be compared to an extended support group with a narrative programme that allowed them to approach one another for emotional and psychological succour. As is the case in support groups, in which members tend to develop a stylised narrative format to speak about addiction, rape or trauma – by borrowing the group's confessional style and tapping into commonly accepted plot structures and themes – coloured forced removees also developed a stylised narrative to convey meaning through their stories. These themes, while seemingly attenuating their narrative options, actually opened up the possibility for meaningful speech in the aftermath of trauma. They formed a common currency that could be traded among removees, allowing for instant intelligibility, despite coming from radically different locales and facing different eviction experiences. As broad meaning-making devices, themes connected coloured forced removees across the Cape Flats without demanding that they sacrifice any of the specificity of their community's or their own experiences. The common themes of their life histories bear testimony to the process of narrative sharing, implicitly connecting these removees despite physical separation, differing opinions and divergent aspirations. Thus, even though many of these themes are used by other township dwellers, the specific functions they serve in removee narratives distinguish them from others. They tie removees together in a loose web of narrative affiliation, giving a remarkable similarity to their stories across the Cape Peninsula. It is easy to predict what kinds of stories removees will offer when telling their life history, so patterned and consistent are they in reproducing this canon of themes through the narrative of descent.

Thirdly, nested below plots and themes are tropes, more intimate meaning-making devices. They are figures of speech carrying symbolic significance far beyond their literal meanings. Tropes condense large amounts of information, emotion and meaning into a memorable, stylised and compact image that is conveyed in a word or short phrase. They allow storytellers to communicate economically and artistically, conveying complex messages in a succinct, symbolic form. As Harold Scheub, in his study of South African storytelling explains: 'Trope implies transformation, from one set of images to another, but without giving up any of the original meanings or perceptions that an audience might have of them.'[64] The use of tropes implies a degree of complicity between speaker and listener, its success being predicated on communicants sharing a cultural vocabulary and an understanding of the relationship between certain symbols and messages. On the Cape Flats, commemorative stories have circulated to the extent that a collective cultural vocabulary has developed so that removees from different destroyed locales can speak meaningfully about their own particular experiences in ways that are collectively understood.

The figure of the gentleman gangster provides a good example of the way tropes work. District Sixers speak lovingly of the 'gentleman gangster', that charming, rough and tough character who is also genteel and civic minded when appropriate. He may fight with other gangsters, or even 'mess' with an outsider, but he would never hurt someone from the community. He is a uniquely District Six figure, a trope evoked by former residents when the theme of gangsterism arises in their narratives. Use of this trope serves two purposes. It locates people's history and identity squarely within District Six and allows them to deal with the current thematic issue of gangsterism through the commemorative narrative. Other removees do not use that trope in their life history for they have their own way of speaking about gangsterism that is more appropriate to their experiences. The specificity of tropes allows removees to identify with and speak in unique ways about their particular communities while linking them at a broader thematic level.

Tropes are drawn from a locally conceived fund of images, characters or events capable of bearing dense symbolic meaning, and have deep resonance for people within that community. People look to their own histories and localities to provide material for symbolic meaning. Certain mores, socio-economic conditions, vocational trends, landscape features, spatial configurations and historical events cue the recall, representation, rehearsal and development of tropes for a community. Linkages between landscape and memory are common in the making of tropes. That is why street life looms large for District Sixers, forests and gardens for Protea villagers, wide-open spaces for Goodwood Acres people and charming cottages for Newlanders. As Simon Schama reveals in his study of ethnic and national memories, landscapes act as a repository for the myths and memories that a community tells of itself: 'For although we are accustomed to separate nature and human perception into two realms, they are, in fact, indivisible. Before it can ever be a repose for the senses, landscape is the work of the mind. Its scenery is built up as much from strata of memory as from layers of rock'.[65] Thus tropes develop from landscape features and other cultural perceptions which offer communities the necessary narrative resources for promoting a unique sense of identity within a context of overwhelming sand-brick-concrete and matchbox house sameness in the townships.

Lastly, anecdotes are personal stories that are unique to a speaker, carving out an autonomous space of experience and action within the commemoration narrative framework. It is a narrative device that often speaks to a host of themes, sometimes utilising specific tropes, but ultimately constituting an assertion of individuality. Anecdotes may use thematic topics or communally defined tropes, but they show the speaker also to be an autonomous subject with personal experiences, emotions and aspirations. They provide personalised proof that the past was better than the present, or that gangsters really were gentlemen, or that money really did go a long way. Thus anecdotes fit into a larger frame of signification, just as individuals fit into larger frames of identification.

It needs to be stressed that the commemoration narrative is not the basis of collective memory. It is a set of guidelines established by removees to help them recount their lives in a culturally appropriate manner in the wake of mass social trauma. The actual memories of any removee life history are singular, the product of that person's own experience, but the way in which those experiences find expression are structured by collectively held narrative conventions. The shared guidelines are what give coloured removee life histories their striking similarity. They are products of the same discursive constraints.

This is not to say that coloured removees never go outside the confines of the commemoration narrative, but when they do, they usually qualify the meaning of their assertions. For instance, some women who were newlywed when forcibly removed say they were happy to get a house of their own and start a family outside of their parents' home. However, lest they appear to be endorsing Group Areas, they quickly say that they wish they could have gotten a house in their old communities, not in the townships.[66] Also, those who were forcibly removed while they were still young do not have a sufficient fund of personal recollections to tap into to give flesh to the commemoration narrative, so they tend to rely on their parents' memories and moral evaluations. Also, the loss is not felt as keenly since they were too young to appreciate the magnitude of what was happening to their families and communities.[67]

Thus, through a shared plot structure and a common endowment of themes, removees identify with each other collectively as removees. Through shared tropes, removees identify themselves as members of particular communities, and through anecdotes, they identify themselves as individuals who have a degree of personal autonomy. Together these devices allow removees to claim collective, communal and individual identities, often tacitly. Identity claims are usually structured into their stories, implicit in how they recall their memories.

Conclusion

The social engineering effected through Group Areas evictions had a fundamental impact on coloured identity. First, population registration grouped those classified coloured into a legally binding racial category which set in motion a host of institutional effects that severely restricted their social and sexual interactions, political and communicative opportunities, and professional and material aspirations. Group Areas substantiated this commonality in a most elemental way, limiting residential mobility to within areas legally prescribed as 'coloured'. It is these institutionally produced effects – not so much the administrative process of classification – that radically reshaped coloured people's experience in the last half-century, giving concrete social, spatial and political expression to the coloured racial category. Group Areas united coloured people as a group in a fashion unprecedented in South African history. The legacy of the Group Areas Act continues to shape coloured self-perception as well as others' perceptions of them.

Secondly, Group Areas residential restrictions allowed coloureds to achieve a level of intra-group interaction unprecedented in their history. Though meaningful inter-group relations between coloured people in newly created townships were anything but assured at the time of dispossession, coming as they did from such varied backgrounds, removee life histories today confirm that substantive social networks have been formed within the racial boundaries legislated under apartheid. The shared conventions of the commemoration narrative by coloured removees tell us much about the nature of these connections. Not quite an imagined community – in which people explicitly identify with a common narrative promoted by elites through mass media[68] – coloured removees form a narrative community in which they implicitly identify with each other through an orally shared narrative structure. The commemoration narrative was constructed and circulated through personal contact, involving tens of thousands of people whose lives became connected through interlocking social networks in a socially and spatially defined area. Though the numbers of each individual's social network were certainly small, these articulated with others, proliferating until they had reached the social limits imposed by Group Areas. Representing the outlook of an oppressed, marginalised community and being in opposition to the interests of the state, this commemorative project was achieved almost exclusively through face-to-face contact. It never enjoyed media support until apartheid was in decline. It was through day-to-day interactions that the narrative gained social purchase.

Furthermore, during the latter part of the apartheid era, many people rejected coloured identity, insisting that it was an artificial racial identification imposed by the government to divide and rule black people. They often signalled their rejection by referring to themselves as 'so-called coloured'. Others, influenced by the Black Consciousness Movement, called themselves 'black', identifying with Africans and Indians who were also oppressed. But the effort remained largely intellectual, a mental stance, for it was difficult to create meaningful relationships beyond racially circumscribed areas. Identification with blackness, or rejection of colouredness, was difficult to sustain in reality because people were spatially and socially disconnected. The majority of coloured people's social networks remained almost completely coloured in character, a point easily missed if the focus is exclusively on overt statements of identification.

Thirdly, the sense of groupness or boundedness felt by coloured people was intensified by Group Areas. Before apartheid, many coloured people had long lived in relatively integrated environments or had belonged to communities that had their own norms, histories and understandings of identity that went beyond race categorisation. Some were absorbed into white society through their appearance, associations, standard of living or nuptials, just as whites and Africans were accepted into coloured circles through the same means. Indeed, coloureds married outside of their putative race group more frequently than any other South African grouping.[69] Though coloured identity was well established socially and institutionally before forced removals, its boundaries were porous. Racial classification and Group Areas segregation together with other apartheid legislation such as the Immorality, Mixed Marriages and Separate Amenities Acts together with the coloured Labour Preference Policy hardened those boundaries as never before. But the response of coloureds, especially forced removes, to state-enforced racialisation gave positive content to their otherwise restricted social world. The trauma of removals compelled victims to seek one another out for sharing, empathy and solace. Their effective social horizon – coloured people in coloured areas – became an affective resource for removees adapting to township life. Through everyday sharing, their intention was not to create a sense of coloured awareness or removee consciousness, but their circumstances enjoined them to constitute their situation affirmatively. The government might have controlled the limits of their social world but it could not determine the content that they would give to it.

The combination of the commonality imposed by Group Areas, the connectivity that was achieved through sharing stories in the wake of mass social trauma, and the reinforcement of a sense of groupness through positive narrative circulation has promoted a sense of coloured self-understanding that goes beyond mere instrumentality. Self-understanding refers to the disposition of having a 'sense of who one is, of one's social location, and of how ... one is prepared to act'.[70] In the post-apartheid era, coloured people have greater freedom to identify without reference to racial categories. But, by and large, they have nevertheless continued to embrace a variant of the identity reminiscent of apartheid-era values, and continue to invest in the social networks they created in the wake of evictions. Part of the reason for this is that they have been able to build rich social lives within those boundaries, creating positive associations through narrative sharing. The depth of understanding that removees have been able to develop through the collective creation of a shared narrative speaks to the sense of intimacy and distinctiveness they feel as coloured people. They have spread the commemoration narrative beyond the confines of the townships to the extent that it has become one of the dominant stories of Cape Town itself.

Although Group Areas removals did much to reconstitute the coloured group as the government intended, the trauma of evictions has set removees apart in important ways. It distinguishes them from their non-removee neighbours in terms of the socialising experiences they created in the wake of their tragedy. They needed, and built, networks of trust, comfort and solace with other removees who faced an uncertain future. This illustrates that race-making projects, like Group Areas social engineering, do more than just unite people under a racial banner. Their trauma can also set them apart and help reconfigure their social identities. While Group Areas social engineering certainly contributed greatly to the reification of coloured identity, it also foisted onto its victims a unique historical and emotional burden which reshaped their understanding of themselves as coloured people. This was partly inspired by narrative strategies they created for coping with their predicament. Their commemorative stories give rich testimony to the ways in which removees have come to understand themselves within and beyond state-sponsored racial categories.

Endnotes

1   I use the term 'coloured' here as an analytical category, not a normative one.
2   Recent books on Cape slavery allude to this historical amnesia in their prefaces. See Loos J. 2004. *Echoes of Slavery: Voices from South Africa's Past*. Cape Town: David Philip; Mountain A. 2004. *An Unsung Heritage: Perspectives on Slavery*. Cape Town: David Philip; Van der Ross R. 2005. *Up From Slavery: Slaves at the Cape, Their Origins, Treatment and Contribution*. Cape Town: Ampersand Press. A historical thesis for how slavery was 'forgotten' by slave descendants is provided by Ward K

& Worden N. 1998. 'Commemorating, suppressing, and invoking Cape slavery', in *Negotiating the Past: The Making of Memory in South Africa*, eds S Nuttall & C Coetzee. Cape Town: Oxford University Press, 201–220. Another commentator claims that coloureds suffer from 'psychological enslavement': Willams B. 1996. 'The power of propaganda', in *Now that We Are Free: Coloured Communities in a Democratic South Africa*, eds W James, D Caliguire & K Cullinan. Cape Town: IDASA, 22.

3   Research was conducted during 2000 and 2001 and in 2004 in Cape Town. I lived in Bonteheuwel, a former coloured township and dumping ground for forced removes. I interviewed 110 coloured and African forced removes, and also interviewed non-removes as a control group. Moreover, I compared the life histories I obtained with those collected by other scholars.

4   Key texts on the state categorisation of coloureds include Du Pre R. 1994. *Separate but Unequal: The 'Coloured' People of South Africa – A Political History*. Johannesburg: Jonathan Ball; February V. 1981. *Mind Your Colour: The 'Coloured' Stereotype in South African Literature*. London: Kegan Paul; Goldin I. 1987. *Making Race: The Politics and Economics of Coloured Identity in South Africa*. Cape Town: Maskew Miller Longman; and Lewis G. 1987. *Between the Wire and the Wall: A History of South African 'Coloured' Politics*. Cape Town: David Philip. For coloured self-identification, see Goldin and Lewis, but especially Adhikari M. 2005. *Not White Enough, Not Black Enough: Racial Identity in the South African Coloured Community*. Athens: Ohio University Press; and Pickel B. 1997. *Coloured Ethnicity and Identity: A Case Study in the Former Coloured Areas in the Western Cape/South Africa*. Hamburg: Lit Verlag.

5   This alternative analytical idiom comes from Brubaker R & Cooper F. 2000. 'Beyond "identity"'. *Theory and Society*, 29, 1–47.

6   For discussion of the settler–native binary in African and South African governance, see Mamdani M. 1996. 'Beyond settler and native as political identities: overcoming the political legacy of colonialism'. *Comparative Studies in Society and History*, 43, 4; and *Citizen and Subject: Contemporary Africa and the Legacy of Late Colonialism*. Princeton: Princeton University Press.

7   Goldin, *Making Race*, 83. See also Norval A. 1996. *Deconstructing Apartheid Discourse*. New York: Verso.

8   Western J. 1996. *Outcast Cape Town*. Berkeley: University of California Press, 121–134; Mesthrie U. 1999. 'Dispossession in Black River, Rondebosch: the unfolding of the Group Areas Act in Cape Town'. Unpublished manuscript, African Studies Collection, University of Cape Town.

9   Scott P. 1955. 'Cape Town: a multiracial city'. *The Geographical Journal*, 121, no. 2, 149–157; Christopher A. 1992. 'Segregation levels in South African cities, 1911–1985'. *International Journal of African Historical Studies*, 25, no. 3, 561–582; and Christopher A. 1994. *The Atlas of Apartheid*. New York: Routledge.

10   Bickford-Smith V. 1995. *Ethnic Pride and Racial Prejudice in Victorian Cape Town: Group Identity and Social Practice, 1875–1902*. New York: Cambridge University Press; and Bickford-Smith V. 1990. 'The origins and early history of District Six to 1910', in *The Struggle for District Six: Past and Present*, eds S Jeppie & C Soudien. Cape Town: Buchu Books, 35–43.

11 For the Sea Point suicide, see Melvin Mitchell, interviewed by Henry Trotter, 12 December 2000; for the Rondebosch one, see Virginia Elissac, interviewed by Henry Trotter, 19 May 2001.

12 Leonard Levendal, interviewed by Henry Trotter, 16 January 2001. For a semi-fictional treatment of eviction leading to death in Claremont, see Schonstein Pinnock P. 1993. *Ouma's Autumn*. Grahamstown: African Sun Press.

13 Norma Solomons, interviewed by Henry Trotter, 30 August 2000.

14 Cecil McLean, interviewed by Henry Trotter, 11 December 2000.

15 There are many studies on removals in Cape Town. On Sea Point removals, see Mesthrie U. 1994. 'The Tramway Road removals, 1959–61' *Kronos*, 214, 61–78; Paulse M. 2001. '"Everyone had their differences but there was always comradeship": Tramway Road, Sea Point, 1920s to 1961', in *Lost Communities, Living Memories: Remembering Forced Removals in Cape Town*, ed S Field. Cape Town: David Philip, 44–61; Paulse M. 2002. 'An oral history of Tramway Road and Ilford Street, Sea Point, 1930s–2001: the production of place by race, class and gender'. PhD dissertation, University of Cape Town. Concerning Mowbray, see Western, *Outcast Cape Town*. On Rondebosch, see Mesthrie, 'Dispossession in Black River'. On Protea Village, Kirstenbosch, see Bantom R. 1995. 'A study in the history of Protea Village and the impact of the Group Areas Act'. BA (Hons) thesis, University of the Western Cape. On Claremont, see Anon. 1983. *United Womens' Organisation, Claremont: A Peoples' History*. Athlone: United Womens' Organisation; and Taliep W. 1992. 'A study in the history of Claremont and the impact of the Group Areas Act c. 1950–1970'. BA (Hons) thesis, University of Cape Town. On Simon's Town, see Boge F. 1998. 'Back to the places of the future?: the transformation of places and local identities in the "new" South Africa: a case study of the land restitution process in Simon's Town'. MA thesis, Free University of Berlin. Sean Field (1996) provides a fascinating study of the Windermere community, in 'The power of exclusion: moving memories from Windermere to the Cape Flats 1920s–1990s'. PhD dissertation, University of Essex.

16 Western, *Outcast Cape Town*, 85.

17 Cape Archives (hereafter CA), Group Areas Board (hereafter GAB), Goodwood K20/1/2 – doc. 82/312/5, 2.

18 For a good example of this sort of justification see the quotation attributed to Joyce Waring, wife of National Party member of parliament, in *Cape Times*, 24 February 1966.

19 Scott J. 1990. *Domination and the Arts of Resistance: Hidden Transcripts*. New Haven: Yale University Press, 17–44.

20 Scott, *Domination*, 111.

21 Scott, *Domination*, 111.

22 *Cape Argus*, 11 May 1962.

23 *Cape Argus*, 25 June 1965.

24 *Cape Times*, 22 May 1981.

25 *Cape Times*, 11 February 1981.

26 CA, GAB, PAA, Proclamation of Group Areas: District Six, Cape Town, ref K20/1/7, 23 November 1964, 11–14.

27 *Cape Argus*, 3 March 1984.

28 CA, PAA, (AK), ref K20/1/15, Group Areas Board meeting on Fraserdale and Black River, 13.

29 CA, G PAA (AK), ref K20/1/15, Group Areas Board meeting on Fraserdale and Black River, 14.

30 See, for instance, letters sent in to the Group Areas Board concerning Claremont. CA, PAA (AK); 18b H6, ref K20/1/8, 1–20.

31 *Cape Argus Weekend Magazine*, 5 June 1971.

32 *Cape Times*, 29 March 1979.

33 These comments pervade my interviews, as well as an apartheid-era study by Maralack D & Kriel A. 1984. '"A streetless wasteland": a preliminary report on Ocean View'. *Carnegie Conference Paper,* no. 10d. Cape Town: Carnegie. See also Zulfa Wagner, interviewed by Henry Trotter, 16 October 2000; Hester Wessels, interviewed by Henry Trotter, 18 January 2001; Leonard Lopes, interviewed by Henry Trotter, 7 December 2000

34 I get this term from Yael Zerubavel's analysis of the Tel Hai legend, in Zerubavel Y. 1994. 'The historic, the legendary, and the incredible: invented traditional and collective memory in Israel', in *Commemorations: The Politics of National Identity*, ed J R Gillis. Princeton: Princeton University Press, 105–123.

35 Katie Pfeiffer, interviewed by Henry Trotter, 6 December 2000. See also Ragmat Mallick, interviewed by Henry Trotter, 18 October 2000; Katherine Fischer, interviewed by Henry Trotter, 29 January 2001.

36 This can be likened to what Bakhtin calls the 'epic past'. He says that 'the epic past is called the "absolute past" for good reason: it is both monochromic and valorised (hierarchical); it lacks any relativity, that is, any gradual, purely temporal progressions that might connect it with the present. It is walled off absolutely from all subsequent time, and above all from those times in which the [speaker] and his listeners are located.' Bakhtin M M. 1981. *The Dialogic Imagination*. Austin: University of Texas Press, 15–16.

37 The Western Cape Oral History Project, now the Centre for Popular Memory at the University of Cape Town, has removee life histories dating back to 1984. Comparison between these older life histories and more contemporary ones show the development of new themes after 1994 such as unemployment, service delivery and corruption.

38 For a discussion on this metaphor of memory resembling a foreign country, see Lowenthal D. 1984. *The Past Is a Foreign Country*. New York: Cambridge University Press.

39 Zulfa Wagner, interviewed by Henry Trotter, 16 October 2000. See also Michael Fischer, interviewed by Henry Trotter, 29 January 2001; Ragmat Mallick, interviewed by Henry Trotter, 18 October 2000.

40 Virginia Elissac, interviewed 19 May 2001.

41 Elizabeth Williams, interviewed by Henry Trotter, 22 January 2001.

42 Recent ethnographic work bears this out. See, for instance, Jensen S. 2006. 'Capetonian back streets: territorializing young men'. *Ethnography*, 7, no. 3, 275–301; and Salo E. 2007. '"Mans is ma soe": ganging practices in Manenberg, South Africa, and the ideologies of masculinity, gender, and generational relations', in *States of Violence: Politics, Youth, and Memory in Contemporary Africa*, eds E Bay & D Donham. Charlottesville: University of Virginia Press, 148–178.

43 Ruth Petersen, interviewed by Henry Trotter, 12 January 2001. See also Ronald and Rachel Lambert, interviewed by Henry Trotter, 16 December 2000

44 Sarah September, interviewed by Henry Trotter, 5 January 2001. See also Daphne Bloom, interviewed by Henry Trotter, 8 January 2001.

45 Sarah September, interviewed, 5 January 2001. See also Hester Wessels, interviewed by Henry Trotter, 18 January 2001; Arthur Morta, interviewed by Henry Trotter, 29 January 2001.

46 For the classic study on how forced removals contributed to the growth of Cape Flats gangs, see Pinnock D. 1984. *The Brotherhoods: Street Gangs and State Control in Cape Town*. Cape Town: David Philip. For his study on Group Areas and protest, see Pinnock D. 1981. *Elsies River*. Cape Town: Institute of Criminology, University of Cape Town. His later book on remedying this problem also reveals how Group Areas destroyed the fabric of family and community. See Pinnock D. 1997. *Gangs, Rituals & Rites of Passage*. Cape Town: Africa Sun Press. Many photo books attempt to describe visually and textually just the kind of community values that abided before removals. See Manuel G & Hatfield D. 1967. *District Six*. Cape Town: Longman; Schoeman C. 1994. *District Six: The Spirit of Kanala*. Cape Town: Human & Rousseau; Greshoff J. 1996. *The Last Days of District Six*. Cape Town: District Six Museum; and Breytenbach C. 1997. *The Spirit of District Six*. Cape Town: Human & Rousseau.

47 Mymoena Emjedi, interviewed by Henry Trotter, 31 October 2000.

48 Sarah September, interviewed 5 January 2001.

49 Sarah September, interviewed 5 January 2001. See also Susanna Williams, interviewed by Henry Trotter, 18 January 2001; Julia Yon, interviewed by Henry Trotter, 16 January 2001; Kathleen Samuels, interviewed by Henry Trotter, 29 September 2000.

50 For an outstanding analysis of the coloured carnival season at New Year, see Martin D. 1999. *Coon Carnival: New Year in Cape Town, Past and Present*. Cape Town: David Philip.

51 Virginia Elissac, interviewed 19 May 2001. For more information on peri-urban amusements, see John Valentine, interviewed by Henry Trotter, 25 October 2000; Brian Sassman, interviewed by Henry Trotter, 23 January 2001.

52 Mymoena Emjedi, interviewed 31 October 2000.

53 For an insightful treatment of how people have relationships with home and mourn those losses if removed, see Porteous J & Smith S. 2001. *Domicide: The Global Destruction of Home*. Montreal: McGill-Queen's University Press. It offers numerous examples of testimony and literature on the importance of home for a healthy and happy life.

54 Boym S. 2001. *The Future of Nostalgia*. New York: Basic Books, xiii.

55 Schwartz B. 1982. 'The social context of commemoration: a study in collective memory'. *Social Forces*, 61, no. 2, 377.

56 Erikson K. 1995. 'Notes on trauma and community', in *Trauma: Explorations in Memory*, ed C Caruth. Baltimore: Johns Hopkins University Press, 183–199; Fivush R, Haden C & Reese E. 1996. 'Remembering, recounting, and reminiscing: the development of autobiographical memory in social context', in *Remembering Our Past: Studies in Autobiographical Memory*, ed D Rubin. Cambridge: Cambridge University Press; Harvey J. 1996. *Embracing Their Memory: Loss and the Social Psychology of Storytelling*. Needham Heights: Allyn & Bacon; Herman J. 1997. *Trauma and Recovery*. New York: Basic Books; Linde C. 1993. *Life Stories: The*

Creation of Coherence. Oxford: Oxford University Press; McAdams D. 1993. *The Stories We Live By: Personal Myths and the Making of the Self*. New York: Guilford Press; Pennebaker J. 1997. 'Writing about emotional experiences as a therapeutic process'. *Psychological Science*, 8, no. 3, 162–165.

57 Scott J. 1985. *Weapons of the Weak: Everyday Forms of Peasant Resistance*. New Haven: Yale University Press.

58 Rive R. 1986. *Buckingham Palace: District Six*. London: Heinemann Educational Books.

59 The relevant documentation is located at the Land Claims Commission (Western Cape), Matrix House, Cape Town.

60 Jackson S. 2005. 'Coloureds don't toyi-toyi: gesture, constraint and identity in Cape Town', in *Limits to Liberation after Apartheid: Citizenship, Governance and Culture*, ed S Robins. Cape Town: David Philip, 209.

61 On coloured identity and annual rituals, see Martin, *Coon Carnival*; Baxter L. 2001. 'Continuity and change in Cape Town's Coon Carnival: the 1960s and 1970s'. *African Studies*, 60, no. 1, 87–105. On linguistic practice, especially code-switching, see McCormick K. 1990. 'The vernacular of District Six', in Jeppie & Soudien, *Struggle for District Six*. On emotions like shame, longing, intolerance, denial and desire for assimilation to the dominant culture, see Adhikari, *Not White Enough*; Gibson J & Gouws A. 2000. 'Social identities and political intolerance: linkages within the South African mass public'. *Journal of Political Science*, 44, no. 2, 278–292. On hair and pigment politics, see Erasmus Z. 2000. 'Hair politics', in *Senses of Culture*, eds S Nuttall & C Michael. Oxford: Oxford University Press, 380–392. On consumer behaviour, see Burgess S. 2002. *SA Tribes: Who We Are, How We Live, What We Want From Life*. Cape Town: David Philip. On humour, see Adhikari M. 2006. '"God made the white man, God made the black man...": popular racial stereotyping of coloured people in apartheid South Africa'. *South African Historical Journal*, 55, 142–164.

62 Somers M. 1994. 'The narrative constitution of identity: a relational and network approach'. *Theory and Society*, 23, no. 5, 606.

63 Somers, 'Narrative constitution of identity', 606.

64 Scheub H. 1998. *Story*. Madison: University of Wisconsin Press, 126.

65 Schama S. 1995. *Landscape and Memory*. New York: Vintage, 6–7.

66 Ruth Peterson, interviewed by Henry Trotter, 12 January 2001; Mary Wyngaard, interviewed by Henry Trotter, 11 January 2001; Ronald and Rachel Lambert, interviewed by Henry Trotter, 16 December 2000.

67 For greater detail on how gender, class and age inflect coloured removee memory, see Trotter, H. 2002. 'Contoured memory: gender, class and generation', in 'Removals and remembrance: commemorating community in coloured Cape Town'. MA thesis, Yale University, 195–219.

68 Anderson B. 1991. *Imagined Communities: Reflections on the Origin and Spread of Nationalism*. London: Verso, especially 44.

69 Sofer C. 1949. 'Some aspects of inter-racial marriages in South Africa, 1925–46'. *Africa: Journal of the International African Institute*, 19, no. 3, 187–203.

70 Brubaker & Cooper, 'Beyond "identity"', 17.

CHAPTER 4

Identity and forced displacement: community and colouredness in District Six[1]

BY

CHRISTIAAN BEYERS

TRENT UNIVERSITY

District Six has been and continues to be one of the principal sites on which coloured identity is symbolically claimed and contested in Cape Town. For much of the 20th century this high-density neighbourhood, adjacent to the central business district of Cape Town, consisted of a largely low-income, 'racially' diverse population of which the majority was classified 'coloured'. After District Six was proclaimed a 'whites-only' area in 1966, most of its approximately 60 000 residents were forcibly removed to the barren and windswept Cape Flats in phases until 1982. African forced removals, however, date back to the turn of the 20th century. Today a large portion of District Six remains undeveloped[2] and subject to a land claims process under the post-apartheid Land Restitution Programme.

District Six has emerged as an exemplary site in the post-apartheid urban landscape for re-imagining community as a counterpoint to racial segregation, forced removals and social dislocation. While District Six prior to forced removals is commonly remembered as culturally and racially diverse, this image is underscored by a subtext which privileges an understanding of the area as primarily a 'coloured space'.[3] District Six holds a status of particular symbolic significance for popular perceptions of colouredness in Cape Town. John Western argues that due to their marginalisation, '[p]lace of origin – home – has become an essential element of self-definition for Coloured people... if there has been any place, any space that Coloureds have looked upon as "our territory", it is – or was – District Six'.[4] Whether or not one agrees with this view,[5] it does appear to be the case that, more than any other ethno-racially defined group, District Sixers – and indeed many Capetonians – self-identifying or identified as coloured feel their roots to be in District Six, and memorialise and sentimentalise this lost 'community'. Their sense of attachment has been bolstered by a mushrooming cultural industry around District Six from the latter part of the 1980s.

This chapter examines the relationship between identity, community and loss in the context of forced removals from District Six. How is the sense of commonality that underpins the notion of coloured identity posited within the fictional and autobiographical literature on District Six? And what forms of social exclusion occasion the assertion of such identity claims? These themes are explored in a reading of Richard Rive's conception of community in District Six in his novel, *Buckingham Palace*, as implicitly coloured. This sets the stage for a critique of some contemporary accounts of District Six, which construe the community as accommodating diversity, but do so within a frame of reference that corresponds to the particular conditions associated with being classified 'coloured'. Even the most reflective scholarly work on District Six arguably reinforces these tendencies by, for example, seeing cultural hybridity as fashioning a kind of unity out of a deeply differentiated socio-cultural and ideological field. In an effort to tackle the question of the exclusionary effect of this coloured-centric discourse, the present chapter closes with an examination of the most significant literary effort to date to redress the exclusion of Africans from the communal landscape of District Six. Nomvuyo Ngcelwane's *Sala Kahle, District Six: An African Woman's Perspective*[6] advances a highly distinct understanding of community which carries within it an implicit critique of current constructions of District Six as an essentially coloured space.

A key dilemma for any social constructionist approach to racialised identities is how to analyse identity formation without reinscribing 'race' in naturalised social or cultural categories.[7] In apartheid's system of racial classification, one's racial designation had overwhelming effects on almost all aspects of one's life. Moreover, within District Six's dense social fabric, people classified as 'coloured' not only tended to share certain social possibilities and constraints in common, but also certain cultural and linguistic points of reference. These were not necessarily as resonant among 'African' people (classified as 'Native', 'Bantu', or 'Black'), for example, who generally went to different schools, spoke Xhosa in addition to English or Afrikaans, worked at different kinds of jobs, travelled to different places and established different kinds of social networks. It is thus possible to speak *interpretively* of a coloured-centric perspective in District Six, if only for the purpose of revealing how identity formation was racialised in socially contingent and site-specific processes. This, of course, does not mean that socio-cultural formations always corresponded with racial categories – even under the auspices of 'separate development'. Rather, racial ascription was one, albeit very important, dimension of several in patterns of identification and exclusion.

Interpretive reliance upon the ordinary language of 'race' is problematic because it assumes a correspondence between racial ascription and self-identification. Consider, for example, people who do not self-identify as coloured – in fact, who consciously disavow the category – but are nevertheless widely perceived to be coloured in the society in which they live and work. This is significant in District Six, where political movements guided by a philosophy of non-racialism, such as the Non-European Unity Movement (NEUM) and the Anti-Coloured Affairs Department organisation, had substantial support. Nonetheless, the relevant point for the current analysis is that one is often socially included or excluded from a racially defined group based on how one is perceived in society at large, and regardless of one's self-definition to the contrary – even if this self-definition is echoed by a considerable minority. The analysis in this chapter thus strategically deploys racial markers in order to reveal the exclusionary dimensions of social conventions of discourse and practice. This is not by any means to endorse these conventions, and the attempt here is ultimately to undermine the apparent 'objectivity' of racial terms by revealing how they have been used in socially contingent ways to ground many stories or analyses of District Six. 'Coloured-centric', then, is not intended to presuppose the existence of an unchanging essence or 'centre' of colouredness which narratives of District Six approximate, but rather to highlight the underlying presumption of the existence of such a centre in these narratives. My argument is that this presumption allows difference to be rendered as sameness in the construct of community.

Approach to coloured identity

In *Coloured Ethnicity and Identity*, Birgit Pickel provides a good starting point for analysing coloured-centric constructions of community that is in keeping with the current trend of social constructionism in studies of identity.[8] Pickel sees coloured identity as consisting of a loosely fitting set of heterogeneous cultural elements that have come into being as a result of its segregated condition and middle position within colonial and apartheid society, and which derived an apparent coherence largely from the definition of out-groups.[9] This approach is broadly consonant with Fredrik Barth's classic treatment of 'community' as a situationally based form of identification whereby putative cultural differences are organised according to social boundaries that are established between 'us' and 'them'.[10] Some Neo-Barthians argue that the significance and the intensity of these differences arise largely from the social ideologies and means of classification of the state. Thus, Katherine Verdery argues, 'the practices of government in the modern state ... not only produce difference but also institute it in the form of "identities"'.[11] The weakness of this general approach is that it reduces individual agency to consciously manipulated categories that are received from the state. It fails to take adequate stock of the ways in which identity formation is determined by social and cultural codes and practices handed down from the past.[12] More significantly for this chapter, it fails to consider how identity is shaped in response to traumatic historical events. An inquiry into the dynamics of social inclusion and exclusion has to begin by asking what is fundamentally at stake in claiming an identity.

The aim of this chapter is not to advance a particular version of coloured identity to be situated among other approaches on offer, or to endorse a move to reclaim the proper name 'coloured' in order to affirm an overarching socio-cultural identity. It rather endeavours to say something useful about identity formation – how the self comes to be defined in relation to others – in a specific context. The object of analysis is not so much collective identity per se, but a range of claims made in the name of identity by different authors. What is called identity – and this applies not just to coloured identity – is seen as consisting of a range of truth claims. Moreover, different kinds of truth claims under the rubric of the same identity work according to different perceptual and cognitive criteria. The question then becomes how such a range of claims comes to exist under the same name.

This is not merely to endorse relativism or methodological individualism. Identity-based truth claims can over time cohere, in more or less durable ways, in patterns of narrative and symbolic meaning, and become materially embodied in social practices and institutional forms. They can fundamentally shape other basic value orientations such as an individual's organisation of the flow of experience into episodes, criteria for judging character, or standards of success or failure in life. Moreover, 'fixed' in various relatively stable representational forms, identity claims not only inform agency, but also figure as subjection by which externally imposed identities are internalised.[13] Notwithstanding these points, the question of how identity-based claims come to be stabilised in broader and more durable patterns of identification and subjection cannot be understood in abstraction of the social dynamics and symbolic struggles in which a concept of identity first takes root.

In the present case, the task is thus to analyse how ethno-racially inflected identity claims are used to assert commonalities of traumatic experience. Moreover, it is to understand how this occurs according to more or less authoritative representations that respond to the specific conditions and dilemmas of particular contexts and localities. In District Six, the impetus for identity construction comes from the deep sense of injustice of forced removals, and a rupture with a past way of life, as well as the possibility of restitution. This chapter thus tries to understand how a sense of community is generated by District Sixers in a historically mediated way. The aim is to discern how the formation of an identity through a traumatic history consists of partial characterisations of the past that carry certain socially exclusionary dimensions.

Loss and identity

Since the early 1980s, the particular context of identity formation around District Six has been one of traumatic loss due to forced removals. Discourses about District Six and the field of District Six politics have been dominated by coloured voices in part because the majority of the population of District Six was coloured, overwhelmingly so after the earlier removal of African people. Whereas most coloured and Indian residents were removed between 1968 and 1981 under the Group Areas Act, the majority of African District Sixers were removed well before this. Most recently, Africans were removed between 1958 and the early 1960s through a variety of legal mechanisms – most typically slum clearance legislation – under the auspices of the coloured Labour Preference Policy in the western Cape.[14] The coloured Labour Preference Policy, in tandem with laws controlling the influx of Africans into the western Cape, was designed to exclude African people from living and working in the western Cape, and Cape Town in particular, and thus protect coloured people in the region from African competition in the labour market. By institutionalising a relatively privileged citizenship status for coloureds, their political acquiescence was encouraged in the face of black resistance. The objective was to secure white dominance in the western Cape with the compliance of the coloured majority.[15] According to W M Eiselen, 'the Western Cape was the natural home of the Coloured people, and they have the right to be protected against the competition of Natives in the labour market'.[16] The result was that Africans were deported to ethnic homelands or driven to seek emergency accommodation in townships or informal settlements on the outskirts of Cape Town.[17]

The presence of Africans in Cape Town was thus precarious, transient and controlled, and to the extent that they managed to live there for any length of time, they maintained a low profile.[18] Africans were generally poorer than coloureds and faced different kinds of social and legal constraints. Writing of the broader context of Cape Town, Sindiwe Magona reveals some of the ambivalence with which African people consequently viewed coloureds:

> Were coloured people less oppressed because more was given to them than had been given to Africans? Coloured people did not carry passes. They had better houses which they could even own. Their salaries, while not equal to the salaries of whites, were far above what Africans earned. However, coloured people were not fully fledged citizens in South Africa.[19]

As will be discussed in the final section of the chapter, although African District Sixers often remember their relationships with coloured neighbours in highly amicable terms, their primary ties of affiliation tended to be with fellow African Capetonians.

Symbolic constructions of District Six generally reflected coloured privilege vis-à-vis African people in the western Cape. Before District Six was declared 'white', it was regarded as 'coloured' by the ruling establishment. When District Sixers were forcibly removed and their houses bulldozed, the liberal press lamented the loss of a 'coloured homeland'. The *Cape Times* averred that '[i]f there ever was an area in which Coloured people were entitled to live by tradition, by occupation, and by human right it is District Six'. It used a minority rights discourse to lament coloured people's loss of territory to which they had a historic claim, ostensibly their most solid foothold in an otherwise sparse cultural tradition.

The Department of Community Development, which was directly responsible for implementing the Group Areas Act, paternalistically rationalised the removals according to what would be in the presumed best interest of 'the Coloured population', which, it was argued, would be 'uplifted' by being moved from a 'slum' to the new housing developments on the Cape Flats.[20] It is thus not surprising that public responses to the 1966 proclamation of District Six as a 'white' area were articulated in terms of the coloured community being the victim of a gross injustice. A general memorandum of protest in September of 1974 is typical of sentiments of coloured District Sixers at the time:

> It is an indisputable fact and it should at all times be kept in mind that of all the people in South Africa the coloured South Africans are the only ones who cannot be traced back to an overseas country of origin. We were born and bred here. We were nurtured on the soil of this country, the only country we know. The origin of our people cannot be traced to before 1652 … We are deeply attached to our country and are intensely hurt by the fact that foreigners, who are not even citizens of this country, have an open sesame to everything this rich country has to offer with facilities and incentives which we have never received, while we, whose blood and sweat form the foundation of their riches, are rejected and must be satisfied with the crumbs which convenience drops our way. The law which has deprived the people of District Six of what was formerly theirs is evidence of this.[21]

The memorandum claims to be 'representative of the current thinking of the vast majority of coloured South Africans on the position of District Six'. In keeping with a liberal tradition going back to the African Political Organisation, its plea was framed in terms of the 'inalienable right of any person to have the freedom of owning and buying property in any area amongst people according to his financial means'. It is worth noting its overwhelming sense that coloured people had been wronged: 'we are the victims of what appears to be a vendetta against step-children who were not in a position to prevent their being brought into this world'.[22] The injustice was perceived to have arisen as a result of the violation of a relationship of trust between whites and coloureds, in terms of which the latter could look forward eventually to being lifted to a status equivalent to that of whites under white guardianship. Significantly, the memorandum appealed to whites to recognise that coloureds share a familial relationship with them as 'stepchildren'. Moreover, the possibility of tracing the roots of colouredness to pre-colonial Africa is excluded.

The memorandum explicitly uses coloured identity to posit an equivalence in the face of a historical wrong, and to call for some sort of justice. The various experiences of removals of people designated coloured are understood to be essentially the same. 'Community' is claimed for the first time at the point that it becomes necessary to talk about a collective entity that has been wronged.[23] This is an imminently political act of voicing a grievance in the name of others within the community who are taken as equal. As racialised others, people classified as 'African' are not fully incorporated within the rubric of community. This process of identity formation and exclusion has much to do with the spatial segregation of people officially designated 'coloured' and their relative privilege vis-à-vis other people designated 'African'. As Pickel remarks, '[s]ocialization in segregated group areas has left persons formerly classified as coloured with a distinct in-group perception that differs from that of whites and Africans'.[24] In the words of one African claimant, the removals 'made everything change between the coloured and black people', as this is where 'people came to know themselves [as different]'.[25] This is illustrated in Richard Rive's novel, *Buckingham Palace*, where community is constructed as a subject of loss that is implicitly coloured, and where the figure of the African District Sixer remains conspicuously absent.

The birth of community in *Buckingham Palace*

Richard Rive's novel, *Buckingham Palace*, which has become a standard component of the post-apartheid school curriculum in Cape Town, is an extended commemoration of community in District Six.[26] The novel is divided into three parts – Morning 1955, Afternoon 1960 and Night 1970 – which are intended to reflect 'the story' of forced removals in District Six. The structure of the novel is of a fall from an age of innocence before forced removals to a dreadful and lonely life on the Cape Flats. The bulk of the novel recounts the experiences of characters who live in or near a house called Buckingham Palace. Their reflection on 'the spirit of the community' is provoked by their own forced removal as coloureds. Significantly, the prior removal of Africans is not registered. After all, the 'Morning' of the novel would be late evening for African

District Sixers. Each of the sections of the novel begins with an italicised introduction narrated in the first person, and cast in the register of a reflective autobiography. It is not clear who the narrator of the story is, but this voice seems to reflect Rive's personal outlook, particularly towards the end of the novel.

Tellingly, the term 'community' does not figure in the dialogue of the characters until their imminent eviction, although the first section of the book tries to paint a picture of close communal living filled with characters and incidents that reinforce their sense of affinity. Following the announcement of planned removals under 'the Group Areas'[27] with the advent of 'Evening', the novel shifts into an explicitly commemorative and nostalgic register. The idea of community is evoked most strongly when contrasting residents' 'life in common' in District Six with their atomised existence on the Cape Flats after their eviction. For instance, in the introduction to the final part, Rive writes:

> *Many were forced to move to small matchbox houses in large matchbox townships which with brutal and tactless irony were given names by the authorities such as Hanover Park and Lavender Hill to remind us of the past they had taken away from us. There was one essential difference between the old places and the new ones. District Six had a soul. Its centre held together till it was torn apart. Stained and tarnished as it was, it had a soul that held together. The new matchbox conglomerates on the desolate Cape Flats had no soul. The houses were soulless units piled together to form a disparate community that lacked cohesion.*[28]

In the absence of social cohesion and solidarity on the Cape Flats, and the loss of a 'past that they had taken away from us', District Six is imagined as uniform in essence. It is visualised as having a 'centre', and yet there is no sociological conception of what this centre was or how the different parts of the community cohered.

The introductions to each of the novel's three parts are used to provide an evaluative framework for locating the characters morally and understanding the historical relevance of the plot. The author's opinions intrude progressively through the novel in both the consciousness of the narrator and of other characters. Towards the end of the novel, character dialogue directly corresponds with Rive's personal reflections, where the idea of community serves to unify the experience of loss. Thus Mary, the brothel keeper, tries to persuade the 'respectable' Mrs Knight to refuse state-provided accommodation in a township: 'One place might be like another, but one community is never like another. A community is not just a place where you live. It is not just another locality like Hanover Park or Bonteheuwel.'[29] Here, the concept of community is expanded from a close-knit neighbourhood around Buckingham Palace and the 'Casbah' brothel to an entire municipal district encompassing tens of thousands of residents. The whole of District Six is now represented as 'community' and as 'home'. The catalyst for this change is residents' sense of solidarity as victims of racial injustice. The spiritual fusion of part with the whole becomes clear when the main character, Zoot, pays homage to Mary:

> She is leaving us to look after her father, but I know that her heart will always be here. Buckingham Palace will be razed next week, but Mary will still be here. And even when District Six is gone, there will still be Marys here. Because they can never destroy our Marys. Mary is District Six.[30]

Mary comes to represent solidarity in loss.

Towards the end of the novel the author's viewpoint asserts itself to the extent that he begins to speak through Zoot:

> We cannot fight this thing alone. We must join up with others who are already fighting, with those who are losing their houses and are afraid of also losing their manhood. We must join up with all other so-called *untermenschen*. Only that way we can win. We lost because we tried to fight this thing alone. It's not a Buckingham Palace thing. Not only our houses are being demolished, it is not District Six that is being thrown down, but the whole country. I know what I will do. I know with whom I will work.[31]

If the spirit of community is feminised in the figure of Mary, the cause of justice is embodied in a 'fight for manhood'. Most of the other characters acknowledge that Zoot is right, and the cause of unified black resistance to apartheid is made to triumph. However, this rise to political consciousness of the main character introduces a tension within the book between its concept of community, which is implicitly understood as coloured, and a vague anticipation of a unified black South Africa. While Zoot muses that '[w]e are all those who suffer in this sad land',[32] the novel lacks any recognition of Africans having suffered forced removal from District Six. Curiously, in the very last pages, 'a huge Xhosa' suddenly makes an appearance in the figure of the night watchman guarding the area for white bosses as it is being demolished. But while there is dialogue with the white demolishers in this final chapter, and with other white characters earlier on, the Xhosa remains voiceless and in the background. He is described as making a fire in 'a galley from his hut'[33] around which the now bereft inhabitants of Buckingham Palace gather one final time. The author tells us that the night watchman is the last to salute Zoot – 'in Xhosa' – before he walks from the fire, a gesture presumably meant to underscore Zoot's resolve to fight.

Buckingham Palace's commemoration of a community in loss contrasts sharply with Rive's earlier writing, which consciously disavowed the tendency to romanticise 'the slum'. In his novel, *Emergency*, published in the mid-1960s and banned in South Africa until 1988, Rive summarises life in the District: 'The filth, the grime. Prostitutes. Street fights. People with no aim in life except to eke out their miserable existences on their Friday night's pay'.[34] Having moved out of District Six, the protagonist, Andrew, 'was determined to blot out the memory of the slums, the dirt, the poverty'. He recalls the 'feeling of shame and humiliation'[35] he felt when his friends from the affluent neighbouring suburb of Walmer Estate came to his old home in District Six.[36] The novel leaves one with a strong sense of the stigma attached to District Six.[37] While Rive self-consciously rejected the notion of race as a basis for identification, Desiree Lewis in an article on the writings of Rive and Zoë Wicomb shows that far from resolving problems of identity, Rive's work stages a compulsive return to matters of racial ascription and identification in an autobiographical 'confessional voice'.[38]

In contrast to *Emergency, Buckingham Palace's* nostalgic commemoration of life in the District rests upon an insular concept of community. District Six is represented in the words of Zoot as 'an island in a sea of apartheid'. He argues that apartheid only becomes visible to the District Sixer 'when the white man comes and forces it on us, when he makes us see it – when the police come, and the council people, and so on – or when we leave the District'.[39] This image of a non-racial and caring community denies the extent to which apartheid shaped life in the District. While the diversity of the neighbourhood is evoked through mention of 'Malay music', the Indian corner shop and the Jewish landlord,[40] Africans do not figure in the consciousness of Rive's characters or even in descriptions of the novel's settings. For *Buckingham Palace*, the burden of history is expressed in a particular way. The formation of a communal identity of those who have been wronged becomes the basis for the emergence of a cross-sectoral political consciousness. However, the cause of unified resistance is betrayed at the outset in the exclusionary construction of identity.

Nostalgic commemoration in autobiographical accounts of District Six

Since the late 1980s, a number of autobiographical and semi-autobiographical works have been published by former District Six residents. This relatively new form of popular cultural entrepreneurship is an outgrowth not only of the heightened awareness of the District as a flagship for redress in the democratic order, but also more concretely of activists encouraging community participation in processes around land restitution. The District Six Museum[41], by promoting the participation of former residents in mounting exhibits, and running artistic projects and writing workshops, has encouraged 'ordinary people … to describe themselves as they wish to be seen'.[42] Autobiographical accounts generally reflect the views of most District Sixers that I interviewed who are currently claiming land rights under the Land Restitution Act, particularly of claimants living in predominantly coloured residential areas.[43]

Buckingham Palace's tendency to commemorate 'the old times' is reflected in these autobiographical accounts. One example of nostalgic commemoration that carries an implicit coloured subtext is the portrayal of gangsterism as having been relatively innocuous. Indeed, giving gangsterism a positive gloss is one of the ways in which community is aestheticised in coloured-centric terms – along with, for example, the Coon Carnival, about which much has been written.[44] Gangs are usually associated with a coloured social milieu and, as Don Pinnock demonstrates in his classic study on the subject, the proliferation of gangsterism in Cape Town is closely associated with the creation of predominantly coloured residential areas on the Cape Flats through forced removals.[45] Indeed, gangsterism is often assumed to be a defining characteristic of colouredness. As one man explained, 'you will never get [gangsterism] out of us, it's innate to the coloured people'.[46] In *Noor's Story: My Life in District Six*, Noor Ebrahim recalls listening to gangsters sing, and enjoying watching gangsters fighting among themselves.[47] In *William Street, District Six*, Hettie Adams claims that '[i]n District Six we had decent skollies' and that gangs 'never harmed you if you minded your own business'. She remembers that 'the leader of the Globe Gang …

had teeth full of gold, he was smart and suave and you'd never think he's a gangster'.[48] Common decency is seen to be upheld by gang leaders, and gangsters are seen as having been gentlemanly towards women and the elderly.[49] In autobiographical texts where gangs are commemorated, African District Sixers are invariably absent.[50]

While racial prejudice is seldom expressed directly in these accounts, there are numerous indications of its existence and there is a lack of concern with the predicament of African District Sixers. When claimants talk about the multiracial, multicultural and cosmopolitan character of District Six, Africans, Indians and especially whites are taken as enriching the mixture, but seldom as offsetting the implicit dominance of the coloured majority. Thus Hettie Adams recounts that she would only visit her brother's wife Ruby and her children in the '*hokkie*' [shack] in which the couple lived in her backyard 'when Dadda was not home; I mustn't go there because they are too black'. Adams confides that Ruby's children 'looked all right when they are small, but when they were three they turned out with big lips like Ruby'. Although Ruby was classified 'coloured', she had to keep a low profile in public. And after a policeman stopped her and her pale-skinned husband in the botanical gardens, he 'never took Ruby for a walk again'. Adams recounts that over time she developed a close friendship with Ruby. She intonates that 'no one said those days, You are a kaffir, or this or that, we were all happy together in the street, all the same'. Nevertheless, Africans figure only anonymously in the book, as 'the Africans on the corner'. Adams also tells of the tragic ordeal of a 'Malay' woman named Siesie who 'married an African' who was eventually deported. This man – who was '[s]uch a quiet man, he didn't fight, never argued, a proper gentleman' – is implicitly set apart from other Africans, for 'though he was from Transkei he had all the coloured ways, he knew nothing else, he grew up with us. I don't know how that happened'.[51]

Linda Fortune's *House in Tyne Street* is somewhat atypical of the genre in that she at least briefly considers the plight of African District Sixers. Fortune describes a shebeen on her street in a double-storey building 'inhabited by "Natives"', and talks about a friend, Lindiwe, who lived upstairs with the 'select' people whom she describes as 'caring and respectable and dressed smartly [and who] ... didn't drink or behave foolishly or make noise'. Lindiwe's voice is at one point manifested directly, when Fortune tells of her determination to avoid her mother's fate of being a domestic servant: 'I know I'll have to work very hard, because there won't be many opportunities for us in future. My parents can't even leave the house now without their passes.' Fortune recalls being upset for some time by the look on Lindiwe's face when she spoke of her plans. Fortune's recollection that the removal of African people living in the building and elsewhere on Tyne Street occurred very suddenly one night, and her inability to understand why Lindiwe had not come to bid her farewell is suggestive of the divide between African and coloured District Sixers.[52]

These memories do not cloud Fortune's otherwise rosy recollection of community life in District Six:

> Different kinds of people lived in these buildings – 'select' people, average families, and gangsters all lived next to each other, and all hung their washing from the balconies. There was no other place. Couples who got married moved in with their families and new babies were born and grew up here. The elderly passed away and younger people took their places. People of all colours and creeds lived side by side. Sometimes a fight would break out, but when it was settled, things would just go back to normal. Here and there a brilliant child would manage to study in these conditions. He or she would finish school and end up being someone of importance. Everyone in District Six would respect such a person.[53]

Her positive gloss on dense urban living is punctuated by the child who rises above the conditions of poverty to respectability. Despite her incantation that 'people of all colours and creeds lived side by side', it is clear that the figure of the 'brilliant child' almost certainly does not refer to an African child. As the difficulties facing Lindiwe attest, African children did not have access to the opportunities, however limited, available to coloured or Indian children. As in other literature of this sort, Fortune's concept of community in District Six is tacitly coloured-centric.

In the post-removals literature reviewed thus far, the trouble with proclamations such as 'the people of District Six shared and cared for each other ... no matter what colour they were',[54] is not only that there is a singular lack of concern with the predicament of African District Sixers, or that they have only a nominal presence in these accounts. It is also that community is aestheticised in terms of cultural reference points that are widely understood to be coloured. Africans are thus excluded in a fundamental way from the symbolic construction of District Six. The silencing of the Africanness of District Six is necessary to a particular cultural construction of the community as a subject of loss. Africans were accommodated in the coloured-centric social rubric on lesser terms than coloureds who were deemed to resemble Africans physically.

Casting race-based exclusion

Crain Soudien's scholarly analysis of District Six as 'a site of social construction' is useful for thinking further about the exclusion of Africans in representations of District Six. Soudien seeks 'to understand *how* District Sixers have written themselves in the range of oral, written and other media'. In what he calls 'critical non-racialism', identity is taken as 'multiplicitous' and its subjects as 'contradictory and inconsistent'. Soudien uses an agent-centred reading of Homi Bhabha's concept of hybridity, and its associations with disavowal of origins, ambivalence and subversion of authority, to interpret the discourses of District Six as revealing a sharing, harmonious and cosmopolitan society. Hybridisation is elaborated as 'cultural synchretism', which is seen as the alternative to racist narratives of miscegenation, such that District Six is presented not as 'Europe, Africa or Asia, but its most generative cultural amalgam'. At the same time, Soudien is attentive to the way in which discourses of non-racism in District Six work to exclude Africans.[55]

By emphasising the pluralistic and performative character of identity formation, Soudien clears conceptual ground for theorising the production of coloured identity in particular sites. District Six is seen as a 'deprivileged symbolic terrain in which symbols overlapped and fused', a 'district … in excess of its parts'.[56] It does indeed appear to be the case that District Six consisted of a comparatively open and inclusionary society, at least in comparison with most of South Africa. The area has come to be known for what might be called its 'ethos of accommodation'. Interviewees describe a tolerance of racial difference and even a colour blindness, and widespread practices of mutual support. These elements are to some extent encapsulated in the term *Kanaladorp*, which signifies both a call for help and a sense of duty. District Six was indeed renowned for its dense associational life, cultural borrowing and improvisation, or 'the spirit of working across boundaries', as Soudien succinctly puts it.[57] This ethos is seen to be based on the street culture and the sense of spontaneity and informality that defined everyday life in the area.

In some respects, Soudien's use of the concept of hybridity does well to evoke the ways in which District Sixers were able to transcend the narrow confines of apartheid-era racial categorisation. This general ethos of accommodation could to some extent be seen as a social expression of being identified as coloured, for although the concept of 'coloured' is racial in origin, the residual social status associated with it appears to have permitted a degree of indeterminacy that allowed for greater accommodation of social, cultural and 'racial' difference than other racial categories.[58] At the same time, it has been demonstrated that not everyone was accommodated in the same way in District Six. The virtue of Soudien's analysis is that it recognises the exclusionary character of this non-racial discourse. He demonstrates that even self-critical intellectual discourse on District Six continues to be symbolically informed by colouredness. The social history of Africans is included, but as an appendage to a historiography defined by a predominantly coloured cultural frame of reference:

> In taking in narratives of Europe, Asia and Africa, and in crafting the linguistic, gestural and symbolic forms which were its hallmark, it left unspoken, or largely so, its umbilical connection to pre-colonial Africa. The figure of this Africa was absent – an unspeakable presence – sublimated within a hybridized discourse which played mainly in the space of its colonial history ... The role accorded to Africa in this hybridization was essentially that of a carrier. Africa carried the district's melding of its European and Asian pasts, and when it had played its role, the carrier was ingested and rendered harmless.[59]

While Soudien's analysis identifies the need to address this historical exclusion, it is debatable whether his theory of identity construction enables the analysis to move beyond a coloured-centric perspective. The concept of hybridisation is used to provide a unifying frame for understanding the construction of a plurality of identities as a continuous socio-cultural formation, a 'unity structured in difference'. He thus speaks of 'people who lived across boundaries and who imbibed and reproduced a culture which was intelligible in what people ate, sang and did'.[60] Is there not an essentialism that is smuggled in under the proxy of hybridisation? Does the 'cultural amalgam' of District Six not privilege certain kinds of difference? Whatever the verdict, a greater emphasis needs to be placed on a concept of socio-cultural *heterogeneity*[61] – the existence of distinct forms of identification and social solidarity involving discontinuous socio-cultural frames of reference. While racial distinction was by no means the only source for such discontinuity in the apartheid era, its importance was considerable indeed.

In attempting to move beyond coloured-centric discourses, it is important not to reify or essentialise the African perspective on District Six, for African identities are of course also multiple and subject to processes of hybridisation. Rather, what is called for is attention to the range of identity claims made from subject positions corresponding to this general racial ascription. For example, one claimant averred that '[non-Muslim] coloureds haven't got culture' – not an unusual assertion – whereas 'Muslims and us [Africans] are very similar'[62] due ostensibly to their adherence to established rituals and cultural practices. In contrast, other African claimants characterise Muslims as being similar to coloureds. Thus one 90-year-old man claimed that 'Moslem people … they took the style of the coloured people … because they only come from other countries'.[63] The point is that neither hybridisation nor racial identification are unitary processes, which warrant the assertion of a common culture, or a set of internally consistent frames of reference for the expression of identity, in District Six.

'An African woman's perspective'

Nomvuyo Ngcelwane's *Sala Kahle District Six*[64] provides a unique perspective on community in the area. A former District Six resident of African descent, Ngcelwane was surprised when she found out in March 1996 that Africans also qualified for compensation from the government, since it was rarely recognised that Africans had lived in District Six. As she puts it, 'it is often forgotten that we hold the same sentiments about the place as [our coloured neighbours]'.[65] When she visited the District Six Museum for the first time, she resolved to write about her own experience as an African woman living in District Six.

As a child, Ngcelwane lived in a building on Cross Street, a family crammed into each room. She recalls that:

> [t]he whole building, from No. 22 to No. 28, was occupied by Black tenants. It was quite unusual that most of us shared the same clan name: ama-Bhele …. [A]ccording to our Xhosa culture, the men were all brothers by virtue of having the same clan name, and this was how they treated each other. The

other family groups who stayed in our building did not belong to the Mbele clan, but still they were treated with love and respect. There was no doubt that these people were Christians and that their motto was 'Love thy neighbour'.

By Ngcelwane's account, the strongest ties of solidarity among Africans were along lines of kinship. She thus recalls that among African District Sixers, *ubuntu*, '[t]he deep sense that kinship controlled the social relationship between the Black inhabitants of District Six in the same way as it did in the country', corresponded to the value of *kanala* in the coloured population. While Ngcelwane remembers playing in the street with a group which she describes as a 'crazy mixture of a lot of Coloured and a few African children', she does not convey the same degree of blending between home and street in the social life of her community as found in the rest of the literature. Ngcelwane also remembers that her name varied between these two spheres; at home her parents and other African residents addressed her as Nomvuyo whereas the coloured friends she played with in the street used her 'English name', Marjorie or Marge.[66]

Although the general image of relations between African and coloured District Sixers in *Sala Kahle* is congenial, the book helps to correct the image of District Six as an island of racial tolerance in apartheid South Africa. The legal and social constraints faced by Africans elsewhere applied in District Six as well. Some public facilities were segregated, and there are indications that coloureds sometimes thought of African people as essentialised racial others. In *Sala Kahle*, these indications are usually subtle and implicit. For example, coloured onlookers of a stick-fighting game during the festivities at a wedding remarked of the African young men that '[t]hese people really have hard heads'. Another example is provided by the story of Mzwandile, one of Ngcelwane's neighbours, who, along with an 'other illegal man', was arrested, presumably under influx control legislation. Upon their release, they 'were advised to go elsewhere or back to Qoboqobo as the police were aware of their presence and would now increase their raids of Cross Street'. Mzwandile was further counselled by his friends that the easiest way that he could gain residence rights would be by joining the police force, which he decided to do. Ncelwane recalls that

[t]he Coloured neighbours were amazed when they saw him in police uniform for the first time. Because the pass laws did

not affect them, they did not understand that Mzwandile had no choice. That he could actually maintain law and order in the area surprised them too. They did not believe it possible that a Black policeman could arrest a Coloured person.

Clearly empathising with Mzwandile's predicament, Ngcelwane draws the reader's sympathy by describing how as a police officer, Mzwandile would intervene with coloured boys who were tormenting mating dogs. The coloured boys would in turn taunt Mzwandile, saying that he could not arrest them.[67]

Ngcelwane demonstrates how social bonds formed among African District Sixers. She recalls that

> [s]chool was quite a social place, because here we had the opportunity of meeting other Black children. The Black families lived spread out amongst the Coloured and other families in District Six, and as most grown-ups worked outside District Six, our parents mostly met one another through the friends we made at school.

The primary social ties constituting a sense of community were not confined to the boundaries of District Six, but reached into other areas of central Cape Town and often further afield to places such as Langa and Nyanga on the outskirts of the city. Ngcelwane claims that some African children that attended coloured schools passed for 'coloured', and '[b]ecause most of our parents did not want us to lose our identity, we were all sent to the Methodist School in Chapel Street. It would not be long before we would visit the friends we made at school during weekends, meeting their families and starting to invite one another to birthday parties'. Once parents had met one another through their children, community building occurred in other ways as well: 'Because our parents regularly met in church, after this, we all came to know each other really well, and the Black residents of District Six became a very tight-knit community.'[68]

Ngcelwane increasingly grew apart from her coloured friends as she grew older. After standard 2 (grade 4), most African children would have to travel by train to the Langa Methodist school. Prior to this move, she recalls a blissful time in her 'small group' of mostly coloured friends in Cross Street, and tells of her best friend Gladys, a coloured girl with whom she was 'very close'. Things would inevitably change after she started attending school in Langa, 'because the different race groups had to attend different schools, only African pupils could be members of our study group. I became closer to my Langa school mates and saw less and less of my old Coloured friends'.[69]

There are many other references to African communal life in Ngcelwane's book. *Sala Kahle* refers to frequent visits by African residents to other parts of the city, but also to far-flung rural areas. She describes *ukugoduka*, the practice of going to the country during the summer holidays to visit family. Someone undertaking such a trip would be sent off with an *umkhwelo* (house party) to which 'African people from all around District Six would be invited', and where money would be collected for the traveller through an *umgalelo* – 'a club for pooling of funds and mutual support, usually organized in rotation at members' homes'. She indicates that the African community had internal mechanisms for establishing and maintaining authority and order: 'The adults formed a united front when it came to the disciplining of children', and in the case of a husband caught battering his wife, a meeting of the *ibhunga* ('disciplinary committee') would be called, usually resulting in a fine. According to Ngcelwane, '[s]ince the group structure was so important to everybody, the offender would conform fully to its laws'.[70]

Later in the book, Ngcelwane incidentally mentions that many of the African residents of District Six were *amaMfengu*. Ngcelwane's brief discussion of her ethnic identity and its placement late in the book may be due to ethnic solidarity being overridden by a broader African identity. A more likely reason that ethnic identity is downplayed in the book is that the *amaMfengu* 'were unpopular with the other Africans living in the Eastern Cape' on account of their historical 'closeness and co-operation with Whites, as well as their non-participation in the national suicide of the *amaXhosa* in 1857'. Ngcelwane adds that 'African freedom fighters and political activists were not at all in favour of promoting ethnicity'.[71]

Ngcelwane identifies her primary community in District Six as African. The book's cast consists largely of African characters, and is full of references to formal and informal groups such as choirs, sports teams, musical bands and circles of friends that were almost exclusively African. While social relations with coloured co-residents are generally represented as amicable and caring, coloured people are rarely identified by name, and their characters remain undeveloped. That solidarity along racial lines should figure prominently in the formation of community among African residents in District Six is not surprising given that they formed a racially prescribed minority with a lower citizenship status than other South Africans. *Sala Kahle* is significant not only because it establishes the presence of African people in District Six and their deep sense of attachment to the place, but also because it frames their presence as a collective and distinctive one. It is noteworthy that, despite the aforementioned differences, there is in *Sala Kahle* a sense of mutual sympathy between African and coloured District Sixers. While there was evidently a greater degree of tolerance of social difference in the District than elsewhere, the advent of forced removals no doubt heightened a sense of solidarity against a common external enemy. Ngcelwane recalls that when Africans received notice of their imminent forced removal, 'the Coloured neighbours were concerned, because we had stayed together and shared so much for so many years'.[72]

That individuals can make multiple identity claims is by now a well-rehearsed truism in social constructionist analyses of identity. It is more interesting to ask by what social and political logic various identity claims are sometimes connected. While Ngcelwane identifies her primary community as African, she also finds common cause with coloureds in her oppression by a common enemy. And yet, in addition to cultural heritage, her identification with other Africans turns on the specific character of her oppression due to her racial categorisation. The burden of history manifests itself in combination with cultural heritage in a markedly different way from the coloured-centric narratives of District Six considered earlier, and this has important implications for how District Six is defined, both as a historical symbol of relative tolerance, and as a social and political project of redressing a historic injustice.

Conclusion

Narratives of identity in District Six carry the burden of a traumatic history of forced displacement. Assuming that the social reality to which talk of identity refers is inherently heterogeneous, the question is: How does identity talk posit a unity of experience in the face of a traumatic past? In most of the post-removals literature, various identity claims function by positing an implicitly coloured concept of community. Claiming a coloured collective identity is about rendering the various experiences of removals of people thus designated coloured as essentially the same. In Rive's *Buckingham Palace*, as in much autobiographical and popular testimony, identification assumes the character of a fall from innocence, and Africans figure as silent bystanders. Moreover, community is aestheticised according to socio-cultural reference points that correspond to the realm of experience of being legally classified as 'coloured'. The edifice of community is thus symbolically predicated upon a silence, which manifests the history of social exclusion of Africans in the region. The specific character of 'African community' in Ngcelwane's *Sala Kahle* suggests that District Six cannot adequately be conceived of as a continuous socio-cultural formation, even in hybridised form. Instead, District Six consisted of a heterogeneous order that included fundamental social and cultural differences. Such differences were, of course, reflected in various forms of social identification, but the idea of 'race' often constituted an overarching frame of reference. District Six's ethos of accommodation, and cultural and racial tolerance did not extend to all District Sixers in the same way, and this is first of all evident in the way that District Six has been and continues to be remembered.

Endnotes

1   I am grateful to Mohamed Adhikari and Kerry Bebee for their invaluable comments on earlier drafts of this paper.

2   It remains undeveloped due to concerted popular resistance as well as opposition from developers and corporations that did not want the mark of District Six against their names. See Soudien C. 1990. 'District Six: from protest to protest', in *The Struggle for District Six: Past and Present*, eds S Jeppie & C Soudien. Cape Town: Buchu Books.

3   Soudien C. 2001. 'District Six and its uses in the discussion about non-racialism', in *Coloured by History, Shaped by Place: New Perspectives on Coloured Identities in Cape Town*, ed Z Erasmus. Cape Town: Kwela Books, 117.

4   Western J. 1981. *Outcast Cape Town*. London: George Allen & Unwin, 146, 149.

5   Z Wicomb, for example, criticises 'the myth of our collective birth in Cape Town's District Six', and calls for 'a strategy of relocating and rehistoricizing our situation'. See Wicombe Z. 1998. 'Shame and identity: the case of the coloured in South Africa', in *Writing South Africa*, eds D Attridge & R Jolly. Cambridge: Cambridge University Press, 91–107.

6   Ngcelwane N. 1999. *Sala Kahle District Six: An African Woman's Perspective*. Cape Town: Kwela Books.

7   See Gilroy P. 1991. *There Ain't No Black in the Union Jack: The Cultural Politics of Race and Nation*. Chicago: Chicago University Press; and Nayak A. 2006. 'After race: ethnography, race and post-race theory'. *Ethnic and Racial Studies*, 29, no. 3, 411–430.

8   Pickel B. 1997. *Coloured Ethnicity and Identity: A Case Study in the Former Coloured Areas in the Western Cape/South Africa*. Hamburg: Lit Verlag.

9   Pickel, *Coloured Ethnicity*, 108.

10 Barth F. 1970. *Ethnic Groups and Boundaries: The Social Organization of Cultural Difference*. London: Allen & Unwin; Verdery K. 1994. 'Ethnicity, nationalism, and

state-making: ethnic groups and boundaries: past and future', in *The Anthropology of Ethnicity: Beyond Ethnic Groups and Boundaries*, eds H Vermeuten & C Govers. Amsterdam: Het Spinkins, 34–35.

11 Verdery, 'Ethnicity, nationalism, and state-making', 47.

12 See Jackson S. 2006. 'Coloureds don't toyi-toyi: gesture, constraint and identity in Cape Town', in *Limits to Liberation after Apartheid: Citizenship Governance and Culture*, ed S L Robins. Athens: Ohio University Press, 206–224.

13 According to D T Goldberg, '"[r]acial subjection" seeks ... to turn imposition into self-assumption, assertive charge into autonomy, self-imposed choice ... '. Goldberg D T. 2002. *The Racial State*. Oxford: Blackwell, 106.

14 See Barnett N. 1993. 'Race, housing and town planning in Cape Town, c.1920–1940, with special reference to District Six'. MA thesis, University of Cape Town, 154–158; Posel D. 1991. *The Making of Apartheid, 1948–1961: Conflict and Compromise*. Oxford: Clarendon Press, 88, 219–220.

15 Humphries R. 1989. 'Administrative politics and the Coloured Labour Preference Policy', in *The Angry Divide: Social and Economic History of the Western Cape*, eds W James & M Simons. Cape Town: David Philip, 169–179.

16 Cited in Posel, *The Making of Apartheid*, 87.

17 Unterhalter E. 1987. *Forced Removal: The Division, Segregation and Control of the People of South Africa*. London: IDAF.

18 African people nevertheless continued to form a significant minority in District Six until the early 1960s. Census figures on the proportion of Africans in District Six are not credible, as many would not have wanted to be identified in such data given the legal prescriptions against them. According to Lauren Waring, head of the District Six Team at the Regional Land Claims Commission Office in 2002, there are approximately 400 African land restitution claims out of a total of some 2 200 in 2002, a number which she claimed to be disproportionately small when compared with rough estimates of their respective original resident populations in District Six. Lauren Waring, interviewed by Christiaan Beyers, 17 June 2002.

19 Magona S. 1992. *Forced to Grow*. Cape Town: David Philip, 134.

20 *Cape Times*, 14 February 1966.

21 The memorandum is signed by Rev J F Forbes of Zonnebloem College, and 'four other people/groups' (District Six Land Claims Unit files, Regional Land Claims Commission Office, Cape Town).

22 Memorandum, September 1974.

23 Rancière J. 1995. 'Politics, identification, and subjectivization', in *The Identity in Question*, ed J Rajchman. New York: Routledge, 63–72.

24 Pickel, *Coloured Ethnicity*, 108.

25 D Ncube interviewed by T Nxumalo, 18 January 2002, District Six Museum Sound Archives.

26 Rive R. 1986. *Buckingham Palace*. Cape Town: David Philip.

27 Rive, *Buckingham Palace*, 183.

28 Rive, *Buckingham Palace*, 127. (Italics in the original)

29 Rive, *Buckingham Palace*, 159.

30 Rive, *Buckingham Palace*, 191.

31 Rive, *Buckingham Palace*, 187–188.

32 Rive, *Buckingham Palace*, 188.

33 Rive, *Buckingham Palace*, 196.
34 Rive R. 1964. *Emergency*. Cape Town: David Philip, 89.
35 Rive, *Emergency*, 86.
36 This sentiment is expressed in Rive's own autobiography, *Writing Black*, where he claims that he grew up in an 'atmosphere of shabby respectability, in a family chafing against its social confinement to dirty, narrow streets in a beaten-up neighbourhood'. Cited in Lewis D. 2001. 'Writing hybrid selves: Richard Rive and Zoë Wicomb', in *Coloured by History*, ed Z Erasmus, 135.
37 An even more forceful counterpoint to nostalgic commemoration is to be found in La Guma A. 1968. *A Walk in the Night: Seven Stories from the Streets of Cape Town*. Oxford: Heinemann; and Dangor A. 1995. *Waiting for Leila*. Randburg: Ravan Press.
38 Lewis D. 2001. 'Writing hybrid selves: Richard Rive and Zoë Wicomb', in *Coloured by History*, ed Z Erasmus, 135, 136.
39 Rive, *Buckingham Palace*, 96.
40 Rive, *Buckingham Palace*, 2, 3, 40, 144–153.
41 The museum was founded by a highly committed group of activists and intellectuals in the late 1980s in order to memorialise the former neighbourhood and its destruction. According to a banner hanging in the museum, it was also their intention 'to repossess the history of the area as a place where people lived, loved, and struggled'. The 'repossession' is framed as a participatory and interactive process – as a process of active incorporation – in which 'community members' are called upon to reveal the past. See Jeppie S & Soudien C (eds). 1990. *The Struggle for District Six: Past and Present*. Cape Town: Buchu Books; Rassool C & Prosalendis S (eds). 2001. *Recalling Community in Cape Town*. South Africa: District Six Museum; and Beyers C. 2008. 'The cultural politics of "community" and citizenship in the District Six Museum, Cape Town', in *Anthropologica, Special Issue: Citizenship, Politics and Locality: Anthropological Perspectives*, 50, no. 2, 359–373.
42 Prosalendis S. 2001. 'Punctuations: periodic impressions of a museum', in *Recalling Community*, eds Rassool & Prosalendis, 84.
43 A series of autobiographical works produced in Canada are much less representative, although their approaches are coloured-centric and commemorative. These works are inflected with issues relating to the immigration of these authors and with Canadian social concerns. See Maart R. 1990. *Talk about It!* Toronto: Awomandla!; Maart, R. 2006. *Roza's District 6*. Cape Town: David Philip; and Kester N G. 2000. From *Here to District Six*. Toronto: District Six Press.
44 Autobiographical accounts generally contain rich descriptions of the carnival. For an academic analysis, see Constant-Martin D. 1999. *Coon Carnival: New Year in Cape Town, Past and Present*. Cape Town: David Philip.
45 Pinnock D. 1984. *The Brotherhoods: Street Gangs and State Control in Cape Town*. Cape Town: David Philip.
46 Mr Hendricks, interviewed by Christiaan Beyers, 4 August 2001.
47 Ebrahim N. 1999. *Noor's Story: My Life in District Six*. Cape Town: District Six Museum, 42–43.
48 Adams H & Suttner H. 1988. *William Street, District Six*. Cape Town: Chameleon Press, 65.

49 In *Buckingham Palace*, 'the Jungle Boys' relish defending the stand against dangers from outside. They defend 'the Girls' in the community from, for example, Portuguese sailors 'looking for girls and waving bottles of wine and money' and narrowly save the teenager Faith from the clutches of the white sexual predator nicknamed 'Elvis'. Rive, *Buckingham Palace*, 104–105, 115–125.

50 The obvious exception is Ngcelwane's *Sala Kahle*. At one point she refers to *tsotsis* (31), and although this term usually is associated with African gangsters or petty criminals in popular discourse, it is not clear whether this is the intention in the text.

51 Adams & Suttner, *William Street*, 47, 51, 59, 60, 75.

52 Fortune L. 1996. *The House in Tyne Street: Childhood Memories of District Six*. Cape Town: Kwela Books, 95, 99.

53 Fortune, *The House in Tyne Street*, 84.

54 Ebrahim, *Noor's Story*, 16.

55 Soudien, 'District Six and its uses', 115, 116–117, 124.

56 Soudien, 'District Six and its uses', 121.

57 Soudien, 'District Six and its uses', 121.

58 A similar case is South End in Port Elizabeth. See Agherdien G & Hendricks S. 1997. *South End: As We Knew It*. Port Elizabeth: Western Research Group.

59 Soudien, 'District Six and its uses', 128.

60 Soudien, 'District Six and its uses', 125.

61 Soudien at certain points describes the District as heterogeneous, 'as consisting of a wide spectrum of different kinds of people', but does not fully consider its implications for defining District Six; Soudien, 'District Six and its uses', 121.

62 Ncevu McDonald interviewed by Thulani Nxumalo, nd, District Six Museum Sound Archives.

63 Mr Mpumezo, interviewed by Christiaan Beyers, 8 June 2002.

64 For a more tough-minded account of the conditions under which African people lived in Cape Town during this time, see S Magona's (1990) two-part autobiography, *To My Children's Children* and *Forced to Grow* (published in Cape Town by David Philip). Magona grew up in Nyanga West/Guguletu, where her family was removed to from Retreat rather than District Six, but has much to say of broader relevance for the kinds of material, legal and social hardships suffered by Africans in Cape Town.

65 Ngcelwane, *Sala Kahle*, 9.

66 Ngcelwane, *Sala Kahle*, 15, 32, 67.

67 Ngcelwane, *Sala Kahle*, 66, 67, 97. Quote on page 97 translated from Afrikaans.

68 Ngcelwane, *Sala Kahle*, 21, 22, 84.

69 Ngcelwane, *Sala Kahle*, 25, 29, 32, 53.

70 Ngcelwane, *Sala Kahle*, 54, 78, 81, 136.

71 Ngcelwane, *Sala Kahle*, 100 explains that the *amaMfengu* originated in Zululand, and gradually moved towards the Transkei during the great wars of Shaka Zulu. They then moved farther south, where they secured a land base by cooperating with the Methodist Church, which on 14 May 1835 had them take an oath to 'worship the living God, ... educate their children, ... and always abide by the laws of the government in place.'

72 Ngcelwane, *Sala Kahle*, 131.

CHAPTER 5

Collaboration, assimilation and contestation: emerging constructions of coloured identity in post-apartheid South Africa

BY

MICHELE RUITERS

DEVELOPMENT BANK OF SOUTHERN AFRICA

The ending of apartheid provided opportunities for people to self-identify as they wished and to experiment with their identities. All South African identities are thus in the process of reconstruction as citizens adapt to new relations of power. This chapter examines contemporary reconstructions of coloured identity among elites[1] in the Western Cape and focuses primarily on reconstructions linked to Khoisan, slave and creole understandings of that identity. This study draws extensively on interviews with members of the coloured elite engaged in public debate about the nature and future direction of coloured identity. It juxtaposes these with analyses of political texts emanating from ruling party discussions around identity and nation-building.

The emergence of the 'new South Africa' has created new problems for communities that perceive themselves as marginal and who consequently either agitate for recognition or withdraw from political participation. Two processes of identity construction are happening simultaneously. The state is in the process of constructing a national identity while different communities grapple with their specific identities in response to the state's discourse. In post-apartheid South Africa, all identities are in the process of being reconstructed particularly in opposition to their apartheid-era incarnations, presenting themselves, among other things, as not racist, not divisive and not isolated. South African citizens are redefining their identities on their own terms, both in relation to an emerging national identity and in relation to other identities within the South African context.[2] This chapter focuses specifically on attempts by coloured leaders and opinion makers to create meaning out of a previously imposed status within the new dispensation.

Under apartheid, many people previously defined as 'coloured' argued that they were not 'white enough' to enjoy the benefits of citizenship, and now in the post-apartheid era they claim that they are not 'black enough' to access programmes that address social inequalities. The Western Cape has a racial and political configuration different to the rest of the country. For example, the African National Congress (ANC) won landslide victories in the 1994, 1999 and 2004 elections nationally, but the Western Cape has always been fiercely contested. Coloureds constitute more than 50 per cent of this province's population and occupy the majority of positions in the service industry and civil service due to the legacy of the apartheid government's Coloured Labour Preference Policy.[3] Many coloured people continued to support the New National Party until it was disbanded in 2005, and the Democratic Party despite strenuous attempts on the part of the ANC to win their support. The media portrays coloured people as having been 'bypassed by the reconstruction and development programme' and as a result, see themselves as the 'step-children of SA'.[4] Reality argues against this perception as many senior and successful public figures regard themselves as coloured, or reject the identity but are nonetheless perceived to be coloured. However, perceptions of marginalisation persist. How has the state responded to groups that perceive themselves as marginalised in the new order?

A rainbow nation?

The end of apartheid afforded people new political and social freedoms which allowed them to determine their own identities. Stan Simmons, an ANC member of parliament formerly of the New National Party, and who defines himself as a 'brown person' explains that as a result of the democratic transition suddenly 'everyone is South African … With our history we need to build a nation to improve our way of living, rather than to fight. We can differ but need to work together, not be enemies'.[5] In the post-apartheid period, the nation-building project is vital for the construction of a unified South African identity. It rejects difference and emphasises similarities between South Africans. In an address to the first sitting of the National Assembly of South Africa, Archbishop Desmond Tutu prematurely exclaimed: 'We of many cultures, languages and races have become one nation. We are the rainbow children of God'.[6] However, this imagery has not been as successful as both Tutu and Nelson Mandela had hoped.

Firstly, the imagery of a rainbow makes reference to difference, and especially the continued existence of racial differences in the post-apartheid era. Coloured people commonly argue that brown does not appear in the rainbow, which also evokes the image of the opposite ends of the spectrum not meeting. Neville Alexander argues that '[i]n the South African case, the, perhaps unintended, stress placed on coexisting colour strata or groups by using the rainbow image is to my way of thinking counterproductive'. He instead proposes the image of the Gariep, or Orange River, which crosses most of the country and moves us away from the 'sense of unchanging, eternal and god-given identities'.[7]

Multiculturalism is promoted as a way of celebrating difference and uniting the nation in its diversity. Multiculturalism maintains that all communities should have equal access to resources, be equally recognised by the state and have equal space for the expression of their cultural practices.[8] A disjuncture exists in South Africa as coloured elites claim that the dominant discourse and imagery of the ANC government fosters a national identity that is narrowly black African.[9] It is not possible for a multicultural society to succeed when race and ethnicity continue to mark identities in particular and unequal ways, and where they continue to play an important role in groups' access to political power and resources.[10]

The South African approach to multiculturalism implicates people in subtle power relations within a framework of intersecting identities. The tourism industry, which markets South Africa as consisting of people, cities and sites affording the consumer 'multicultural' experiences, is an example of a failing policy based on difference. Other dimensions of inequality such as caste, class, gender, and rural versus urban, which determine power dynamics in unequal societies, are sublimated in an effort to achieve cultural equality.[11] Communities are encouraged to promote their cultural heritage in the name of development and tourism. In an attempt to draw tourists, rural areas often maintain a 'traditional' state in order to capitalise on their differences. It is for this reason that Spinner argues against the call for 'cultural rights' because 'the language of culture should not displace the language of power and wealth'.[12]

Former president Thabo Mbeki created a national discourse around identity and power but while he attempted to construct a common South African identity, he also continued to use the divisive apartheid-defined identities of white, African, coloured and Indian.[13] A national identity needs to be cognisant of localised identities that 'continue to constitute and reconstitute the mainstream'.[14] An official ANC document argues that the concept of the rainbow nation could 'fail to recognize the healthy osmosis among the various cultures and other attributes in the process towards the emergence of a new African nation'.[15] For this reason the rainbow metaphor has since been discarded as a viable political tool to unite South Africans. Subsequently, the ANC proposed a 'New Patriotism' that remains vaguely defined but could ultimately forge a national identity that is South African, with an emphasis on the African.[16] Politically this translates into the recognition of identity differences that remain in play in contemporary South Africa and also recognises that those differences would need to be suspended for the sake of creating a homogeneous nation state.

Peter Mokoena, director in the Department of Arts, Culture Science and Technology in the Western Cape provincial government, concedes that 'a collective identity ... supersedes everything' but warns against the creation of a common identity that 'trample[s] over individual and group identities ... Nation-building is a political not a cultural process'.[17] Mokoena's distinction between political and cultural identities is useful in that strong cultural identities could support a secure national identity. However, if localised identities do not feed into a national identity, many South Africans would only identify as South African when referencing their geographical origin and fail to identify with the nation in their day-to-day existence.

Mbeki's seminal 'I am an African' speech provides an all-inclusive myth of origin for South Africans and those who identify as African.[18] His discourse rejects a narrowly defined meaning of African and emphasises a shared geographical and historical experience that unites people of this continent. Racial particularities are excluded except that they all combine to make us who we are. His speech, however, opens itself to unintended interpretations based on prior understandings of the term 'African'. Under apartheid, 'African' was understood to be 'black African' rather than an all-encompassing term referencing a shared political and continental identity. Many political activists previously defined as coloured self-identified politically as black or African, and continue to do so, in an attempt to reject coloured identity. Grant Farred, a South African cultural studies scholar, originally from the Cape Flats but now based at Cornell University, writes that '[w]hereas "full blackness", or Africanness has translated into full citizenship of and belonging to the post-apartheid state, colouredness has retained its historic ambivalence'.[19] Many communities which perceive themselves as marginal continue to retain a narrow understanding of the concept 'African' despite these attempts at broadening its meaning.

That ANC documents utilise both the narrow and broad definitions of African in their documents complicates matters. For example, one document affirms 'our Africanness as a nation ... in recognition of a geographic reality and the awakening of a consciousness which colonialism suppressed' and simultaneously refers to 'coloured', 'white', 'black', and 'Indian' communities as a means of distinguishing between the benefits obtained and roles played by each group in the liberation struggle.[20] Similarly, in the realm of culture, the term 'African' is understood by some coloured people to imply an 'authentic' black African culture. Race continues to hold sway in common and official discourse even though new opportunities have emerged for self-identification.[21] These different discourses have led to divisions within South African society that are either inadequately addressed, or ignored, by the ruling party in its drive to create a national identity.

Official projects have tried to create national pride through, for example, the *Proudly South African* campaign that promotes products and services produced in South Africa. The South African Broadcasting Corporation also exclaims '*Simunye* – We are one!' while the City of Cape Town markets itself with the slogan 'One city, many cultures' in an attempt to promote unity despite its divided historical past and continued racism. These attempts to construct a common identity among South Africans have produced varied results. The main problem is that the differences entrenched during the apartheid era are proving to be highly resilient in the face of largely superficial strategies to eradicate them. Communities struggle to come to terms with their former identities while they try to redefine themselves socially in the post-apartheid environment. Their attempts at rejecting the old have often resulted in a reconstruction of the old in new terms. It is thus evident that apartheid-era senses of colouredness continue to influence current expressions of the identity. Perceptions that the post-apartheid state favours Africans help reinforce coloured separatism.

Tensions between the legislated identity categories of apartheid and current constructions of those identities continue to exist because these identities are reconstructed within boundaries that are familiar to people. In the coloured community, as in the case of others, apartheid-era parameters continue to define the construction of colouredness in a myriad of ways, drawing on past experience and shared geographies. Apartheid constructions of colouredness merged very different groups of people into a legislatively defined administrative category. The state identified coloureds loosely as people who were neither white nor black. With forced removals, the state pushed together people who would not otherwise have lived in the same area or have mixed socially. This process led to closer identification between neighbours and within neighbourhoods, cementing a closer sense of colouredness. Individuals and communities adopted elements from the state-legislated category of coloured, but also added other social and cultural aspects to their personal identifications as coloured. The identity was thus based on the 'neither white nor black' concept but incorporated distinctive religious, linguistic and class-based elements as well. The boundaries of the legislated category proved to be porous as some individuals were able to find ways around state restrictions and managed to pass for white because they bore the physical and cultural markings of whiteness.

The post-apartheid period removed racist legislation but the social identities built around it persisted because of the shared trauma of forced removals and being confined to coloured residential areas. For these reasons, strong identification with the South African nation has failed to emerge within the coloured community. Instead, old identities are being revisited, leaving the impression that new ones are unattainable and limited to re-imaginations of existing ones. Through 'new forms of imagining', it is not the identity that changes, but the ways in which it is constructed.[22] This imagining points to the difficulty of constructing entirely new identities, even though the physiognomy of power has changed. The new power relations influence the ways in which people interact in public spaces. All identities are constructed relationally, meaning that people act in response to political and social realities when they define or redefine who they are.

Citizens reconfigure boundaries of inclusion and exclusion according to their perceptions of whose needs and aspirations are being represented in government. Those people or communities who continue to feel marginalised on the basis of race or class baulk at the idea of an all-inclusive national identity, against which they feel they need to protect their limited access to resources.[23] In those societies where communities claim an insufficient level of service delivery, there is a 'marked upsurge in ethnic identities among coloured and African populations'.[24] If citizens are more likely to identify in localised terms, then it is important that a national identity encompasses all those differences or finds a way to create cohesion between groups. For many communities in the Western Cape, a racial identity remains the primary source of self-definition despite the removal of apartheid legislation because it indicates in social and political shorthand who they are, where they come from and their cultural distinctiveness. Apartheid legislation created correlations between race, space, language and class, and communities who struggle for meaning in the new South Africa continue to cling to these familiar configurations. Jordan is of the opinion that similarity because of difference could work well for national identity in South Africa but asks whether the ANC is 'leaving those of our people who identify ethnically to the political wolves of ethnic entrepreneurship by continuing to discourage ethnicity and favouring an inclusive nationalism?'[25]

The state argues that those people who continue to identify ethnically are racist or ethnicist, and aim to derail the national project. The ANC's return to a black or African identity has revived a conservative conception of those identities and has returned the debate to issues of 'authenticity' which were found in 'traditional' societies prior to their supposed cultural and genealogical hybridisation. There are no 'authentic' cultures and traditions because identities and cultures evolve.[26] Even imposed identities are reconstructed to reflect the daily experiences and realities of a community and individuals, and this process could entail a reconstruction of an ethnic identity.[27] People's reconstructions of their ethnic and, by extension, racial identities in the post-apartheid period point to the process of creating their own self-understanding because of a shared history and space, and their own version of identity. This process, however, is affected by prior constructions of identities and the power relationships that undergird that structure, therefore the new constructions need to negotiate a space for themselves within a structure that still functions along the lines of race and ethnicity.

Elite reconstructions of coloured identity

Coloured elites who are calling for a new identity are not only driven by a desire for increased access to material resources but also by the need for political and social recognition, and healing in some cases. The process of reconstructing coloured identity is an elite process because it is driven by

pe. This both angered coloured voters who
vated as other voters by issue-based politics,
ommunity around a common identity under
the Western Cape have tried to find ways to
tical identity through mass identification with,
-class issues.[44] Political representatives such as
immons have employed their colouredness as
re coloured voters who have expressed feelings
he advent of democracy.

coloured identity in the Western Cape is directly
al that community feels in the post-apartheid
nts in a 2005 *Afrobarometer* poll have shown a
fy as anything other than 'coloured'.[45] Ethnicity,
safe space in which coloured people feel they can
maintain a particular lifestyle they had under the
ny organic intellectuals in the coloured community
ho identified as black during the latter decades of
ir support of the liberation struggle led them to
was seen to be conservative and racist in favour of
erstanding of blackness. Because coloured identity
loser to whiteness than blackness, it was regarded as
ced coloured activists to show their allegiance to the
by denying coloured identity in its entirety.

belonging

the coloured community does not easily accept the
can, despite some attachment to Khoisan identities,
define as not being black African. One finds that, in
rica', educated and middle-class coloured people tend
of the new government and its policies, but do not
because they see the state's conception of Africanness
rooted. Hence there is a reluctance within the coloured
entify as African or even South African.[47] It is not a
enship but a yearning for full citizenship that drives the
inity's demand for recognition and acknowledgement.
ht that South Africans resist a universal citizenship and
to people as coloured, black African and white. Cheryl
demic and ANC activist originally from the Eastern Cape

people who have the ability to generate public debate around coloured identities. In the post-apartheid period, these elites have begun to question their identities and to reconstruct their old identities in order to move away from a negative representation of coloured identity. A process of conscientisation has taken place, where people have become aware that they can be agents for change in their own lives.[28] This awareness has led to a movement to renegotiate the position of coloured people in South African society.

Coloured elites have, through public debate and letters to the press, complained about their in-between identities, demanded state recognition for the Khoisan as the First Peoples of South Africa and claimed a 'new' colouredness. Through this ethnographic self-fashioning,[29] these elites have discovered in themselves what Homi Bhabha refers to as 'depth of agency'.[30] The coloured community has never lacked agency but has been forced to act and react within the bounds of the apartheid system. In the post-apartheid period, coloured people are no longer confined to the options of assimilation or countering apartheid policies.[31] They are able to choose identities with which they wish to be associated. The media's reduction of issues concerning the coloured community to 'the coloured vote' in 1994 showed a lack of understanding of the debates around difference within the coloured community. Under the guidance of coloured elites, people have begun personal journeys around the questions of identity and now engage vibrantly in the media about their position in contemporary South Africa. Coloured elites argue that theirs is not a social movement, but a process that has taken root throughout the community, a social process which has been adopted by small groups of people in an attempt to refashion their identities.[32]

The process of self-identification has been painful, because it forces people who have denied a part of themselves to come to terms with painful histories. For many, says Henry Cupido, an Afrikaans-speaking Capetonian and a leading figure in the African Christian Democratic Party, it is a confusing process: 'The brown people are confused because they must now self-identify'.[33] Many people who have chosen to redefine their personal identities are often ridiculed because they have revived and adopted Khoisan and slave identities which have historically been negatively stereotyped. Many coloured people have been 'socialized by seeing the photo's [sic] of ... white ancestors, not the black ones'.[34] Ironically, some white individuals flaunt newly 'discovered' African ancestry to show that they 'belong' to the continent and to the nation.

Afrikaners also tend to stress that they are African because they have been born and raised on the continent.

The ending of apartheid has 'significantly expanded the range and vitality of racial significations'.[35] Many coloured elites consciously use the term 'coloured' to show that they have reclaimed it and imbued it with new political meaning. Simultaneously they acknowledge that coloureds may have internalised the imposed identity and made it their own. Coloured people now have the agency to 'negotiate and reinterpret their mixed feelings and fragile identities in empowering ways'.[36] For many elites in the coloured community, the term 'coloured' is still inadequate and problematic for describing their identities, and they have thus embarked on constructing new understandings of their colouredness.

New conceptions of colouredness have emerged which include historical identities such as those of the Khoisan, creole and slave communities throughout South African history. These identities are linked to colouredness because, to date, it is largely coloured people who have claimed them. Mbeki, in his 'I am an African' speech, for example, claimed Khoisanness as part of his identity but this acknowledgement is not widespread in the African or coloured communities because Khoisan identities have been denigrated throughout colonial and apartheid history. Its reconstruction has highlighted the heterogeneity of coloured identity which, in the past, has always been represented as homogeneous, as if a stereotypical 'Cape coloured' identity existed. Many individuals who have chosen Khoisan identities have undertaken a highly personal process of self-definition and attachment to various ethnic or 'tribal' groups such as the Damaqua, Outeniqua, Griqua, and so forth. Even though people have come together to define their identities collectively, it is a personal process in which people renegotiate their relations with one another in the South African context.

Coloured identities are multiple, fluid and hybrid. Muslim, Christian, English, Afrikaans, rural, urban, rich, poor, educated and uneducated were grouped under the limited apartheid identity of colouredness, which continues to weigh on contemporary forms.[37] Soli Philander, a coloured comedian, points out that 'it is impossible to make the leap from just being an "old coloured" to an emancipated, evolved and free person'.[38] This statement serves as justification for those coloured people who wish to self-identify as coloured despite the advent of a new political dispensation. The 'evolved and free person' to which Philander refers has to be open to different identities and different hierarchies, and be a fully participative,

non-racia
existing s
among co
Africans. I
one needs t

Gail Sr
feels that for
'brownskin id

We need
celebratin
my work a
this negati
mixed bloo
the animosi
make sense.
need to celeb
things about l
word, phrase,

Smith's reference to
her inability to descri
found within everyon
identity does not neces
a space, history and exp
Her resistance to stereo
both personal and politi
community.

Chris Nissen, a form
1996 boldly stated that he
am coloured'.[41] Nissen's re
to his reclamation of the ter
to harness a collective identi
around new conceptions of
Oliphant, explained that 'Colc
people' are the 'true rainbow
coloured identity is multiple an

Generally, people resort to
faced with a crisis.[43] Analyses o
a discourse that identified the 'c

victory in the Western Ca
claimed they were as mot
and rallied the coloured
threat. Coloured elites in
lobby for a collective poli
and support for, working
Chris Nissen and Stan
political draw cards to lu
of marginalisation since

The persistence of
related to how margin
era. Coloured responde
reluctance to self-identi
in this case, provides a
express themselves and
apartheid regime.[46] Ma
were ANC activists w
the 20th century. Th
deny an identity that
a more inclusive und
was perceived to be
anti-African. This fo
Congress movement

Difference and

Broadly speaking,
idea of being Afri
which they tend t
the 'new South A
to be supportive
identify as Africa
as being narrowly
community to i
resistance to citi
coloured comm
Also, it is evide
continually refe
Potgieter, an ac
explains:

> Whites and Africans pigeonhole and see us as 'coloured'. Theoretically I don't know how we should engage with this. Do we talk about building a South African identity, but then there's something lost. I do know that the ordinary working class person in Bonteheuwel, Mitchells Plain, and Eersterus says 'we are coloured'.[48]

Potgieter's statement that coloured people are forced to be coloured by those with whom they interact shows the limitations imposed on that community in the post-apartheid era but warns against a South African identity that hides the particularities of citizens' experiences and contributions to the anti-apartheid struggle.[49] As a result, coloured people are 'possessed of a more fragile sense of belonging ... engaging in contradictory projects: they are simultaneously trying to write themselves into and against post-apartheid sameness'.[50] The Janus-like face of the coloured person shows both the agency of the individual in relation to identity choices that they make throughout their day and the lack of choice in terms of the range of identities that are available to them.

Despite the fact that many members of the coloured elite have embraced a broad conception of African identity, one that is as inclusive as that outlined in Mbeki's 'I am an African' speech, continued racism persists within sectors of the community towards black Africans and as a result coloured elites reject the narrowly defined conceptions of 'African' that still continue to appear in ANC documents. This appears to be the result of the perception that the ANC has embarked on a project in which South Africa was to become Africanist in its policies, outlook and culture. In recent letters to the editor in the *Cape Argus*, three readers confirmed these fears. The first claimed that 'President Mbeki's speech on Africanism to parliament was the turning point. It was not to uplift the African spirit but to impose a new brand of "black" African elitism'; another that '[w]e so-called coloureds are not in general black or, in particular, African. So what/who are we?'; and the third was of the opinion that '[t]he ANC is here to protect and entrench the rights of the blacks to the exclusion of coloureds, Malays and Indians'.[51] All three argue that they do not fit Mbeki's description of African. For more conservative elements in the community, coloured identity is being threatened by Africanness and as a result they call for a protected and defined coloured ethnic identity which is defined in terms of language, religion and historical experience. These views are being propagated by an array of organisations that sprang up after the 1994 elections.

Coloured essentialists

In February 1995, a new coloured organisation, the *Kleurling Weerstandsbeweging vir die Vooruitgang van Bruinmense* (KWB) was established in Johannesburg.[52] Its leader, Mervyn Ross, argued:

> We are proud that we are ethnic. And once we are ethnic and being recognized by various other people, we can also go further and say 'Look, we are ethnic. We have our own language, our own culture, our own land and we want to govern ourselves'. We are not prepared to be governed by the white man anymore – he made a mess of it for 300 years. We are not prepared to be governed by black people.[53]

Ross did not clarify who his constituency was, thus it is not clear who he represented. He spoke as though he represented all coloured people, which was clearly not the case. His claim to an ethnic identity has alienated many in the coloured community who associated ethnicity with tribalism and black African identity. The KWB has lobbied for support around issues of land claims, recognition of Khoisan languages and protection of their culture, and the right to coloured self-determination.[54] In the light of these claims, the KWB represented 'the most extreme ethno-nationalist portrayal of Coloured identity'.[55] Ross's attempt to mobilise around an ethnic identity has not garnered much support, nor has his use of Afrikaans been sufficient to mobilise coloureds to join the organisation. Despite many coloured people claiming Afrikaans as their mother tongue, the English language has been a marker of status in the coloured community. Mervyn Ross also invokes Small's conception of 'brown Afrikaners' to afford 'our people vision, economic advancement and political power'.[56]

The KWB does not want an ethnic homeland even though it does want the state's land restitution programme to consider claims to land lost prior to 1913. In order to do this the KWB needs to prove that brown people had existed as a group historically, their longevity qualifying them as an indigenous population.[57] Ross cannot claim that brown identity has always existed in South African society as it is an identity that has drifted in and out of constructions of coloured identity since the early 1900s. However, since 1994 there appears to have been a growing trend for people to identify as brown. For groups like the KWB, people are born with their identities and because brown people always lived in southern Africa they belong to the land and are indigenous. Some coloured leaders such as Stan Simmons and Henry Cupido refer to themselves as *'bruin'* (brown). Cupido and Simmons' denial of colouredness reveals the highly contested nature of the identity. Ultimately, the KWB's ethnic mobilisation in the coloured community did not succeed but it did reach a particular sector of the community which has identified with that organisation's call for an ethnic politics and a coloured party to represent coloured interests.

This dual process of engaging in contradictory projects was evident during the election period in the Western Cape in 1994. Former United Democratic Front (UDF) activist David Abrahams explains that the success of the UDF in the western Cape in the 1980s had given them a false sense of confidence regarding the outcome of the election: 'We expected [support for the UDF in the 1980s] to translate smoothly into an ANC election victory. It never happened and we didn't spend time to find out why it didn't happen'.[58] He argues that it was clear that the ANC was not willing to engage coloured voters as coloureds during the election campaign and had chosen to concentrate on predominantly African areas where the majority of their support was situated. There were class differences in voting patterns with middle-class coloured voters predominantly supporting the ANC and working-class voters supporting the National and Democratic parties.[59] Wilmot James explains that the ANC lost because it dealt with the coloured community as a homogeneous group.[60] David Abrahams clarifies this as follows:

> [T]he way coloured people voted ... was a combination of fear, ethnic racial difference, them–us, representation of the ANC that primarily represents African people. We thought the [ANC] policies would inform people's decisions. The issue was not about who the National Party put up. In 1994 it wasn't about policies – it was about fear, ethnic mobilization and them–us.[61]

This short-sightedness proved to be the downfall of the ANC in that region. Father Michael Weeder, a Cape Town-based cleric and historian of Cape slavery, explains that the ANC lost the Western Cape as a result of an 'uncritical application of the national question' that did not 'contextualize' the issues or the 'revolution' in those areas. Weeder believes that the ANC's attention to differences between its voting communities cost it the opportunity to win over the *'bruinmense'* (brown people).[62] The resultant backlash and ridicule of the 'coloured vote' then created a perception within sectors of the coloured community that they were being alienated from mainstream political life. Zoë Wicomb refers to it as a 'shameful vote'.[63]

The December First Movement and slave identities

In 1994, when the ANC lost the Western Cape to the National Party, many coloured political activists expressed shock that their constituencies had voted for their former oppressors. On July 26 1995, three coloured leaders, the well-known educationist Richard van der Ross, Afrikaans-language poet Adam Small and activist Chris April, launched the Coloured Forum in Delft, a coloured township on the Cape Flats. The Forum was established to provide a mouthpiece for coloured people in the Western Cape. It was premised on the idea that coloured identity is primordial and should be recognised within existing political and social structures. It was not established as an alternative to existing political parties but rather to encourage debate within, and about, coloured communities. Wilmot James, former executive director of the Institute for Democracy in South Africa, was instrumental in facilitating debate both about the Forum and coloured identity in 1995. James posited that:

> [T]he Forum positions itself unmistakably in the main stream. It was to engage with, and not erode, democratic institutions. It purports to draw on, not supplant, the party-political framework. It encourages introspection, self-evaluation and self-criticism, as a way of energizing coloured people into the main stream. The social-psychological benefits of this approach are not to be underestimated for building self-esteem and confidence, as the Black Consciousness Movement of the 1970s demonstrated.[64]

Many coloured intellectuals were of the opinion that through self-analysis their communities would gain self-esteem and confidence and thereby become fully engaged in the democratic process. The Forum did not 'create a particularly vocal or popular platform' in 1995 and 1996, but it did 'inspire' the formation of the December First Movement, named after the emancipation date of slaves in the Cape Colony in 1834.[65] The failure of the Coloured Forum was due to the conservative politics of its founder members. Like the KWB, the Forum's politics were problematic because colouredness was constructed in essentialist and fixed terms.

The December First Movement (the Movement) was established in 1996 to inform coloured people of their history and culture, which, due to apartheid education, was largely unknown. The Movement was to be 'a political cultural formation' which has as its central focus the 'political awakening of coloured people'.[66] For David Abrahams, the rationale behind the formation of the December First Movement was as follows:

> The movement originated because firstly, why did 1994 happen in the Western Cape? What is it about the coloured community that led to this? Secondly, what is it about politics inside the ANC in the Western Cape that needs to be addressed? ... We need to start putting the notion of understanding the political, social and demographic realities on the top of the agenda in the ANC.[67]

The Movement was intellectually based, and engaged with debates on colouredness and coloured identity within an ANC-dominated political milieu. The leaders of the Movement had been UDF activists and supported the ANC. They did not distance themselves from it but wished to introduce the debate on coloured identity into ANC structures. This was an attempt to foreground the particularities of the Western Cape within a larger debate on identity in post-apartheid South Africa. Abrahams said that they wished to 'demythologize [colouredness] and to take it out of the realm of reactionary coloured ethnic group identity'.[68] The Movement attempted to create a deeper understanding of coloured identity that was not tied to an ethnic understanding of identities. For them colouredness was tied to a history of slavery and shared experience, rather than a primordial identity.

For the leadership of the Movement, material benefit for coloured people was not the primary focus of their project. They aimed to inform people of their past in an attempt to foster feelings of belonging and esteem. Weeder explains that 'the December First Movement pursued an agenda that said "this is the way we are African". We have equal access [to Africanness]'. He argues that the coloured stake was 'devalued' because coloured people are seen to be 'not fully African' or 'not having suffered fully'. Weeder explained that his interest in slave history motivated his role in the Movement because he wished to inform coloured people of their roots and origins, which could lead to a better understanding of their place in contemporary South Africa.[69] Trevor Oosterwyk defined the Movement as 'completely a cultural organization'.[70] The Movement wished to lobby and advocate for an end to the political and social marginalisation of coloured people, to develop and encourage an intellectual and political understanding of non-essentialist culture through a politics of difference, and to organise among coloured communities to restore their right to self-determination and participation in the transformation of South Africa.[71] Much criticism could be directed against it for promoting coloured identity, politics and culture, and in a later document the Movement recognises this essentialism. It explains it as follows:

> There seems to be an obvious contradiction between wanting to 'bring coloureds into the political and economic mainstream' and yet also in the same breathe [sic] to talk about the 'development of a non-racial project'. My response to this is that we have to admit, as many other people have argued, that the so-called non racialism of the 1980s was largely a failure ... because it never moved beyond being an organisational ethic and principle which for many reasons never permeated to the masses in a fundamental way.[72]

Weeder explains the failure of the Movement in the following terms:

> December First was demonized and the biggest hatchet men in this thing were the coloureds in the unions and the ANC to show how much African they are within the image of Nguni African: the African as noble and the African as pure. They had to show how they went for these narrow coloureds. So to show how big I am, I have to go against my own people. I'm just saying how the December First initiative was aborted for ethnic politics' celebration of the First Nation in an idealized rewritten way.[73]

The ANC did not support the continued existence of the Movement because it appeared to highlight differences between communities in the Western Cape. The Movement acknowledged that similarities existed between communities in the region and that racial differences were constructed as part of the apartheid government's 'divide and rule' strategy, but they opted to operate within the ANC structures which still recognised racially based differences. Abrahams also argues that 'the ANC is more comfortable with dealing with ethnicity [and the belief that] "coloured people are different"' but it fails to address those differences and fears and instead produces broad-stroke policies that define citizenship in terms of Africanness with which the broader coloured community does not identify.[74]

Khoisan identities

Khoisan identity has emerged strongly from within the coloured community, but is not seen as a black African identity. Mervyn Ross is of the opinion that '[w]e were the first to have fought against colonialism; it was the Khoisan, our ancestors. Where was the black man then?'.[75] For this reason Michael Weeder rejects Khoisan identity as colouredness 'by another name. It is a post-modern tribalism that is driven by the impulse of separateness and quest for purity. It looks like a politics of ethnicity on appearance and doesn't look at power'.[76] Reaching back into history for a sense of belonging and differentiation shows a need for people to connect coloured identities to what they would regard as an authentically African identity that predates black African identities.

Like all identities, the Khoisan revivalist movement is instrumentalist as it links the identity to land rights and land restitution, and the political recognition of its leaders by national and international bodies.[77] Khoisan activists such as chief Joseph Little, chief Jean Burgess, chief Harleen Sassman, Hendrik van Wyk, Ron Martin, and chief Joseph Marks mostly argue that their movement aims to engage people in a more personal process of self-determination. These key individuals began to debate Khoisan identities in the public sphere in the period immediately after 1994. The link between Africa and Khoisan identities is strong as the Khoisan are seen to be the First People of southern Africa.

Khoisan chiefs generally do not wish to be included in the Congress for Traditional Leaders in South Africa (Contralesa), a body consisting of African chiefs that is afforded limited political power and recognised by the Constitution. Khoisan activist John Witbooi, on the contrary, demands that Khoisan chiefs be recognised as traditional leaders and join Contralesa, thereby giving them access to political representation in parliament, a stipend and power at local government level.[78] For chief Jean Burgess, a Khoisan activist from the Eastern Cape, the creation of a sense of belonging is of utmost importance to the Khoisan revivalist movement.[79] She finds humility in belonging to a continent and a place, humility that is connected to her belonging to an ancient people who always lived in Africa and therefore have a right to be in South Africa as equal citizens. Many Khoisan activists wish to highlight their attachment to a historical identity that could be traced to the period prior to the arrival of the Dutch. It could be argued that this is a search for purity, a purity that cannot be achieved through a hybrid coloured identity. Land rights are foremost in Khoisan politics because Khoisan land rights were not open to negotiation as the ANC had identified 1913 as the cut-off date, thereby nullifying many coloureds' claims to land that their families had lost under British rule and during the early years of the Union.

Other Khoisan identities survived apartheid, and the Griqua one is still being practised in separate communities in Klaarwater, Ratelgat and Kranshoek. Cecil le Fleur, chairperson of the National Khoisan Consultative Conference (NKCC), said as much during his speech: 'Griqua culture and tradition survived despite the regime's attack on Khoisan people. It is through our doing that the Khoisan flame burns'.[80] Le Fleur explains that the apartheid government's 'purposeful attempts to transform our people [Griquas] into a coloured identity disempowered our people. There was forced registration by officials based on phenotype'.[81] Under colonial and apartheid rule, the Griquas sought a separate existence that protected and maintained their culture within a racialised system that ignored their particularities and treated them the same as it did other coloured communities. The Griquas' search for separate development and self-determination and, more generally, the Khoisan revivalist group's project, renewed discussions around ethnic and racial identities.

In 1997, the Khoisan Identities and Cultural Heritage Conference was held in Cape Town to discuss the future of Khoisan identities in the new South Africa. The holding of the conference was prompted by two developments. Firstly, the declaration of the United Nations' Decade of Indigenous Peoples in 1995 highlighted issues around Khoisan rights and identity, and situated debate around them in an international context. Secondly, in 1996, Thabo Mbeki's 'I am an African' speech opened up a debate around who is 'African'. Mbeki stated the following:

> I owe my being to the Khoi and the San whose desolate souls haunt the great expanses of the beautiful Cape – they who fell victim to the most merciless genocide our native land has ever seen, they who were the first to lose their lives in the struggle to defend our freedom and dependence [sic] and they who, as a people, perished in the result.[82]

The ANC government's claim that the Khoisan had 'as a people, perished' pushed the leadership to make surviving Khoisan communities more visible.

Unlike the KWB and the December First Movement, the Khoisan revivalist movement has entered the debate related to group rights of indigenous peoples. The NKCC's definition of 'indigenous' follows the

United Nations' understanding, which de-links the term from native or aboriginal identities:

> The Khoisan people say they are indigenous. That is the basic argument about UN indigeneity. It's not about racial purity. Indigenous identities are mixed, but it doesn't mean that they cannot take on a specific identity. It's about the principle of self-identification.[83]

Le Fleur talks about *volksregte* (people's rights), thereby removing Khoisan identity from the liberal conception of individual rights. The Khoisan movement wishes to obtain recognition for language and cultural rights, which Le Fleur claims are not protected by group or community rights. The Khoisan do not only need protection of their cultural, linguistic and religious rights but also need those cultural expressions to be constructed, reconstructed and corrected before they can be protected. He calls for a separate process through which the Khoisan could catch up with other groups, and argues that this is the reason why they need recognition first before they call for protection.[84]

Efforts to revive the language and cultures of the Khoisan groups have emerged in the Western, Eastern and Northern Cape provinces. Social constructions of Khoisan identities are important because the culture has largely been eradicated through cultural assimilation into coloured communities. Ron Martin, a Khoisan activist in the Western Cape, explains that he is 'fighting the Khoi awareness cause'.[85] Another cultural activist, John Witbooi from the Eastern Cape, refers to this process as a 'reawakening and demystification of Khoisan identity'.[86] Martin calls for 'constitutional accommodation' of the Khoisan and the 'restoration of [Khoisan] identity and dignity as a people'. He has played a pioneering role in the restoration of the Nama language through the promotion of Nama language classes. Martin's purpose is to show that 'culture can be embraced by everybody'. For him 'coloured is Khoisan' and through knowledge and experience of that culture, stereotypes will be destroyed: 'we put it out there that these people are not nonentities, cultureless bastards; the working class of the Western Cape'. Martin distinguishes between cultural identity and racial identity by arguing that 'cultural groups are not ethnic or racial'.

Culture can transcend racial and ethnic barriers constructed in society. Evidence abounds in South African schools and universities, where students from all 'racial groups' share similar tastes in music and fashion, and have a preference for the English language.[87] John Witbooi assisted with the establishment of the Khoisan Awareness Initiative (KAI) in the Eastern Cape that promotes an understanding and knowledge of the Khoisan groups in that area. 'How do we decide what is our authentic culture?' he asks. His answer is that 'KAI is not interested in political issues. We're interested in language, culture, history. KAI is non-partisan'.[88]

Issues of authenticity are important to black Africans in the post-1994 period for particular social and political reasons related to access to resources. Ethnic identities such as Xhosa, Zulu and Sotho are grounded in historical writings, and can prove their belonging to Africa in terms of shared language and culture. Because of its rootless nature, coloured identity has not attained the same level of authenticity as the Nguni cultures. For this reason the Khoisan revivalist movement could be accused of attempting to define identity in 'pure' terms by relating Khoisan-ness to a past, prior to colonialism. Kwame Anthony Appiah equates the search for authenticity with the peeling of an onion as people try to find the essence of their identities. He warns that cultures constantly change and '[s]ocieties without change are not authentic: they're just dead'.[89] The search of an 'authentic' African identity that is tied to the land, such as Khoisan identity, will not prove those members' authenticity because society, and the state, has not attached any value, other than tourism value, to that identity.

Creoles and Africans

In 2002, Father Michael Weeder and ANC stalwart Reg September launched the Roots and Visions Forum in Cape Town 'to promote enquiry, information sharing, debate, cultural activity, engagement with issues of Africa, and proud celebration of our African heritage along with the full tapestry of our Creolised culture'.[90] The Roots and Visions Forum was to be inclusive, regardless of political affiliation or status within the society with the proviso that participants subscribe to a 'non-racist, non-ethnicist and non-sexist approach'. It rejected ethnic definitions which divided people, and called for a society in which there was gender equality. The Roots and Visions Forum's aim was to engender debate about identity in the coloured community to encourage it to engage with contemporary politics and the nation-building project. 'We use terms like "creole" and "creolisation", but we do not use these terms normatively where "creole" refers to people who have multiple ancestral roots'.[91] Patric Tariq Mellet, an identity activist in Cape Town, asked the participants at the Roots and Visions meeting in 2003 to '[g]o back and read President Mbeki's "I am an African" speech. I am also creole, the sum total of what I am, I am not what others say I am ... The more of us who proudly say "I am an African", the more of a movement there will be'.[92] The nature of the debate around creole identities is not very different from that of the December First Movement. Both analyse identities and processes related to social change in post-apartheid society. It is important to note that the founders of these movements acknowledge the intellectual nature of the debate, and concede that not many of the objectives will be shared by the broader coloured community.

Mellet explains his use of the term 'creole' in the context of coloured identity, and manages to incorporate debates around who was an African and the position of coloured people within history.

> The language that developed was made up of a whole array of languages. It was a hybrid language, a creole language, Afrikaans, emerged from slave population. There was contestation around Afrikaner creole identity versus Afrikander creole identity. For most of the 1700s and 1800s the term coloured did not feature. If you look at the first political organizations, the first recorded coloured organization was the Kimberley Afrikander League in 1880 and the APO 1903. There was a period when coloured people said proudly that I am an African.[93]

Mellet also argues that African nationalism in South Africa came from the coloured people. He provides the examples of the South African Native National Congress, the Afrikander League, and the African People's Organisation, which he claims had moved black identity away from a racially imposed native identity towards a broader Africanness as had been imagined in African-American writings at the turn of the 20th century. Mellet advises nation-builders to adopt his Africanness and not to 'run away from creole-ness or mulatto-ness'.[94] For Mellet, the multiple identities found in an African context would form a part of the nation-building project. The national naming process should not engulf minor identities under a suffocating national identity, which will ultimately lead to dissatisfaction and increased tension within South African society.

The term 'creole' has not been well received in post-apartheid South Africa and has often been viewed as 'both racist and suspect'.[95] Some scholars have used 'creole' to explain that coloured identities are based on 'cultural creativity [and] creolized formations shaped by South Africa's history of colonialism, slavery, segregation and apartheid'.[96] Zimitri Erasmus, a sociologist at the University of Cape Town, posits that creolisation 'involves the construction of identity out of elements of ruling as well as subaltern cultures' and that 'coloured identities are made and re-made by coloured people themselves in their attempts to give meaning to their everyday lives'.[97] Again, this is an intellectual debate which fails to gain a footing in the broader coloured community.

Many coloured people believe strongly that their 'mixture' occurred so far back in history that it does not feature in their contemporary consciousness. As a result, 'mixed' has new connotations in a post-apartheid South Africa in that it denotes children born of 'mixed' couples. Johannesburg journalist Bongiwe Mlangeni asks: 'What identity do you give a child of mixed race in post-apartheid South Africa?' because coloured is an 'inadequate definition ... "What am I?" is the question many children need answered without feeling they are the result of an immoral act'.[98] Here Mlangeni, like others, favours the remnants of an apartheid-era sense of colouredness. She misses the point that in the new South Africa, children 'of mixed race' could define themselves as they choose. This does not, however, preclude people defining such a child as coloured or 'other'. Terms such as 'creole' and 'hybrid' hide the negative stigmas attached to a coloured identity while signifiers such as 'brown' or 'mixed' would more likely appear in ordinary conversations that have consciously moved away from the use of the term 'coloured'. Neville Alexander refers to it as a 'cultural domain without boundaries' in which people can experiment with different computations of identities and cultural practices.[99]

Conclusion

While accusations of race-based voting are well founded in some cases, issue-based politics have always been important in the coloured community. Racism does exist within the coloured community for reasons mentioned above. However, as this chapter argues, the coloured community has always sought a political and social home that best represents its interests. It is imperative that, in addition to addressing material and social needs, the state should be cognisant of the different histories and conditions of each community and acknowledge these differences. The nation-building project cannot succeed if certain identities are valorised and others are not.

People in post-apartheid South Africa are reconstructing their identities but are doing so within an apartheid mental framework. Coloured identity continues to occupy a space between whiteness and Africanness even though it moves through a continuum comprising Khoisan, coloured, creole and mixed people. Time, space and institutional structure feed into constructions of identity, therefore coloured people still create meaning within their communities and through experiences that are still tainted by apartheid. On a positive note, however, the group has begun to interrogate its own constructions of itself and to debate its conceptions of its 'authenticity'. By claiming an 'authentic' African identity, coloured people can claim to belong in South Africa and to be tied to the land. Constructions of 'authentic' indigenous identities cement the divide between black Africans and coloureds, which needs to be eliminated in order for South Africa to be truly democratic.

The ANC government is calling for a national identity at a time when specific identities are being sought. Fears of ethnic nationalism underlie the caution against localised identities. The argument is that in order for a young democracy to thrive, internal strife and differences should be minimised. This chapter argues the contrary. In order for a democracy to survive, specific identities are necessary so as to provide individual citizens with the ability to say, 'This is who I am' and to vote on their beliefs. This is not a call for searches for primordial linkages; rather, it is a call for 'imagined communities' to emerge according to the needs of each community and group. Coloured people are culture brokers in that 'what [they] have to offer ... in their deliberations of identity is the resilience entailed in crossing all types of boundaries rather than in simply forging negotiated agreements which harmonize interactions, but essentially allow the boundaries to remain'.[100] If coloured people continue to search for discretely recognisable identities, they will lose their resilience and ability to cross the boundaries to which Simone has referred.

The politics of identity in South Africa since 1994 have shown that this country is still beset by issues of difference. In turn these differences, in the present political milieu, determine whether groups gain access to resources and recognition, or are rendered politically or socially invisible. Coloured, brown, Khoisan, creole and slave identities have highlighted the nuances within the coloured community, thereby revealing individuals' agency in the process of choosing their individual and collective identities. Coloured elites have managed to find new ways to construct coloured identities that conform to the discourse around Africanness, authenticity, indigeneity and belonging. The motives of elites could be instrumental or spiritual, but they have engaged in these debates in the public sphere that is dominated by the ANC. Steven Robins conceives of identity reconstruction as a 'recuperation of social memory'.[101] It is a recuperative process but it is also one through which new memories are made and which responds directly to the nation-building project and the call for democracy in South Africa. Sharp suggests that the reasons for perceptions of marginalisation in the former coloured community 'may be that the dominant metaphors of the nation-building process have a different meaning for this segment of the population than for others'.[102]

The process of constructing a national identity that hinges on conceptions of Africanness needs to be inclusive enough to embody a sense of belonging in its bearers. As Mellet puts it, 'ANC stalwarts – their Africanness is mine. Slave spirits are mine. Identity is not singular, it's plural'.[103] Perhaps this is the true hybridity which post-colonial writers have theorised. Sharp argues that '[cultural] hybridity involves a reflexive awareness of multiple subject positions rather than a simple "mixing" of two or more cultures'.[104] A society with multiple identities will bolster democracy unless the hegemonic identity conforms to old racialised divisions within South African society. Various identities within an individual that are recognised in particular contexts could provide for and reinforce participatory democratic practices.

Endnotes

1   In this chapter, coloured elites are taken to be those people who are leaders and opinion makers in their communities and who use their access to the media to theorise and shape debate about coloured identity in South Africa. These individuals, many of whom played leadership roles in the liberation struggle, are what Gramsci called 'organic intellectuals'. They maintain strong links with their communities and engage in, and influence, issues that affect their constituencies with the intention of creating a counter-hegemonic discourse.

2   See Steyn, M. 2001. *Whiteness Just Isn't What It Used to Be: Whiteness in a Changing South Africa*. Albany: State University of New York Press. For debates on Indian identity in a post-apartheid South Africa, see Ramsamy E. 2007. 'Between non-racialism and multiculturalism: Indian identity and nation-building in South Africa'. *Tijdschrift voor Economische en Sociale Geografie*, 98, no. 4, 468–481; and Lemon A. 2008. 'Indian identities in the "Rainbow Nation": responses to transformation in South African schools'. *National Identities*, 10. For debates on changing black African identities, see Scheper-Hughes N. 2001. 'The recovery of spoiled identities in the new South Africa'. *The Multiracial Activist*, April/May http://www.multiracial.com/readers/scheper-hughes.html (accessed 22 September 2004).

3   http://www.capetown.gov.za/home/demographics.asp

4   *Business Day*, 27 May 1999.

5   Stan Simmons, interviewed by Michele Ruiters, 14 February 2004.

6   Alexander N. 2002. *An Ordinary Country: Issues in the Transition from Apartheid to Democracy*. Pietermaritzburg: Natal University Press, 81.

7   Alexander, *An Ordinary Country*, 100, 107.

8   Baines G. 'The Rainbow Nation? Identity and nation building in post-apartheid South Africa', http://www.arts.uwa.edu/MotsPluriels/MP798gb.html (accessed 28 September 2005). See also McAllister P. 1996. 'Australian multiculturalism: lessons for South Africa?' *Indicator SA*, 13, no. 2, 2–78.

9   Most South Africans claim to be tolerant of each other, but are not. See Gibson J & Gouws A. 2003. *Overcoming Intolerance in South Africa: Experiments in Democratic Persuasion*. Cambridge: Cambridge University Press, 41–115.

10 See Taylor C. 1992. 'The politics of recognition', in *Multiculturalism and the Politics of Recognition*, ed A Gutmann. Princeton: Princeton University Press; Kymlicka W. 1995. *Multicultural Citizenship: A Liberal Theory of Minority Rights*. Oxford: Clarendon Press; and Adam H. 1995. 'The politics of identity: nationalism, patriotism and multiculturalism'. *Anthropologie et Sociétés*, 19, 87–110.

11 See Moller Okin S. 'Is multiculturalism bad for women?' *Boston Review Online*. http://www.bostonreview.net/BR22.5/okin.html (accessed 26 January 2006).

12 Spinner J. 1994. *The Boundaries of Citizenship: Race, Ethnicity, and Nationality in the Liberal State*. Baltimore: Johns Hopkins University Press, 136. See also Habib A. 1996. 'Myth of the Rainbow Nation: prospects for the consolidation of democracy in South Africa'. *African Security* Review, 5, no. 6.

13 Mbeki T. 1998. 'Statement of Deputy President Thabo Mbeki at the opening of the debate in the National Assembly, on "Reconciliation and nation-building"'. National Assembly, Cape Town, 29 May, http://dfa.gov.za/docs/speeches/1998/mbek0529.htm (accessed 22 February 2006).

14 Alexander, *An Ordinary Country*, 107.

15 Anon. 'Nation formation and nation-building – the national question in South Africa, 1997', http://www.anc.org.za/ancdocs/discussion/nation.html (accessed 27 July 2005), 4. According to this document, coloureds are 'somewhere in the undefined middle of the rainbow'.

16 Mbeki T. 2001. 'New patriotism for a new South Africa'. *ANC Today: Online Voice of the African National Congress*, 1, no. 4, 16–22 February, http://www.anc.org.za/ancdocs/anctoday/2001/text/at04.txt (accessed 22 February 2006).

17 Peter Mokoena, interviewed by Michele Ruiters, 14 February 2004.

18 'Statement of Deputy President T Mbeki, on behalf of the African National Congress, on the occasion of the adoption by the Constitutional Assembly of the Republic of South Africa Constitution Bill 1996', http://www.anc.org.za/ancdocs/history/mbeki/1996/sp960508.html (accessed 22 February 2006).

19 Farred G. 2001. 'Where does the Rainbow Nation end? Colouredness and citizenship in post-apartheid South Africa'. *The New Centennial Review*, 1, no. 1, 182–183.

20 Anon. 'Nation-formation and nation-building – the national question in South Africa', http://www.anc.org.za/ancdocs/discussion/nation.html (accessed 27 July 2005).

21 Nuttal S. 2004. 'City forms and writing the "now" in South Africa'. *Journal of Southern African Studies*, 30, no. 4, 738.

22 Nuttal S & Michael C. 2002. *Senses of Culture: South African Culture Studies*. Oxford: Oxford University Press, 2.

23 Jordan P. 'The national question in post-1994 South Africa – a discussion paper in preparation for the ANC's 50th National Conference, 1997', 10, http://www.anc. org.za/ancdocs/discussion/natquestion/html (accessed 27 July 2005).

24 Habib, 'Myth of the Rainbow Nation', 4. See also Mattes R, Taylor D & Poore A. 1997. 'The role of identity in building a democratic culture in South Africa'. Paper presented at the conference 'Multicultural citizenship in the "new" South Africa', Cape Town, 15–17 December.

25 Jordan, 'The national question', 12.

26 Sharp J. 1997. 'Beyond exposé analysis: hybridity, social memory and identity politics'. *Journal of Contemporary African Studies*, 15, no. 1, 7–21; Robins S. 1997. 'Transgressing the borderlands of tradition and modernity: identity, cultural hybridity and land struggles in Namaqualand, 1980–94'. *Journal of Contemporary African Studies*, 15, no. 1, 23–42.

27 Cornell S & Hartmann D. 1998. *Ethnicity and Race Making Identities in a Changing World*. Thousand Oaks: Pine Forge Press, 30.

28 Abdi A. 1999. 'Identity formations and deformations in South Africa: a historical and contemporary overview'. *Journal of Black Studies,* 30, no. 2, 150.

29 This term is borrowed from Wicomb Z. 1998. 'Shame and identity: the case of the coloured in South Africa', in *Writing South Africa: Literature, Apartheid and Democracy, 1970–1995*, eds D Atteridge & R Jolly. Cambridge: Cambridge University Press, 92.

30 Bhabha H. 1994. *The Location of Culture*. London: Routledge, 69.

31 Adhikari M. 2002. 'Hope, fear, shame frustration: continuity and change in the expression of coloured identity in white supremacist South Africa 1910–1994'. PhD dissertation, University of Cape Town, 24–33.

32 For further discussion on identity within social movements, see Stryker S, Owens T & White R (eds). 2000. *Self, Identity and Social Movements*. Minneapolis: University of Minnesota Press.

33 Henry Cupido, interviewed by Michele Ruiters, 14 February 2004.

34 Jordan P, Jaffer Z & Maré G. 2002. 'The formation of national identity: summary notes from debate of 9 November, 2002'. *Goedgedacht Forum for Social Reflection*, 14, accessed via http://www.goedgedacht.org.za/view.asp?pg=archive.

35 Simone A M. 1994. 'In the mix: retaking coloured identities'. Cape Town: Foundation for Contemporary Research, 2.

36 Field S. 2001. 'Oral histories of forced removals', in *Lost Communities Living Memories: Remembering Forced Removals in Cape Town*, ed S. Field. Cape Town: David Philip, 98.

37 See Erasmus Z & Pieterse E. 1997. 'Conceptualising coloured identities: preliminary thoughts'. Paper presented at the conference 'National identity and democracy', Cape Town, 14–18 March, 8.

38 *Cape Argus*, 28 May 2002.

39 Crenshaw K. 1991. 'Mapping the margins: intersectionality, identity politics, and violence against women of color'. *Standford Law Review,* 43, 1241–1299.

40 Gail Smith, e-mail to author, 25 March, 2005. Smith is an identity and gender activist who was instrumental in the making of the 1998 Sarah Bartmann documentary, *The Life and Times of Sarah Baartman, the Hottentot Venus* by Zola Maseko. She also played a major role in the repatriation of Sarah Bartmann's remains to South Africa in 2002.

41 *Cape Times*, 18 March 1996.

42 *Rapport*, 12 June 2005. Translated from Afrikaans.

43 See Bekker S, Leildé A, Cornelissen S & Horstmeier S. 2000. 'The emergence of new identities in the Western Cape'. *Politikon*, 27, no. 2, 231.

44 Trevor Oosterwyk, David Abrahams and Michael Weeder are prominent examples of former UDF activists who tried this strategy.

45 Mattes R, Chikwanha A & Magezi A. 2005. 'South Africa: after a decade of democracy: a summary of results'. *Afrobarometer*. Cape Town, IDASA.

46 See Dubow S. 1994. 'Ethnic euphemisms and racial echoes'. *Journal of Southern African Studies*, 20, no. 3, 355–370; Van den Berghe P. 1970. *Race and Ethnicity: Essays in Comparative Sociology*. New York: Basic Books; and Heese H. 1988. 'Ras en etnisiteit: perspektiewe van 1938 en 1988'. *Kronos*, 12, 42–51.

47 Klandermans B, Roefs M & Olivier J (eds). 2001. *The State of the People: Citizens, Civil Society and Governance in South Africa, 1994–2000*. Pretoria: Human Sciences Research Council, 101–102. In 1998, only 10 per cent of coloureds claimed a strong national identity.

48 Cheryl Potgieter, interviewed by Michele Ruiters, 2 April 2004. The former two suburbs are working-class coloured areas of Cape Town and the latter a coloured area in Pretoria.

49 For discussion on limitations of an overarching South African identity, see also Erasmus Z (ed). 2001. 'Introduction', in *Coloured by History, Shaped by Place: New Perspectives on Coloured Identities in Cape Town*. Cape Town: Kwela Books.

50 Farred, 'Where does the Rainbow Nation end?', 182.

51 *Cape Argus*, 28 July 2006.

52 The name translates as 'Coloured Liberation Movement for the Advancement of Brown People'.

53 Caliguire D. 1996. 'Voices from the communities', in *Now that We Are Free: Coloured Communities in a Democratic South Africa*, eds W James, D Caliguire & K Cullinan. Cape Town: IDASA, 10.

54 Jackson S. 1999. 'The South African public sphere and the politics of coloured identity'. PhD dissertation, University of Chicago, 178.

55 Hendricks C. 2000. '"We knew our place": a study of the constructions of coloured identity in South Africa'. PhD dissertation, University of South Carolina, 239.

56 *Mail & Guardian*, 24–30 March 1995.

57 Jackson, 'The South African public sphere', 180.

58 David Abrahams, interviewed by Michele Ruiters, 18 February 2004.

59 Seekings J. 1996. 'From independence to identification', in James, Caliguire & Cullinan, *Now that We Are Free*, 35.

60 James W & Caliguire D. 1996. 'Renewing civil society'. *Journal of Democracy*, 7, no. 1, 43.

61 David Abrahams, interviewed 18 February 2004.

62 Michael Weeder, interviewed by Michele Ruiters, 12 February 2004.

63 Wicomb, 'Shame and identity', 93.

64   James W 1995. 'The South African public sphere'. *Cape Times*, 4 August. See also Jackson, 'The South African public sphere', 178–184.

65   Jackson, 'The South African public sphere', 182.

66   Oosterwyk T. 1997. 'December First Movement'. Report on a conference arranged by the Cape Town Heritage Trust, 2–4 April (unpublished document in the possession of Oosterwyk.)

67   David Abrahams, interviewed 18 February 2004.

68   David Abrahams, interviewed 18 February 2004.

69   Michael Weeder, interviewed 12 February 2004.

70   Oosterwyk, 'December First Movement'.

71   Abrahams & Oosterwyk, letter to the editor, *Cape Times*, date unknown (copies in the possession of Oosterwyk and the author).

72   Anon. nd. 'December First Movement: statement of intent' (unpublished document, in possession of the author).

73   Michael Weeder, interviewed 12 February 2004, Cape Town.

74   David Abrahams, interviewed 18 February 2004.

75   Mervyn Ross quoted in *Mail & Guardian*, 24–30 March 1995.

76   Michael Weeder, interviewed 12 February 2004.

77   See Sharp J & Boonzaier E. 1994. 'Ethnic identity as performance: lessons from Namaqualand'. *Journal of Southern African Studies*, 20, no. 3, 405–416.

78   John Witbooi, interviewed by Michele Ruiters, 28 October 2004.

79   Jean Burgess, interviewed by Michele Ruiters, 16 October 2004.

80   Cecil le Fleur's speech entitled 'Die stryd om erkenning van Suid-Afrika se eerste inheemse mense in 'n nuwe demokrasie' (The struggle for recognition of South Africa's first people in a new democracy), delivered on 19 October 2004, University of Port Elizabeth, C J Langenhoven Lecture Series, translated from Afrikaans by author.

81   Le Fleur, 'Die stryd om erkenning van Suid-Afrika'.

82   'Statement by Mbeki on Constitution Bill, 1996'.

83   Le Fleur, 'Die stryd om erkenning van Suid-Afrika'.

84   Le Fleur, 'Die stryd om erkenning van Suid-Afrika'.

85   Ron Martin, interviewed by Michele Ruiters 18 February 2004.

86   John Witbooi, interviewed 28 October 2004.

87   Ron Martin, interviewed 18 February 2004.

88   John Witbooi, interviewed 28 October 2004.

89   Appiah K. 2006. 'The case for contamination'. *New York Times*, 1 January.

90   Roots and Visions Forum, http://www.inyathelo.co.za/roots.about/main.html (accessed 15 August 2005)

91   Roots and Visions Forum, http://www.inyathelo.co.za/roots/about/main.html (accessed 2 August 2005).

92   Roots and Visions Forum, minutes of meeting, 5 April 2003, 10 http://www.inyathelo.co.za/roots.about/main.html (accessed 15 August 2005).

93   Patric Tariq Mellet, interviewed by Michele Ruiters, 12 February 2004.

94   Patric Mellet, interviewed 12 February 2004.

95   Nuttal, 'City forms', 733

96   Erasmus, *Coloured by History*, 14.

97   Erasmus, *Coloured by History*, 16.

98   Mlangeni B. 'Racial identity is greyer than ever in the new South Africa, 2003', http://www.sundaytimes.co.za/articles/TarkArticle.aspx?Id=857478 (accessed 7 February 2005).

99   Alexander, *An Ordinary Country*, 207.

100 Simone, *In the Mix*, 21.

101 Robins S. 2000. 'Land struggles and the politics and ethics of representing "Bushman" history and identity'. *Kronos*, 26, 69.

102 Sharp, 'Beyond exposé analysis', 15.

103 Patric Mellet, interviewed 12 February 2004.

104 Sharp, 'Beyond exposé analysis', 17.

CHAPTER 6

'We are the original inhabitants of this land': Khoe-San identity in post-apartheid South Africa

BY

MICHAEL BESTEN

UNIVERSITY OF THE FREE STATE

This chapter examines the dynamics of Khoe-San identity in post-apartheid South Africa. It begins by providing historical background and discussing some of the effects of colonial racial categorisations in legislation and censuses on Khoe-San identities. It is then argued that, with the ending of apartheid, the coloured category, under which many Khoe-San descendants had been classified prior to 1994, lost much of the psychological, socio-economic, ideological and political value it previously conferred on its bearers. This predisposed coloured people to distance themselves from the identity and to affirm an indigenous Khoe-San heritage. The shift was largely motivated by an attempt at finding identity terms that were useful for promoting broader coloured social and political concerns rather than those of people who had historically espoused Khoe-San identities. This tied the articulation of Khoe-San identities to colouredness at the same time that it challenged the premises on which coloured identity has been based.

Terminology and identities in flux

The term 'Khoe-San' is used to refer to the indigenous peoples of southern Africa who inhabited the area before the arrival of Bantu-speaking agro-pastoralists 2 000 years ago. It was appropriated after 1994 by people who regarded themselves as descended from these indigenous peoples. This specific form is preferred to 'Khoisan' partly because 'Khoekhoe' is a more appropriate linguistic rendering than 'Khoikhoi'. Hunter-gathering communities tended to be referred to as San by Khoekhoe herders. Hunter-gatherers who spoke a language other than Khoe historically did not refer to themselves as San but used more narrowly based group names to refer to themselves.[1] Hyphenating the two terms also reflects the view among some academics and people who identify themselves as Khoe-San that although the early hunter-gathering and herding indigenes of southern Africa had a shared ancestry and some cultural commonalities, there were differences in language, culture, livelihood and identity between the two. This configuration also takes account of the objection that the San should not be subordinated to, or subsumed within, Khoekhoe groupings. Many San reject 'the idea of the Khoisan people, terming it a political ploy by non-San-speaking people', particularly the Nama and the Griqua, 'to continue subjugating their unique culture'.[2] They would also reject the term 'Khoe-San', preferring to identify as a separate group.

The hunting, gathering and herding livelihoods of the early Khoe-San communities encouraged multiple and relatively fluid group identities. The impact of colonialism led to the fragmentation of Khoe-San communities and further erosion of traditional Khoe-San cultures and identities. The application of the terms 'Bushman' and 'Hottentot' to these people by colonists and subsequent self-referential usage of these categories fostered overarching group identities within Khoekhoe and San communities. San who were incorporated into the colonial labour force were also liable to be categorised as Hottentot[3] and thus to develop a Hottentot identity. Captured San, especially children taken into the colonial labour force as servants on farms in the interior during the 18th and 19th centuries, were likely to assume a Hottentot identity.[4] By spawning categories such as 'coloured' and 'Aboriginal Native', colonialism engendered a broader group consciousness among Khoe-San underclasses.

The terms 'Bushman' and 'Hottentot' did not, however, feature in the pre-1994 South African constitutional and legal dispensation as legitimate communities with identities, cultures and historical claims worthy of respect. Racial discrimination and the association of the

Bushman and Hottentot categories with inferiority and primitivism led to people of Khoe-San ancestry distancing themselves from Khoe-Sanness and assuming alternative identities. Many such people found Christian and Bastaard identities more attractive than being categorised as Bushman or Hottentot as these were associated with higher status in the colonial value system. Bastaard and Christian identities allowed Khoe-San descendants to assert a status that suggested closer proximity to Europeans and Western culture and helped distance them from their Khoe-San heritage. This is apparent from William Burchell's 1812 account of Van Roye and Cornè, two servants accompanying him on his travels:

> None were more lazy than these two … yet, on account of their being *Christemensch*, they rated themselves so high, that they actually regarded it as degrading, to do the same work as a Hottentot. They carried this ignorant mischievous pride so far, as to deny all knowledge of the Hottentot language… It was disgusting, though ridiculous, to hear these two woolly-headed men, call their companions, *Hottentots*, as an appellation of inferiority....[5]

Most Khoe-San descendants were officially classified as coloured and Native during the 19th and 20th centuries. As long as the coloured category subsumed the Native category, as was the case for much of the 19th century when the term 'coloured' was used broadly to refer to people not considered European,[6] Bushmen and Hottentots could unproblematically be designated both coloured and Native. A growing distinction between these two categories from the late 19th century onwards resulted in some ambiguity in the categorisation of people referred to as Bushmen and Hottentots.[7] This was especially the case with the Griqua. Some colonial laws explicitly lumped Griqua and Khoe-San together with Bantu-speaking communities as Aboriginal Natives.[8] Other laws that classified Bushmen, Hottentots, Korana and Namaqua as Aboriginal Natives did not include Griqua in this category. The perception that Bushmen and Hottentots were racially mixed often caused them to be seen as a subset of the coloured category.[9] At other times, the perception that people with Bushman and Hottentot ancestry were indigenous meant that they were regarded as Native. The chance that they might be included in the Native category and subjected to discrimination imposed on Natives inclined many to invoke a coloured identity and to valorise a non-indigenous heritage.[10]

Categorisation, both in law and in official censuses, was very much tied to the colonial state's imperative to maintain social order. Preserving order under white rule required a neat demarcation of population groups. This was made difficult by a lack of consensus over, and shifting meanings of, racial terminologies within the colonial establishment itself. The water was further muddied through social networks cutting across official categories, and colonial subjects contesting the applicability of certain terms to their particular groups.[11]

In the 20th century, government officials used racial categories inconsistently in both legislation as well as in censuses. For example, in censuses between 1921 and 1970 the terms 'Bantu' and 'Native' were used interchangeably.[12] Hottentots and Bushmen, on the other hand, were excluded from the Native category and included together with Griqua in the coloured category in censuses between 1904 and 1946.[13] During this period they were also referred to as Aboriginal Natives in some laws.[14]

The census classification of Khoe-San, with the exception of the Griqua, changed in 1951. Viewed as 'aboriginal races', people regarded as Bushmen, Hottentots, Korana and Namaqua were classified as Natives in the 1951 census so as to be in line with the Population Registration Act of 1950. The Act did not explicitly refer to Khoekhoe or San but defined a Native as 'a person who is in fact or is generally accepted as a member of any aboriginal race or tribe of Africa'.[15] The exclusion of the Griqua from the Native category in the 1951 census reflected the strong association of Griqua with the coloured grouping. The Population Registration Act defined a coloured person as 'a person who is not a white person or a native'.[16]

Since Bushmen and Hottentots were to be classified as Natives in censuses from 1951 onwards, these two categories were effaced from subsequent censuses. Many Khoe-San descendants, were, however, in practice treated as coloured, a category of people that became increasingly associated with racial mixture in the course of the 20th century. This was very much as a result of the widely held perception among government officials that there were few 'pure' Hottentots and Bushmen left, and that most who had previously been identified as Hottentot were racially mixed.[17] It was mentioned in the 1911 census report that 'the term "Hottentot" ... [was] colloquially applied to many persons who, though their forebears in the distant past may have belonged to the Hottentot race, should strictly speaking be classed ... as of the Mixed Race'.[18]

From 1961, population censuses generally used the term 'Bantu' in place of 'Native', and this meant that people considered Bushmen and Hottentots were now liable to be classified as Bantu. Bantu were defined in the 1961 census as persons 'who in fact are, or who are generally accepted as members of any aboriginal race or tribe of Africa' referred to in 'previous census reports ... as "Native"'.[19] A 1961 circular from the Department of Bantu Administration and Development made it clear that those considered Bushmen or Hottentots were to be classified as Bantu:

> Some district officers may encounter difficulty due to the fact that certain groups such as Nama-Korana and Bushmen may claim classification as coloureds. It must be emphasised that although the abovementioned groups are lighter of skin than the typical Bantu, they belong to an aboriginal race of Africa and are regarded as Bantu for the Population registration purposes.[20]

The subsequent use of the term 'black' in place of 'Native' would similarly have resulted in some Khoe-San being classified 'black'.

Official usage of population categories in legislation and censuses tended to limit the identity choices of people, inducing them to locate themselves and others in terms of official categories. These categories and their meanings were, however, subject to contestation both within dominant and subordinate communities. The divergent ways in which these categories were deployed within the dominant classes, especially government officials, gave subordinate people some leeway in the identity choices they could make and the meanings they could give to population categories.

Terms such as 'Hottentot', 'coloured' and 'Native', introduced by colonisers, were not necessarily accepted by all people thus designated or, when accepted, were not necessarily imbued with the same meaning. Although the term 'Hottentot' connoted primitiveness for many whites, it could be affirmed with a measure of pride by some Khoe-San people, as occurred in the Kat River settlement between 1825 and 1851. Khoe-San heritage and memory, especially around pre-colonial landownership, was invoked by Khoe-San descendants in the eastern Cape to mobilise against colonial restrictions.[21] In the 20th century, Griqua leader Andrew Abraham Stockenström le Fleur I (1867–1941) attempted to turn coloureds into proud Griqua subjects. Le Fleur also invoked categories such as Hottentot and Namaqua with a measure of pride.[22] While there was a general proclivity during the era of white supremacy for Khoe-San to distance themselves from their disparaged heritage, some people openly acknowledged having Khoekhoe and San ancestry.

Post-apartheid Khoe-San revivalism

The demise of apartheid together with anxiety about the future caused some coloured people to re-evaluate their social identities and to affirm, even invent, an indigenous heritage. This contributed to a broader rethinking in South African society of what it meant to be indigenous and African. There was renewed discussion within coloured communities after 1994 about the appropriateness of espousing a coloured identity in the new order as many saw it as an artificial imposition of the apartheid establishment. Many felt the need to develop a more appropriate identity. A relatively small but growing number opted to promote a Khoe-San or one or other narrower indigenous identity.[23] This they presented as the 'real' identity of coloured people, embracing what for many had previously held unpalatable associations. They asserted that there needed to be a rethinking of what it meant to be Khoekhoe and San in post-apartheid South Africa. Educated elites featured prominently in Khoe-San revivalism and assumed leadership roles in many Khoe-San organisations. A number claimed to be chiefs of long extinct Khoe-San tribes to attract support and bolster their legitimacy. It was largely members within the educated coloured elite who assumed a leadership role within the movement because they were able to harness the mechanisms of power and influence in the new South Africa.

The resurgence of Khoe-San identities in South Africa in the 1990s coincided with a number of international developments that stimulated growing Khoe-San organisations and the affirmation of their culture and identity. The United Nations (UN) declaring 1993 as the Year of Indigenous People and the subsequent declaration of 1995–2004 as the International Decade for the World's Indigenous People focused greater attention on the rights of indigenous peoples or First Nations. Renewed Western fascination with, and romanticisation of, indigenous cultures and the attendant boom in cultural tourism encouraged the assertion of Khoe-San identity.

These developments contributed to the realignment of identities within communities such as the Griqua, which had long acknowledged a

Khoekhoe heritage. This in turn contributed to identity realignments among coloureds. During apartheid, Griqua were inclined to project themselves as being of mixed Khoekhoe, slave and European descent. They were prepared to acknowledge part 'Hottentot' ancestry but did not represent themselves as Khoekhoe. Griqua, especially the most Westernised segments outside of Griqualand West, were also not inclined to view traditional Khoekhoe culture in a positive manner. By 1995, however, Griqua were increasingly claiming that they were Khoekhoe. The view that they were of mixed descent was now de-emphasised. They were also now prepared to affirm traditional Khoekhoe culture, and projected themselves as Khoe-San. In rearticulating their identity, Griqua reasserted a longstanding aspiration for official recognition of Griqua identity and culture, gaining constitutionally entrenched political representation and the restoration of lost land.[24] The public articulation of these objectives was encouraged by an accommodationist official ideology and a growing international First Nation rights discourse. Since most of these aspirations could not feasibly be met within the current constitutional framework, it reinforced their sense that Griqua were being marginalised in the new order.

The perception that the post-apartheid government was not sensitive to the needs of Khoe-San communities caused activists to try to gain First Nation status, both from the United Nations and the South African government. Griqua organisations together with the South African San Institute (SASI) and its mother body, the Working Group for Indigenous Minorities in Southern Africa (WIMSA), an NGO that specialises in promoting San interests across southern Africa, became the principal catalysts in the assertion of an indigenous status and in the agitation for First Nation rights among Khoe-San. These demands were highlighted by post-1994 campaigns for the restitution of Khoe-San land and at academic conferences on Khoe-San history and identity. The new discourse of indigenous rights found resonance among some coloured people in search of empowering post-apartheid identities. These developments together with the changed constitutional order provided an impetus for the emergence of a Khoe-San identity outside of longstanding Khoe-San communities.

Khoe-San and indigeneity in South Africa

Affirmation of Khoe-San identities and claims that they were the 'real' indigenes had the potential to yield a range of benefits. This fostered a deep sense of rootedness in South Africa as well as a sense of entitlement to socio-economic resources. After the transition to democracy, segments of the coloured population were more open to acknowledging an African heritage. A number opted not only to proclaim their Africanness but also that their indigeneity entitled them access to resources. Many, however, sought to distinguish themselves from Bantu-speaking communities.

In projecting themselves as indigenous, claimants to Khoe-San identity appropriated a status generally associated with Bantu-speaking communities in South Africa during the apartheid period. Within Khoe-San organisations, Bantu-speakers were not regarded as indigenous to southern Africa. Khoe-San claimed their ancestors to have been in southern Africa before any other peoples, and their claims to indigeneity to be more authentic than anyone else's. This logic encouraged Khoekhoe to also position themselves as Khoe-San as the San were acknowledged to be the earliest people to have inhabited the region.

The rights claimed for First Nations at the United Nations contributed much to the popularity of the term 'indigenous' within Khoe-San organisations. The International Labour Organisation's Convention no. 169 of 1989, Concerning Indigenous and Tribal Peoples in Independent Countries, was seen as particularly significant because it had far-reaching implications for the treatment of Khoe-San across southern Africa. It required ratifying states to institute special measures, in collaboration with indigenous people, to safeguard their rights, cultures and institutions, and the ownership of land that they traditionally occupied. To be defined as an indigenous people the Convention required a group to have been in existence before colonial conquest. Regarding the Khoe-San as the only indigenous people of South Africa was controversial as African politicians were inclined to reason that all 'black Africans' were indigenous to Africa, thus making the ratification of the Convention 169 by African states problematic.[25] The terms 'First People' and 'First Nation' could be used as alternatives to 'indigenous' in restitution campaigns.

Demands for restitution, especially of land, within longstanding Khoe-San communities such as the Griqua, Kalahari San and Nama, provided some incentive for the affirmation of Khoekhoe and San identities among people who were not part of these communities. A host of new organisations claiming to represent Khoe-San interests emerged after 1994.

The drive for land restitution was particularly evident among the Griqua from the Northern Cape, who made extensive demands for land and monetary reparation. The view that the British were responsible for Griqua impoverishment and the confiscation of their land in Griqualand

West and East Griqualand gained new life. In 1996 the Griekwa Volks Organisasie sued the British government for £1.4 billion for 'robbing and driving our ancestors off their land and property'. It also sued De Beers Consolidated Mines for R8.7 billion for royalties on the mineral rights of the company's Northern Cape and Free State diamond mines situated on historic Griqua land.[26]

Renewed Khoe-San activism: WIMSA and SASI

As with the Griqua, the affirmation of a ≠Khomani San identity in the Northern Cape was also influenced by the prospect of land restitution in the Kalahari Gemsbok National Park (KGNP). The activities of organisations such as WIMSA and SASI also played an important role in the reaffirmation of San identities and awareness of indigenous rights.[27]

In 1994 a !Xun and Khwe delegation from Schmidtsdrift, supported by whites later involved in the creation of SASI, attended the proceedings of the United Nations' International Working Group for Indigenous Affairs (IWGIA) in Geneva. The delegation not only attended discussions on the need to protect indigenous peoples but also delivered two speeches appealing for international recognition of their indigeneity and for the conservation of their cultures. The visit by the !Xun and Khwe delegation to IWGIA and subsequent delegations from other Khoe-San groups was important in facilitating contact with First Nations from elsewhere and for familiarising themselves with First Nations rights discourse.[28] The visit by the !Xun and Khwe delegation also provided inspiration to other Khoe-San and neo-Khoe-San groups to assert claims to First Nation status.

Greater international sensitivity to First Nations rights contributed to the emergence of an industry around the protection of indigenous rights in South Africa. Highly educated and skilled individuals, largely white and usually contracted as consultants, became involved in San educational, cultural and economic development projects, especially the promotion of San land rights. These efforts drew a fair amount of funding from international sources for their activities, suggesting that activists skilfully exploited international sympathy for the plight of the San people.[29] According to WIMSA the organisation was established in January 1996 in Windhoek, Namibia, after San representatives from southern African countries expressed the need for representation at local, national and international levels. They sought effective channels through which to exchange information among their communities and through which they could participate in regional developmental processes.

San delegates defined a number of objectives for WIMSA. It had to help the San gain political recognition, secure access to natural and financial resources, and raise a general awareness of their rights so that their communities could become self-sustainable through development projects. WIMSA was also expected to assist San communities regain their identity and pride in their culture. WIMSA provided training courses at its Windhoek office for San youths, and conducted a series of workshops with San traditional authorities on land tenure, income-generating possibilities and specific community problems. The organisation provided opportunities for San delegates from southern Africa to participate in regional workshops and international conferences.

SASI was established by WIMSA as a specialist service organisation.[30] It mandated SASI to set up multidisciplinary development projects in areas such as education, leadership training, cultural resource management, land rights, intellectual property rights, oral history collection and community mobilisation. SASI aimed to give the San 'permanent control over their lives, resources and destiny'.[31] Although SASI, at its inception, was very much a white-controlled organisation, it insisted that it was acting in the interests of the San, who were being guided to take control of their own destiny.[32] San now play a more visible role in the organisation and its leadership than before.

To secure funding for their activities, SASI and WIMSA were inclined to use a discourse that presented the San as a primordial people whose hunter-gathering lifestyle and ancient way of life was threatened. This discourse played on the strong interest of international donors in the survival of 'vanishing cultures'[33] and was invoked to support the ≠Khomani claim for land in the KGNP.[34] During the land-claims process, the ≠Khomani were projected as a highly marginalised but homogeneous and cohesive hunter-gathering community with historical links to the KGNP. The ≠Khomani land claim not only stimulated a reaffirmation of ≠Khomani identity but also boosted the profile of SASI as a San developmental organisation.

Neo-Khoe-San and Neo-Khoekhoe revivalism[35]

The presence of Griqua, Nama and San as longstanding communities in the Northern Cape allowed coloureds in the region to be more open to accepting a Khoe-San heritage and embracing Khoe-San revivalism.

The same applied to coloured people living in the Free State since they had strong historical associations with the Griqua and Korana peoples. While Khoe-San revivalism within these communities rubbed off onto coloureds who had no such attachments, the broadening of the revivalist movement to such people in turn fed revivalism within longstanding Khoe-San communities.

Though not as attractive an option as espousing a Khoekhoe identity, some revivalist segments in the Northern Cape opted for a specifically San identity, as embodied in the San Diaspora, an organisation formed shortly after the 1994 democratic transition by Pastor Johannes Lawrence of Kimberley. Claiming to be a !Xam descendant, Lawrence assumed the title of San paramount chief.[36] The presence of longstanding Khoe-San communities in the Northern Cape facilitated a positive reception of this initiative among coloured people in the region. Lawrence's positioning suggested the opportunism that might be involved in claiming Khoekhoe and San identities, especially chieftainship of one or other group. Lawrence at first espoused a Griqua identity but later opted to present himself as San after falling out with his Griqua counterparts. He claimed, however, to have been born San.[37] Lawrence's shifting identities suggest opportunistic use of multiple ethnic heritages. Claiming to be San allowed him to exploit their association with innocence, vulnerability, marginality and colonial genocide, that is, with ultimate victimhood, in appeals for reparation and aid.

Lawrence's San Diaspora issued a media statement in 2000 in which it asked the government to prevent museums from removing 'San title deeds', by which it meant rock art, from their original locations and placing them in museums. The San Diaspora reasoned that rock paintings were the only proof the San had of their land rights and heritage. The organisation also asked for government assistance in retrieving their ancestors' skins and skulls from museums in other countries so that they could be buried at an appropriate place. Playing on the notion of the San as the ultimate victims, the San Diaspora appealed to the public to help protect its heritage from further exploitation. It also solicited donations of office equipment, old clothes, tinned food, furniture and blankets, and any other articles that may be of use. The media statement, in addition, called for San representation at provincial and parliamentary levels and for their participation in government decision-making structures.[38]

While there were many organisations claiming Khoekhoe and Khoe-San identities, there were far fewer that associated themselves exclusively with the San despite the perception that they were the original inhabitants of the region. The lower status associated with the San as hunter-gatherers as opposed to Khoekhoe pastoralism contributed to this. The historical marginalisation of the San was thus replicated in post-apartheid Khoe-San revivalism. A scarcity of detail on specific San groups may, however, also have played a part.

Joseph Little and the Cape Cultural Heritage Development Council (CCHDC), which registered as a Section 21 non-profit company in 1996, played an important role in the organisation of neo-Khoekhoe in the Western and Eastern Cape.[39] Joseph Little, chief executive officer of the CCHDC, in 1997 claimed to be the chief of the Hamcumqua people and to be a Khoekhoe descendant through his grandmother, who was a member the 'royal tribe' of the Hamcumqua.[40] He later positioned himself as chief of the Chainoqua. Little and his associates were inspired by the South African constitution's various provisions for protecting and promoting the nation's cultural diversity to establish the CCHDC.[41]

Explicitly coloured concerns as opposed to Khoe-San or neo-Khoe-San interests were evident in the formation of the CCHDC and in the formulation of its objectives. At the Khoisan Identities and Cultural Heritage Conference held at the South African Museum in Cape Town in July 1997, Joseph Little explained that:

> Our very first objective in the Cape Cultural Heritage Organization is to create a spirit of unity among all South Africans, especially those under the statutory title as Coloured South Africans … In 1994 everybody got a shock and everybody was in a subdued mode because all of a sudden we were going to have a black government. … [T]he coloured people were looking for their identity along the Khoisan lines which we, I think at this stage, also are halfheartedly, from my point of view, are willing to accept.[42]

Little also mentioned that his organisation was launched in response to the government's affirmative action policies, 'under the previous dispensation we weren't white enough, with the next we weren't brown enough'. A leading associate of the CCHDC, Jean Burgess, a former United Democratic Front activist who now positioned herself as chief of the Gonaqua tribe, rationalised her acceptance of a Khoekhoe identity as a response to perceptions among Bantu-speaking Africans that coloureds lacked a cultural heritage. Burgess claimed to have been part of the Black

Consciousness Movement and to have always seen herself as black but that on Heritage Day in 1996,

> [a] Xhosa man asked me, in front of all the people in the hall, where my culture and heritage was … It made me feel like nothing. I couldn't answer him. I started searching for it … I wanted it so badly, I would have done anything for it. It's difficult to explain what it means to have one's culture denied.

Upon embracing a Khoekhoe heritage and identity, Burgess suggested that she felt her dignity had been restored and that she saw her role as a 'spiritual responsibility to make coloured people see they aren't just a mixture of black and white'. Little concurred with her views: 'Black people have no respect for us because we have no ancestral roots'.[43]

Coloured insecurities generated by the democratic transition, together with the historical association of coloureds with the Khoe-San, ensured a degree of receptivity to identity entrepreneurs such as chief Joseph Little and his associates, who promoted Khoe-San identities as having psychological, political and material benefits. Re-evaluating the historical association of coloureds with partial Khoe-San ancestry, the CCHDC and its affiliates emphasised their indigenous heritage and played down, at least in public, the notion that the coloured people were the product of sexual liaisons between white settlers and indigenous peoples. Coloureds were now seen as descendants of the Khoe-San, their slave heritage occasionally acknowledged.[44]

The CCHDC aimed, according to Little, to 'foster unity among historically coloured people and give them pride in their origin'.[45] According its spokesperson, David Andrews, the CCHDC sought to restore coloured people's heritage to its pre-colonial glory. The CCHDC opened branches in the Western and Eastern Cape, and subsequently acquired affiliates in Gauteng.[46] Functioning as an umbrella organisation, the CCHDC was presented as consisting of Khoekhoe 'tribes' represented by their respective chiefs.[47] The CCHDC campaigned for the recognition of their 'tribes' as indigenous people, for the recognition of their chiefs as traditional leaders, and for constitutionally entrenched political representation.[48] The CCHDC also planned to identify and claim land that originally belonged to the Khoekhoe 'tribes' and to capitalise on the cultural heritage industry. According to Andrews:

> [i]n many areas, indigenous people are living in squalor while other interested [sic] groups are making money from

their history. We will submit land claims to the Land Claims Court to get the land back and have them declared national heritage sites. We will develop it, with the co-operation of the people, into sustainable hives of activity which would enable the people to economically empower themselves while at the same time tap the tourism potential.[49]

Claims by their chiefs reflected both the material as well as psychological imperatives of the Khoe-San revivalist movement. At a Khoekhoe gathering in Oudtshoorn in May 1999 Jean Burgess criticised the Land Claims Commission (LCC) and the Truth and Reconciliation Commission (TRC) for not recognising the Khoekhoe. She also criticised the TRC for only focusing on cases of injustice committed from 1948 onwards, and the LCC for only helping people who were deprived of land since 1913. Suggesting a basis for Khoekhoe land ownership claims, Burgess stated that 'Harry die Strandloper' (Autshumato) was the first political prisoner on Robben Island and that Eva (Krotoa) died on the island thus 'making the Khoikhoi the owners of it [Robben Island] and we demand that it be returned to us'.[50]

Reasoning that 'coloureds were an apartheid creation', Basil Coetzee, chief of the CCHDC-affiliated Cochoqua 'tribe', also expressed the neo-Khoekhoe desire for cultural renewal as well as for restitution of land on the basis of neo-Khoekhoe aboriginality:

Whoever came here, from wherever, found us here. We are the original inhabitants of this land. We want our land back and our languages recognized. If we can have land, we can end this cultural slavery. We were a sovereign people before the Europeans came here.

The demand for land was, as Coetzee indicated, often qualified or moderated so as to appear reasonable and practicable. The CCHDC did not, according to Coetzee, seek complete restoration of Khoe-San historical land or a homeland or a Khoe-San state: 'How can we ask for a homeland in our own country? But we're not saying all immigrants should leave the country. There's enough land for all of us'.[51]

There were also a few neo-Khoekhoe organisations that operated independently of the CCHDC between 1994 and 2000. Two examples are the Cape Town-based !Hurikamma Cultural Movement and the Khoisan Awareness Initiative (KAI) based in the Eastern Cape. These organisations nevertheless shared much with the CCHDC. They also saw the need for colouredness to be replaced by a Khoe-San identity, and strove for government recognition, land restitution, economic empowerment, cultural revival, promotion of Khoe-San languages and the inclusion of Khoe-San history in the school curriculum.

A number of people in the Northern Cape and Free State also started re-assuming a Korana identity after 1994. Leaders with surnames of historic Korana personalities such as Hoogstander, Katz and Taaibosch came to the fore and asserted First Nation status. They also demanded the restitution of some of their historic land, and rejected the 1913 cut-off date for claims lodged in terms of the 1994 Restitution of Land Rights Act.[52]

Khoe-San revivalism also took root in Gauteng. The Gauteng Khoi-San Tribes Youth Council (GKTYC) was formed in 2002. Its main objective was to re-establish the Khoe-San culture, language, identity and traditions. The Council also strove for government recognition of the Khoe-San and their leaders and for the rights of Khoe-San people to be guaranteed by the constitution.[53] The GKTYC was strongly critical of the perceived marginalisation of the Khoe-San. Phillip Williams, president of the GKTYC, felt that the government was deliberately marginalising the Khoe-San and that '… the arrogance of the present-day leadership in our society is destructive to healthy nation-building. The African renaissance will fail the Khoi-San people and more so Africa'.[54] He reasoned that 'meaningful nation-building' could not take place 'while the Khoi-San were marginalised'.[55] In line with the CCHDC, members of the GKTYC presented coloureds as descendants of the Khoe-San and coloured identity as an illegitimate imposition that undermined their unity. In the words of Williams:

> European immigrants conquered the minds of the Khoi-San to the extent that they suffered from poor self-esteem and had an identity crisis. Khoi-San Africans are misled into focussing on their Eurocentric heritage and 'coloureds' lack a serious sense of creativity, spending most of their time anxious, highly stressed and mostly drunk – with devastating consequences. The 'coloured' suffers from self-hatred and therefore engages in self-destructive behaviour. They are proud of who they are not, but they are the most divided of people who can never unite without their original identity, language and culture. The Khoi-San, in their artificial identity as sophisticated 'coloureds', divide

our people into an antagonistic 'us' (Gauteng, Cape Town, etc) and them (Kalahari desert, Schmidtsdrift community and the Basarwa people of Botswana). We continually divorce ourselves from our African mother and cling to our European father ... It is imperative that we understand that colonialism, the mother of all thefts of all land and resources, is the real cause of societal divisions and conflict. South Africans, we plead with you to assist us in the quest for our 'identity'.[56]

Public expressions of Khoe-San identities were partly driven by the expectation that some demands would be met. However, none of the key demands – most notably that Khoe-San chiefs be accommodated in traditional leadership structures – have yet been met. Protracted negotiations that yielded little and declining hope that their demands would be satisfactorily addressed intensified their sense of deliberately being marginalised.[57] While a decline in the hope that key Khoe-San demands would be met sapped some of the energy behind the public staging of Khoe-San indigeneity, a continued sense of coloured economic and political marginalisation continued to provide an impetus for the affirmation of Khoe-San identity. South Africa's past generated concern within coloured communities that the country could again be ethno-racially ordered, to their disadvantage. Thus, insecurity and fear of especially Bantu-speaking African favouritism and coloured marginalisation, reinforced very much by the perception that affirmative action and black empowerment benefited mainly Bantu-speaking Africans, encouraged individuals and groupings to rethink and redefine their identities, their space, as well as their relations to others,[58] with some opting to invoke Khoe-San identities.

The potential of the ongoing sense of coloured marginality to provide an impetus for the affirmation of Khoe-San identity was exemplified by the creation of organisations such as the Movement against Domination of African Minorities (MADAM). Formed late in 2004 by four senior correctional services officials, MADAM was concerned that Bantu-speaking African correctional services officials in the Western Cape were 'getting promoted into posts without the necessary qualification, just because they are African and Xhosa-speaking'.[59] The organisation was formed as a pressure group to oppose 'black dominance' in prisons across the Western Cape. It also promoted a Khoe-San rather than a coloured identity, and sought to recruit Khoe-San to its cause.[60] MADAM seemed as much concerned with the career advancement of its leadership as with the ethno-racial marginalisation of the Khoe-San.[61]

The perception that coloureds in senior positions within government were being sidelined by the ANC was reinforced with the restructuring of the City of Cape Town's management team in 2005 after it came under ANC control. The restructuring resulted in the predominance of Bantu-speaking Africans in the top levels of power in Nomaindia Mfeketo's mayoral committee and the city's directors known as the Ikhwezi (sunrise) team. The Ikhwezi team consisted of six Bantu-speaking Africans, two whites and two coloureds, despite coloureds being in the majority in Cape Town and the Western Cape. The limited representation of coloureds in the top structures of Cape Town's municipal structures caused much bitterness. The mayor justified the restructuring on the basis of the need for representivity in terms of national demographics. The restructuring was also seen as part of Mfeketo's drive to 'Africanise' Cape Town.

While limiting the number of coloureds in top management caused much bitterness among those who felt sidelined,[62] much less concern was expressed about the preponderance of whites in the top management of the preceding Cape Town City Council, which was controlled by the Democratic Alliance (DA). This suggests a particular concern with domination by Bantu-speaking leaders. The DA's selection of coloured mayors might, however, have dampened criticism by coloureds of the ethno-racial makeup of the Cape Town City Council's management under the DA between 2001 and 2002.

Media revelations in March 2006 that Mfeketo's media advisor and head of the City of Cape Town's communications department, Zimbabwean-born Roderick Blackman Ngoro, had articulated offensive generalisations about coloureds on his private website[63] before his employment by Mfeketo reinforced the perception that the mayor as well as some of her close associates harboured prejudice towards coloureds – despite Mfeketo's emphasis that she was a longstanding proponent of 'non-racialism'. Ngoro claimed, inter alia, that coloureds were drunkards and acted as cheerleaders for whites, and that the culture of Bantu-speaking Africans was superior to that of coloureds.[64] Cultural chauvinism expressed by the likes of Ngoro reinforced coloured concerns about their being marginalised, and continued to provide impetus to Khoe-San revivalism.

Conclusion

Coloured insecurity generated by the transition to a democratic order eroded the measure of security they had under apartheid as a group with relative privilege. Neo-Khoe-San identities reflect attempts at adapting to the new order to meet individual and collective ethno-racial concerns. With the ending of apartheid, and the attendant reconfiguration of political, cultural and ideological relations, the coloured category lost much of the psychological, socio-economic, ideological and political value it previously held, predisposing some coloureds to distance themselves from coloured identity and affirm an indigenous heritage. By positioning themselves as African, coloureds suggested that Bantu-speakers were not entitled to special privileges by virtue of being African. A Khoe-San identity further allowed coloureds to outdo Bantu-speaking Africans in claims to indigeneity and entitlement to resources in South Africa. While insecurity generated by the 1994 transition predisposed a number of coloureds to assume a Khoe-San identity, everyone who claimed such an identity was not necessarily uneasy about the transition or driven by fear. It was also not inevitable that once assumed, a Khoe-San identity would be sustained by insecurity. Many other factors fed into the identity. The articulation of a Khoe-San identity also allowed individuals to recreate their personal lives in a way that assumed new significance to themselves and to others. For example, those opposed to prevailing gender and social inequities point to the egalitarian social and gender relations they read into the Khoe-San past as ideals for which they should strive in the present. The past is thus revisited to validate present desires.[65]

Khoe-San identity engendered a range of social and psychological qualities that many desired but which the coloured category could not confer on bearers. These included a geographic rootedness, a sense of belonging, self-esteem, ethno-cultural specificity, legitimacy, integrity, unity and a sense of entitlement to national resources. Although neo-Khoe-San expressed disapproval of the concept of colouredness, the Khoe-San identity that they presented as an alternative was continually invested with elements of coloured identity. The two categories tended to be articulated in a manner that placed them in a similar relationship to other racialised categories against which both were defined. This association and entanglement reflected the coloured background of the neo-Khoe-San and the re-ethno-racialisation of the Khoe-San.[66] Affirmations of neo-Khoe-San indigeneity and its attendant demands are testament to the psychological space opened up by the 1994 democratic transition for coloureds to reassess their identity.

Endnotes

1   The term 'San' has a plurality of meanings depending on the length and tone of the 'a'. It could historically be used to refer to people who lived by foraging, to people with a low socio-economic or lineage status or to robbers. People who lived by hunting and gathering tended to be referred to as 'Bushmen' by colonists who also used the term 'Hottentot' to refer to indigenous herders. 'San' has been used by many scholars to refer to hunter-gatherers in contradistinction to Khoe-speaking herders. Today some people reject the term 'San' and prefer to be called Bushmen. Translated from Nama the singular 'Khoe' suggests man, human or person, and 'Khoekhoe' suggests men of men or people. For discussion on the terms 'Khoekhoe', 'San' and 'Khoisan', see Nienaber G. 1989. *Khoekhoense Stamname: 'n Voorlopige Verkenning*. Pretoria: Academia, 190–212, 616–627, 830–837; Barnard A. 1992. *Hunters and Herders of Southern Africa: A Comparative Ethnography of the Khoisan Peoples*. Cambridge: Cambridge University Press, 8–9; and Elphick R. 1985. *Khoikhoi and the Founding of White South Africa*. Johannesburg: Ravan Press, 23–28.

2   *Mail & Guardian*, 26 April 2001.

3   I have refrained from putting potentially offensive terms such as Hottentot, Bantu, Bushman and Native in inverted commas in certain cases to avoid an unwieldy proliferation of these punctuation marks. My usage of these terms is not in any way intended to offend.

4   Newton-King S. 1999. *Masters and Servants on the Cape Eastern Frontier, 1760–1803*. Cambridge: Cambridge University Press, 120–123.

5   Burchell W. 1824, *Travels in the Interior of Southern Africa, Vol II*. London: Longman, 296.

6   This is reflected in the population censuses of 1865 and 1875. G 20-66. 1866. *Census of the Colony of the Cape of Good Hope*, 1865. Cape Town: Saul Solomon & Co Printers, viii–ix; G 42-76. 1877. *Results of a Census of the Colony of the Cape of Good Hope, Taken on the Night of Sunday, the 7th March, 1875, Part 1 – Summaries*. Cape Town: Saul Solomon & Co Printers, 3.

7   *Kokstad Advertiser*, 16 August 1893, 28 June 1895, 22 May 1896; Bickford-Smith V. 1995. *Ethnic Pride and Racial Prejudice in Victorian Cape Town*. Johannesburg: Witwatersrand University Press, 201.

8   Establishment of Native Township (Cape Colony) Act no. 44, 1908; Native Definition Amendment Act no. 1, 1916; Private Locations (Cape Colony) Act no. 32, 1909.

9   See, for example, the following Acts from the Cape colony: Native Locations Amendment Act no. 8, 1878; Liquor Law Amendment Act no. 28, 1898; Native Locations Amendment Act no. 30, 1899; Native Reserve Locations Act no. 40, 1902.

10 National Archives Repository, Pretoria (hereafter NA), Secretary of Native Affairs (NTS) 1772, 65/276, A S Ruiters, Secretary, East Griqualand Pioneers Council, to General Smuts, Minister of Justice, Cape Town, 17 January 1934; *Kokstad Advertiser*, 24 December 1920.

11 See U G 40–24. 1924. *Third Census of the Population of the Union of South Africa Enumerated 3rd May 1921, Part VIII, Non-European Races*. Pretoria: Government Printer, iv.

12 U G 15–23. 1922. *Third Census of the Population of the Union of South Africa Enumerated 3rd May 1921, Part 1: Population Organization and Enumeration, Number, Sex and Distribution (All Races)*. Pretoria: Government Printer, vi; U G 40–24, iii; U G 21–38. 1938. *Sixth Census of the Population of the Union of South Africa Enumerated 5th May 1936, Volume 1, Population*. Pretoria: Government Printer; U G 12–42. 1942. *Sixth Census of the Population of the Union of South Africa Enumerated 5th May 1936, Volume IX, Natives (Bantu) and Other Non-European Races, Sixth Census Volume IX*. Pretoria: Government Printer; R P 62–63. 1963. *Population Census, 6th September 1960, Volume 1, Geographic Distribution of the Population* (Pretoria: Government Printer, v; Department of Statistics. 1976. *Population Census 1970, Geographical Distribution of the Population*. Pretoria: Government Printer.

13 G 19–1905. 1905. *Results of a Census of the Colony of the Cape of Good Hope, as on the Night of Sunday, the 17th April, 1904*. Cape Times Ltd: Government Printer, xxxiv–xxxv; U G 32–1912. 1913. *Census of the Union of South Africa, 1911*. Pretoria: Government Printer, xxii; U G 40–24, iv; U G 12–42, xxv; U G 51–1949. 1949. *Population Census, 7th May, 1946, Volume 1, Geographical Distribution of the Population of the Union of South Africa*. Pretoria: Government Printer, iv.

14 Some examples include the Establishment of Native Township Act no. 44, 1908; Private Locations Act no. 32, 1909; Native Definition Amendment Act no. 1, 1916.

15 U G 42–1955. 1955. *Population Census, 8 May, 1951, Volume 1, Geographical Distribution of the Population*. Pretoria: Government Printer, v.

16 Population Registration Act no. 30, 1950.

17 G 19–1904, xxxv; U G 57–1937. 1937. *Report of Commission of Inquiry Regarding Cape Coloured Population of the Union*. Pretoria: Government Printer, 7.

18 U G 32–1912. 1913. *Census of the Union of South Africa, 1911*. Pretoria: Government Printer, xxii.

19 R P 62–1963, *Population Census*, v.

20 Cape Town Archives Repository (hereafter CA), Chief Magistrate, Transkei (CMT) 3/1450, 37/C, Part 1, Department of Bantu Administration and Development, Pretoria, General Circular no. 15, 29 April 1961.

21 Ross R. 1998. 'The Kat River rebellion and Khoikhoi nationalism: the fate of an ethnic identification', in *The Proceedings of the Khoisan Identities and Cultural Heritage Conference Held at the South African Museum, Cape Town, 12 July 1997*, ed A Bank. Bellville: Institute for Historical Research, 214–222.

22 NA, NTS 7600, 4/328, Part 2, AAS le Fleur, Kensington, Maitland, to Capt Maryon Wilson, Cape Town 22 March 1920; *Griqua and Coloured People's Opinion*, 9 April 1920.

23 In reclaiming what they projected as their authentic identities, these new Khoe-San identity claimants tended to use names of Khoe-San groups of the early colonial period.

24 For the articulation of Griqua aspirations and demands prior to 1994, see Department of Coloured Affairs. 1980. *Report of the Interdepartmental Committee of Inquiry into the Identity of the Griquas*. 27 October. See also P C 2/1983. 1983. *Report of the Constitutional Committee of the President's Council on the Needs and Demands of the Griquas*. Cape Town: Government Printer.

25 South African Human Rights Commission (HRC). 2000. 'Research project: indigenous peoples' rights'. Pretoria: HRC, 4–5.

26 *Cape Argus*, 8 October 1996; *Daily News*, 18 June 1998; *Cape Argus*, 18 June 1998; Leader, 3 July 1998.

27 SASI. 1999. *Annual Review, April 1998 – March 1999*. Cape Town: SASI, 4; WIMSA. 'WIMSA background', http://www.san.org.za/wimsa/backround.htm (accessed 2002). Though SASI was formally established in 1996, individuals like Roger Chennells who became involved with the organisation were already working among the San by 1995. Robins S, Madzudzo E & Brenzinger M. 2001. *An Assessment of the Status of the San in South Africa, Angola, Zambia and Zimbabwe*. Windhoek: Legal Assistance Centre, 7. See also references in endnote 34 for more information on Chennells' activity among the San.

28 Douglas S. 1997. 'Reflections on state intervention and the Schmidtsdrift Bushmen'. *Journal of Contemporary African Studies*, 15, no. 1, 57.

29 SASI. 1998. *Annual Review, April 1997 – March 1998*. Rondebosch: SASI, 36.

30 SASI, *Annual Review, April 1997 – March 1998*, 3, 33.

31 *Cape Times*, 9 December 2002.

32 See SASI, *Annual Review, April 1998 – March 1999*, 16.

33 See Robins S. 2001. 'Whose culture, whose "survival"? The ≠Khomani San land claim and the cultural politics of community and "development" in the Kalahari', in *Africa's Indigenous Peoples: 'First Peoples' or Marginalized Minorities?*, eds A Barnard & J Kenrick. Edinburgh: University of Edinburgh, 229–253.

34 The ≠Khomani land claim was lodged in 1995 with the assistance of Roger Chennells, who became a SASI legal representative from its inception in 1996. From 1997 onwards he was also involved in negotiations for ≠Khomani land restitution in the KGNP. The ≠Khomani land claim was settled on 21 March 1999. SASI, *Annual Review, April 1998 – March 1999*, 10; *Cape Times*, 22 March 1999; *Cape Argus*, 22 March 1999.

35 While some appreciate the analytic value of terms such as 'neo-Khoe-San', 'neo-Khoekhoe' and 'revivalist Khoe-San', others find them offensive because they perceive them as suggesting that these identities are not authentic. The terms are useful in accounting for transformations in identity and are not in any way used here to impute inauthenticity.

36 *Volksblad* (Noord Kaap), 1 March 2000.

37 IOL. 30 March 2000. 'Deep divisions amongst SA Bushman groups', http://ww.iol.co.za/index.php?set_id=1&click_id=13&art_id=qw954440461440B252 (accessed December 2004).

38 *Beeld*, 25 April 2000.

39 *Cape Argus*, 20 September 1996. Little and his associates formed two related structures that are easily confused, namely the CCHDC and the Cape Cultural Heritage Development Organisation (CCHDO). The CCHDC was the more prominent of the two. On the CCHDO, see Brink G. 2000. 'A historical analysis of the constitutional development of groups within the Cape Cultural Heritage Development Organisation'. Research paper for the Department of Constitutional Development, especially 19–20, 51–53.

40 *Mail & Guardian*, 25 July 1997.

41 Brink, 'A historical analysis', 19–20. See especially sections 6, 31, 185 and 235 of the South African Constitution.

42 Bank, *Khoisan Identities & Cultural Heritage Conference*, 7, 35.
43 *Mail & Guardian*, 25 July 1997.
44 *Cape Argus*, 20 September 1996.
45 *Mail & Guardian*, 25 July 1997.
46 In 2004, the CCHDC changed its name to the Khoe Cultural Heritage Development Council.
47 *Cape Argus*, 20 September 1996; *Financial Mail*, 7 January 2000; ILO. 1999. *Indigenous Peoples of South Africa: Current Trends*. Geneva: ILO, 10.
48 *Rapport*, 6 June 1999.
49 *Cape Argus*, 20 September 1996.
50 *Burger*, 13 May 1999. Translated from Afrikaans. Autshumato was leader of the Goringhaicona Khoekhoe people and uncle to Krotoa. Both were key mediators between the Dutch and the Khoekhoe.
51 *Financial Mail*, 7 January 2000.
52 *Diamond Fields Advertiser*, 30 August 2002.
53 *Sowetan*, 6 December 2002.
54 *Sowetan*, 8 December 2002.
55 *Sowetan*, 6 December 2002.
56 *Sowetan Sunday World*, 15 December 2002.
57 See *Rapport*, 15 February 2004 for an example of Khoe-San frustration expressed by Cecil le Fleur.
58 Caliguire D. 1996. 'Voices from the communities', in *Now that We Are Free: Coloured Communities in a Democratic South Africa*, eds W James, D Caliguire & K Cullinan. Cape Town: IDASA, 6.
59 *Cape Argus*, 3 December 2004.
60 *Cape Argus*, 7 July 2005.
61 One specific grievance expressed by MADAM was the allegedly irregular replacement of the former Pollsmoor prison's maximum security division head, Johnny Jansen, chairperson of MADAM. Jansen was relocated to Goodwood prison where he was made prison head. Jansen, however, aspired to be director of Pollsmoor prison after the post was created in 2004. He expressed concern about attempts to prevent him from filling the position and through MADAM raised the subject of ethno-racial marginalisation in prisons. *Cape Argus*, 3 December 2004; 7 July 2005; information from Basil Coetzee, 6 August 2005.
62 *Cape Argus*, 27 April 2005; 9 May 2005; 11 May 2005; 27 July 2005.
63 http://www.asiaafrorights.org.za
64 *Cape Argus*, 21 July 2005; *Cape Times*, 22 July 2005.
65 See Abrahams Y. 2000. 'Colonialism, disjuncture and dysfunction: Sarah Baartman's resistance'. PhD dissertation, University of Cape Town; Langeveldt W. 1999. *Aluta Continua! Ons Stryd Duur Voort!* Vryburg: Khoisan Gemeeskapsforum.
66 With Khoe-San revivalism, South African Khoe-San were, to a degree, subject to dissociation from somatic and cultural features associated with the historical Khoe-San, and reinvested with colouredness, with the latter being reinvested with a Khoe-Sanness that drew on aspects of traditional Khoe-San culture. There has been a slow acceptance that individuals, especially those from the coloured communities, could be Khoekhoe or San even though they did not fit old stereotypes of authentic Khoekhoe and San.

CHAPTER 7

Race, ethnicity and the politics of positioning: the making of coloured identity in colonial Zimbabwe, 1890–1980

BY

JAMES MUZONDIDYA

HUMAN SCIENCES RESEARCH COUNCIL

This chapter examines the growth of a distinct coloured group consciousness in Zimbabwe. The history of this group has not only been marginalised in political and academic discourses but has also been subject to widespread popular misconception.[1] One of the most prevalent fallacies is the notion that coloured identity is a biologically determined, inherent quality derived from miscegenation. Another projects coloured identity as an invention of the colonial state, arguing that coloureds did not exist as a distinct racial or ethnic group beyond state categorisation and dismissing it as nothing more than false consciousness. This chapter will argue that the growth of coloured identity resulted from definitions both internal and external to the group involving a wide range of actors that included the colonial state, the white public and the subject people themselves who, through self-identification, not only negotiated the dynamics of coloured group creation, but also gave coloured identity its shape and tenure. The identity was continually contested and redefined by various groups both within and outside of the culturally diverse coloured community.

Colonial institutions and the growth of coloured identity

The growth of a distinct coloured identity began with the onset of colonial rule in the 1890s. The development of this ethnic group consciousness was shaped by the complex interaction of both internal and external factors. Among the more important external factors was the Rhodesian state which, like the colonial state in many other parts of Africa and the world, sought to differentiate between natives and non-natives, and between majorities and minorities among subject groups.[2] It also tried to construct and reconstruct people's identities by compartmentalising them in biological, cultural and geographic terms. Laws passed from the earliest days of colonial rule – such as the Firearms Act of 1891, which prohibited the possession and use of firearms and ammunition by all black people; the 1898 Liquor Act, which prohibited the buying or consumption of liquor by coloureds and Africans; and the 1900 Census Act – defined black subjects into three major categories: Native, Asian and coloured. The Firearms Act, for example, defined 'Native' as 'any person being, or being a descendant of, any aboriginal native of Africa' while 'Asian' referred to 'all Chinese, Indians and Malays or their descendants' and 'coloured' referred to 'any person other than an Asiatic or native who has the blood of an Asiatic or native'.[3]

Classification of this sort did not necessarily lead to the assumption of ethnic identities on the part of those categorised. It did, however, set parameters within which the production and reproduction of ethnic identities – coloured identity included – could occur. The way officials defined colonial subjects in their day-to-day implementation of the law was particularly significant in the production and reproduction of coloured and other black identities. To take one example, under the Vagrancy Act and the Registration of Natives Regulations, only 'natives' were obliged to carry passes, while under the Town Location Regulations 'natives' alone were compelled to stay in locations. Furthermore, when the first location was opened in Salisbury in 1892, only 'aboriginal natives of Southern Rhodesia' were forced to live there. Coloureds and Indians, together with other non-autochthonous African groups, were only moved to segregated residential areas in the 1930s after the Land Apportionment Act of 1930 was passed. This meant that officials such as location inspectors, police officers and magistrates were called upon to make potentially life-changing distinctions among people defined as native, Asian, coloured and European.[4]

Colonial categorisation was indeed arbitrary, not simply because there were no easily perceivable phenotypical or cultural traits denoting coloureds as a group, but also because there was no precise definition of coloured in the law which clearly set them apart. Even in the absence of clarity of definition, government officers still had to distinguish between 'natives' and 'non-natives' on the one hand, and 'aboriginal natives' and 'non-aboriginal natives' on the other. Within this context of categorisation and discrimination based on colonial legislation, some people found themselves being ascribed new identity labels. Some people regarded as being of 'mixed race', for instance, suddenly found themselves defined 'coloured' upon entry into Rhodesian towns, simply because their colour and physical characteristics made them indistinguishable from people categorised as coloured when in fact they had always thought of themselves as African. That some of these people eventually came to see themselves in terms of the ethnic categories set in these definitions is not surprising. Distinctions or definitions made by colonial officials thus in no small way helped to shape ideas about coloured identity in the broader society, while at the same time facilitating the reconstitution of peoples' own identities.[5]

Most importantly, because the law was more restrictive against Africans in general, and indigenous Africans in particular, assimilated colonial blacks, immigrants and locals alike found it convenient, if not advantageous, to assert non-African identities. To take one example, when Thomas Adams, a 'Cape boy' accused of breaching the pass regulations, was brought before a Salisbury court in 1900, he was acquitted after successfully contesting the prosecution's argument that he fell into the Vagrancy Act's category of 'native of central and southern Africa'. Similarly, arguing his case before a Salisbury magistrate in 1902, James Marshall Kelly, a 'Cape boy' accused of forging an order for alcohol, asserted that he was neither a 'native' nor had he the physical characteristics of 'the native tribes of South or central Africa'. By recognising, and in certain cases imposing, distinctions based on colour, language and geographic origins, state institutions such as courts of law became focal points in the process of coloured identity construction.[6]

Churches and missionaries who tended to believe that all coloureds were descended from unions between Africans and whites, and that coloureds constituted a separate and intermediate racial category between Africans and whites, played an important role in the creation of a distinct coloured consciousness. Missionaries also believed that the colonial government was morally bound to provide social services for coloureds. With this in mind, the Catholic Federation, for instance, criticised the government for neglecting coloureds, and proposed a land settlement scheme for them to create a self-sufficient community, which would offer them a sense of economic and social security. Missionaries took it upon themselves to establish homes for abandoned coloured women, orphans and destitute children, such as Embakwe, built in Plumtree in 1921 and St Johns, established by the Catholic Church in Salisbury in 1924. They also advocated the removal of all 'mixed-race' children from rural African environments and for their incorporation into urban coloured communities and institutions. The orphanages and schools that were set up, as Ibbo Mandaza insightfully argues, became an important medium through which the culture that helped define coloured identity was transmitted. The social bonding that occurred in these institutions fostered a sense of group belonging.[7]

The white press and public discourse, through racial stereotyping, further helped to turn these people into a self-conscious social group. From the very early years of colonial rule, white settler discourse, influenced by Social Darwinist thinking, depicted black immigrants as a distinct social group possessing higher forms of civilisation and intellect than local blacks. Partly influenced by this positive stereotyping, a growing number of immigrant blacks increasingly distinguished themselves from Shona and Ndebele speakers using the colonial terminology of 'raw natives' versus 'colonial boys' or 'Cape boys'. Against this backdrop, an incipient group consciousness, in which coloured identity increasingly found expression, developed among immigrant and other assimilated blacks.[8]

Inasmuch as positive stereotyping shaped immigrants' ideas about coloured identity, so did negative stereotyping. In both official and public discourse, immigrant blacks, particularly non-African immigrants from South Africa, were chided for 'seem[ing] to think that they hold the same position as a white man' and for allegedly inciting problems among natives. They were collectively blamed for crimes ranging from prostitution to illegal liquor trading and from robbery to murder. Borrowing from stereotyping of coloureds in the Cape Colony, settler discourse portrayed these non-African immigrants as idle, alcoholic and morally decadent.[9]

By stringing together both negative reports and stereotypes of Asian and other non-African immigrants, settler discourse helped to define them as 'other'. Utilising those same ideas and assumptions underlying settler discourse, some non-African immigrants reinvented and combined them with other distinctive features, such as cultural and phenotypical differences to define colouredness as distinct from Africanness and whiteness. In this respect, settler discourse shaped the symbolic terrain of colouredness and also helped to construct coloured identity. Thus, colonial legislation and white public discourse helped influence coloured people's perception of 'self' and 'other'.

Notions of ethnic group identity among people who came to see themselves, and were seen by others, as coloured were therefore not simply invented or imposed from above.[10] The colonial state, the church and the white public in Rhodesia may have used labels, such as 'coloured', and categorised people accordingly, but they were not solely responsible for giving coloured identity its form, content and endurance. The coloured people themselves were the primary authors of their identity text.

Writing their own text: colonial subjects and self-definition

A distinct coloured group consciousness existed in some parts of South Africa before the founding of Southern Rhodesia.[11] Thus, among the 'Cape boys' who accompanied the white pioneers were persons who saw themselves and were seen by others as coloured. One of Rhodesia's white pioneers, Stanley Hyatt, for example, recalls that 'half-castes from the Cape' resented being treated as natives and wanted to be accorded the same rights and privileges to which coloureds were entitled in the Cape.[12]

With their own sense of shared origins and cultural practices which included an Afrikaans subculture, these coloured immigrants found in Southern Rhodesia a social environment that produced and reproduced old and new African, coloured, Indian and white identities. The gulfs between the languages, cultures, religions and senses of shared historical origins and destiny of the immigrant and the indigenous blacks were not only great, but in its miscellany the immigrant black population was also divided by distinct physical, cultural and linguistic differences.[13] While the mere presence of cultural, religious and physical differences did not necessarily create ethnic or racial consciousness among blacks, they helped make these distinctions more probable. This was particularly the case when these culturally diverse groups began to define themselves in opposition, and in relation, to one another.

From its inception, the various white and black groups constituting Rhodesian colonial society differentiated among one another in terms of origin, colour, physical appearance, language, religion and culture. Among blacks, for instance, a big political and social divide existed between indigenous and non-indigenous groups. From the very outset, local Africans considered immigrant blacks as culturally distinct outsiders and closer to whites than themselves. Though employed mainly as transport riders and personal servants, this perception of immigrant blacks was strengthened by their presence in the pioneer column which the local Shona and Ndebele regarded as an invading force. Above and beyond this, in their collaborative capacities as store assistants, interpreters, messengers and catechists, immigrant blacks often found themselves clashing with local Africans. At the mines there were also endless conflicts between immigrant blacks and local Africans. During the early years of colonial rule, relationships between these groups was thus often tense.[14]

There is also evidence that both Shona and Ndebele communities regarded those descended from unions between white settlers and the local population, popularly referred to as 'mixed-race' people, not only as inferior but as outsiders. The late coloured political activist Joshua Cohen, who grew up in rural Matabeleland during the 1920s, thus points out that he was despised for being of 'mixed race' and felt out of place. The 1932 commission of inquiry into the education of coloured children also heard that 'half-caste' children were sometimes 'jeered at by natives [and] by the time they are 5 or 6 they begin to notice the difference'.[15]

That both black immigrants and people of 'mixed race' were defined by Africans as 'other' was central to the emergence of a distinct coloured identity. At the same time, immigrant blacks, who were to varying degrees assimilated to aspects of Western culture, defined themselves as members of a distinct social group, culturally different from the indigenous population. They saw themselves as part of white immigrant society and identified with various strands of middle- and working-class white ideology. Black immigrants from Mozambique, for example, called themselves 'Portuguese' while some 'mixed-race' immigrants from South Africa described themselves as 'descendants of white men'. Indians similarly thought of themselves as an integral part of colonial society, and considered local Africans inferior. Drawing on Western notions of status and modernity, these immigrants cast local Shona and Ndebele as primitive and uncivilised – in the words of one MoSotho immigrant, 'dirty little hill-savage[s] without trousers'.[16]

Although immigrant blacks categorised themselves and were categorised by others as a single group, they were heterogeneous and saw themselves as such. They also differentiated among one another in terms of colour, physical appearance, language, religion and culture. Processes of self-definition within this group usually revolved around competition for resources, jobs and facilities, and relative privileges conferred on subject groups on the basis of racial or ethnic identity.

The process of self-definition was much more intense in the urban areas, especially in the major towns of Bulawayo and Salisbury, where competition for social resources was more pronounced and distinctions based on historical background, language, colour and culture usually coincided with distinctions of work and residence. In the towns, residential segregation together with virulent customary segregation forced people with partially shared cultures, languages, religions and historic backgrounds to cluster together in defined residential areas. These living spaces were an important site for the construction of coloured identity. In Salisbury, for instance, customary segregation influenced the cadastral development of the town from the time of its founding. As a result, by 1907 the older and less desirable Kopje area was primarily inhabited by Asian and non-African immigrants, a few destitute whites and Africans, while the affluent northern section of the town, the Causeway area, was mainly occupied by white settlers. A similar pattern emerged in Bulawayo, where people defined as Asian and coloured were confined to the less desirable parts of the town around the Railway Station, Lobengula Street and the Market Square.[17]

In these residential areas, closer identification occurred among residents through sexual relationships and intermarriage between people of various racial and ethnic groups, as well as through social and sporting activities, such as evening dances and football matches.[18] New communities with distinctive values and cultural ethos began to emerge. In the case of Salisbury, Richard Parry points out that around 1900, black immigrants and some urbanised local Africans who lived in Pioneer Street, together with white artisans and drifters, had created a community with a unique working-class subculture encompassing, among other things, drinking, gambling and prostitution.[19] Communities, such as the one described by Parry, also provided an important site for the emergence of communal ideologies. Such ideologies reflected the cultural diversity of the various groups comprising these communities. Where there was a strong correlation between colour, language, culture and historical origins on the one hand and living space on the other, as in Bulawayo and Salisbury, the communal bonds forged by the residents tended to take on an ethnic dimension.

Equally important was the workplace, where a strong correlation between colour, physical appearance, language, culture and historic origins on the one hand, and the division of labour on the other, existed. Black immigrants who formed the basis of the skilled black working class filled most skilled positions during the early decades of colonial rule. Laundry, tailoring, and hotel and bar service became the preserve of Asian and coloured people. Immigrant blacks were also employed in the commercial sector, where they became store assistants. Not until the third decade of colonial rule, when urban commercial work was rapidly taken over by white settlers, did they lose their dominance in the sector. Certain jobs thus came to be associated with certain groups, and this division of labour tended to promote greater ethnic awareness among blacks of Southern Rhodesia.[20]

In the workplace, the colonial state also reserved specific jobs for particular subject groups. Settler stereotypes combined with other considerations, such as the skill and experience of labourers, to produce a hierarchy of wage differentials based on ethnic or racial categorisations.[21] The system of job and wage differentiation provided the context in which the adoption and rejection of certain identities occurred. Workers discovered that the assumption of particular ethnic identities could be rewarded in the labour market, and it was not uncommon for individuals to emphasise or claim those identities that opened up opportunities for upward social mobility. Because of the privileges associated with being coloured in relation to other black identities, the assertion of a distinct coloured identity became a means whereby they could earn better wages and escape some social disabilities. Inevitably, some Africans, both immigrant and local, 'passed for coloured'. Some posed temporarily as coloured while others managed to 'pass' permanently in order to secure privileges and opportunities, such as better jobs and higher salaries, accessible to coloureds under Rhodesia's hierarchical society.[22]

In this regard, the racial stratification of Rhodesian society, in which coloured people came to occupy the middle position between whites and Africans, tended to promote the adoption of coloured identity by people who sought to benefit from its status of relative privilege. Those who adopted coloured identity were not passive victims of a racially structured process determined by the colonial state, but were self-aware actors in their own right. As Stuart Hall correctly points out, the identity dialectic, and identity politics in particular, are all about being positioned and positioning oneself to gain some advantage out of that positioning.[23]

The politics of coloured identity in the 1920s and 1930s

Whereas the period from 1890 to the end of the First World War represents the formative stage in the growth of a distinct coloured political identity, the 1920s and 1930s witnessed the heightening of such consciousness. New and extended forms of coloured identity, either reinforcing or challenging existing ones, were developed. During this period of drastic socio-economic change, tensions arising from competition for jobs, housing and educational facilities mounted. These tensions often found expression in racial and ethnic terms as organic intellectuals tried to mobilise politically on the basis of coloured identity, and the various groups within the community fought over who was empowered to police the category 'coloured', as well as the criteria used to police these boundaries. Coloured identity thus remained highly contested. The process was influenced by an individual's ideas on such issues as religion, race and gender. For instance, patriarchal notions of descent led most people to define coloured identity in terms of descent on the father's side. Thus, while coloured men who had married into African communities, and their families, were regarded as part of the coloured community, coloured women who had married African men, and their families, were not.[24]

In Umtali, for instance, by the middle of the 1920s, Indian and coloured parents worried about increased competition for vacancies at Baring Primary, the only school for coloured and Asian children in the town. They formed the Umtali Coloured and Asian School Advisory Committee through which they demanded the removal of 'native' and 'half-caste' children from the school. These parents insisted that admission should be confined to 'pure children of coloureds and Indians only'.[25]

In Salisbury, as competition for jobs, housing and educational facilities stiffened and unemployment grew following the collapse of Southern Rhodesia's tobacco, cattle and maize markets in 1927, group networks were also activated to support their interests. Coloured ethnic organisers in the town formed the Rhodesia Eurafrican Vigilance Association (REVA) in 1925. Alexander McLeod, a coloured builder and lay preacher who had emigrated from Kimberley in 1915, was at the helm of the organisation until its demise in 1931. REVA stood for the promotion of the civil and economic rights of coloured people, and restricted its membership to coloureds only. From 1927 onwards, REVA promoted a Cape coloured political identity by mobilising only coloured people of South African origin. The main reason for this shift was the fear that 'the influx of half-castes and other rural Coloureds' would put pressure on housing, education and employment opportunities for South African-born coloureds and the more-established urban elite. Worried that integration with other coloured groupings might blur the distinction between coloureds and Africans, the 1927 REVA conference resolved to approach the government to have their distinct 'status as Cape Coloureds' recognised. The REVA executive recommended that Cape coloureds be known as Cape Afrikanders to remove any 'ambiguity in our identity'.[26]

In 1929, another organisation seeking to defend the interests of the Cape coloured community, the Cape Afrikander Population of Salisbury, was formed. Bulawayo also experienced renewed coloured ethnic mobilisation when some members of the Bulawayo branch of REVA formed a breakaway organisation called the Rhodesia Cape Afrikander Association (RCAA) at the beginning of 1928. The RCAA restricted membership of the association to Cape coloureds, and banned the use of the more inclusive term 'coloured' when referring to its members.[27]

Concerned about mounting hostility towards locally born coloureds, referred to as 'first generation Coloureds' or 'Eurafricans,' this group began to organise on the basis of their exclusion from existing coloured organisations. By the end of the 1920s, the Rhodesia Coloured Society (RCS) had been formed to represent Eurafrican interests. Describing the RCS as an organisation 'quite distinct from any of the Cape Coloured organizations', the founder members restricted its membership to 'children of white men by native women' only. Organisations that sought to promote the interests of coloured people more broadly defined were also formed in the 1930s. The Rhodesia Teachers' League (RTL), founded in April 1931, and the Coloured Community Service League (CCSL), founded in July of that year, were among the more enduring. These organisations utilised ruling notions of race and civilisation to claim concessions from the colonial government on the basis of their assimilation into Western culture and blood ties to the white settler community.[28]

During this period, coloured ethnic mobilisers were increasingly concerned about intensifying discrimination against Africans. They worried about coloureds being relegated to the same position as Africans, and wanted a clear delineation of social and political boundaries between the two groups. Writing to Howard Moffat, the Prime Minister, in 1931, McLeod protested against what he described as the 'tendency in some [government] quarters to class our people with aboriginal natives' and urged the government to 'draw a distinct line between the Coloured people and aboriginal natives' in its segregation scheme. Other coloured political leaders opposed the Native Registration Amendment Act of 1930 for its use of the 'mode of living' criterion to determine the status of coloured people. In their view, it was bound to condemn some coloureds to the same rank as Africans. They also protested against coloured prisoners being served the same meals and rations as Africans and against the mixing of coloured and African patients in prison hospitals and similar institutions.[29]

In their attempt to widen the social distance between coloureds and Africans, coloured leaders fiercely opposed all policies and practices that blurred distinctions between the two. Concerned about Africans 'passing for coloured', some even proposed that coloureds be given the common-law right to question the identities of persons admitted into their schools, housing schemes and social amenities. Others asked the government to amend the Immorality and Indecency Suppression Act (1903) to include a provision that forbade intermarriage between African men and coloured women.[30] Conspicuously, their demands were silent about marriages between coloured men and African women.

The political strategies of coloured communal organisations displayed a good understanding of how the colonial system with its notions of colour and civilisation could be manipulated to their advantage. This racial aversion towards Africans led many coloureds, both elite and working class, to feel superior to Africans. A 1933 CCSL deputation to the prime minister protesting the prohibition on coloureds consuming liquor argued that '[t]he Coloured man, who lives in a town and has raised himself above the natives' could not be like the 'native'.[31] The objection of coloured communal leaders, such as Gaston Thornicroft and Alexander McLeod, to African and coloured prisoners being housed or working together was based on the premise that it was 'disrespectful for Coloureds to work with their servants [Africans]' or to mix with 'the primitive African' in prison sleeping quarters.[32]

Contestation and redefinition of coloured identity in the 1930s and 1940s

Being a highly contested phenomenon, coloured identity continued to be redefined. For a start, many individuals both white and black rejected the idea that coloureds formed a separate group. They challenged coloured people's attempts to secure special concessions or to mobilise on a racial basis. From the earliest days of the colony, African political leaders attacked the provision of separate facilities for coloureds, and called for coloureds and Africans to be categorised as one group. Rejecting both the validity of coloured identity and the existence of a distinct coloured community in the colony, Aaron Jacha, a founder of both the Bantu Voters' Association in 1923 and the Southern Rhodesia African National Congress in 1934, argued that 'a coloured man is a native ... [because] whenever a coloured man is poor he live[s] and eat[s] together with natives [and it is only] when he has means to support himself he likes to be separated'. Bradford Mnyanda, a leading African activist, argued that there were only two racial communities in the country and hence coloured children 'should not be given separate schools but should attend Native schools'. He further urged those 'leaders of coloured thought (chiefly from the Union) ... clamouring for the removal of half-caste from purely native surroundings so that all coloured people in Southern Rhodesia may receive a higher status than that of natives, as is the case in the Union' to return to South Africa.[33]

Within the coloured community itself, debate continued over the place of coloured identity within a broader black identity. This question was particularly debated in the 1940s amongst activists who favoured black political unity.[34] Radical activists of the time, such as trade unionists Stanley Culverwell and Charles Mzingeli, and school-teacher Francis Graenger Rousseau, called for closer social and political identification between coloureds and other black groups, including Asians and Africans, based on their common experience of colonial oppression.[35] The idea of black political cooperation, however, failed to find popular resonance among the majority of coloureds. It was heavily criticised by some coloured leaders, especially within the Euro-African Patriotic Society (EAPS), who not only lobbied the government to prohibit marriages between African men and coloured women, but also maintained that coloureds were a distinct group with a distinct history and a destiny separate from both Asians and Africans.[36]

Debate and contestation within the coloured community during this period also revolved around the question of whether those born of Indian and African unions and their descendants, Indo-Africans as they were called, were members of the coloured community or not. Leaders in most established urban coloured communities opposed the integration of such people into the coloured community. Using patrilineal notions of descent, these leaders argued that since most of the first generation 'Indo-Africans' were born of Indian fathers and African mothers, they and their descendants should be integrated into the Indian rather than the coloured community. They called for Indo-African exclusion from public facilities and amenities reserved for coloureds. In Salisbury, some of these influential coloureds in 1949 successfully petitioned for the removal of 25 'mixed-race' children of Indian descent from Moffat Primary School, which was reserved for Asian and coloured children. At a subsequent public meeting held by coloured parents, they managed to persuade other parents to resolve to withdraw their children from both Moffat and McKeurtan schools if the government continued to send such children to coloured schools. There were numerous cases of coloureds protesting the admission of Indo-African children to coloured schools, arguing that they were either Indian or African. Ironically, members of the Indian community also refused to accept Indo-Africans. Instead, they saw them as either African or coloured, and often refused them admission into Asian schools, such as Mountbatten Primary in Salisbury and Tredgold Primary in Bulawayo.[37]

The contest over coloured identity was mirrored in opposing views on the integration of people of white and African parents, often called half-castes, into the coloured community. The first generation of Rhodesian-born coloureds, or Eurafricans as some of them liked to refer to themselves, maintained that all Eurafricans were members of the coloured community. Arguing against government definitions based on culture and residence, they urged the government to extend its definition of coloured to all children born of white and African unions, irrespective of whether they lived in rural or urban environments. For them, blood ties were more important in determining one's belonging than language, culture or environment.[38]

This emphasis on blood ties rather than language and culture continued to be opposed by some members of urban coloured communities, particularly Cape coloureds. They denied that people of mixed racial parentage, especially those raised in rural areas, were coloured, and tried to bar their access to educational, health and housing facilities reserved for coloureds. Meeting in February 1932, the Bulawayo Coloured School Advisory Committee, which was dominated by Cape coloureds, formed a sub-committee to decide on the admission of children descended from white and African unions. In making such decisions, the committee was supposed to assess whether the children's 'cultural background' qualified them to be considered coloured or not. Through these developments, coloureds of South African origin, who formed about 36 per cent of the total coloured population but constituted the majority of urban coloureds, tried to appropriate the right to draw group boundaries for the coloured community.[39]

The strongest challenge to the Cape coloureds' attempt to impose their definition on the whole group came from locally born coloureds, particularly those born of white fathers and African mothers. These coloureds constituted more than half of the coloured population and included the first generation who received mission education. Partly influenced by their English and Christian upbringing, they tried to introduce their own definition of colouredness. They emphasised English culture and Christianity as defining characteristics of colouredness, as opposed to Afrikaans culture and adherence to Islam, as found among some Cape coloureds. Accordingly, they urged the government to exclude Cape Malays from its definition of 'coloured', and argued that Muslims were not part of the coloured community.[40]

Throughout the 1930s and the early 1940s, conflict over the status of children born of mixed marriages between whites and Africans on the one hand, and Asians and Africans on the other, dominated coloured politics. At the organisational level, this conflict expressed itself in the form of a battle for control of the CCSL, the main coloured communal organisation of the time. Under the leadership of Thornicroft, who took over the presidency in 1933 and was born of an African mother and a white father, the CCSL increasingly became a vehicle through which the Eurafrican elite tried to redefine coloured identity to suit their agenda. Eurafrican leaders fought to integrate 'mixed-race' people in native reserves into urban coloured communities, and tried to assert political ascendancy over the Cape coloured elite. They even tried to have the term 'Euro-African' adopted as an officially sanctioned label for coloureds. This, according to Ronald Snapper, a prominent Eurafrican leader, was thwarted by the 'Cape Coloured-dominated RTL'.[41]

Consensus over what it meant to be coloured remained elusive, and competing interests, based on linguistic, religious and cultural differences within the community, continued to dominate coloured politics. The various factions used these distinctions to legitimise their ideologies and denigrate opponents. Eurafrican intellectuals argued that coloured people born of white and African parentage were not only superior to all other coloured groups but deserved higher privileges because they were direct descendants of white settlers. They cast Cape coloureds as 'descendants of slaves' and immigrants not committed to the future of Southern Rhodesia but to South Africa. In counterclaims, Cape coloured ethnic mobilisers rejected the charge that Eurafricans were coloureds. Resorting to the same logic of blood, Cape coloured leaders cast Eurafricans as inferior beings with 'native blood in their veins'. Eurafricans, they argued, were 'half kaffirs ... used to the kraals as opposed to their 300 year tradition of western civilization'.[42]

The rivalry between the Cape coloureds and Eurafricans, mirrored at the organisational level by the rift between the CCSL and the EAPS, became so intense that it came to form one of the major dynamics of coloured politics during this period. The EAPS had been formed in 1943 by a breakaway group of CCSL members, mainly Eurafricans, who were not happy with what they perceived to be the Cape coloureds' political dominance in the CCSL, and the Bulawayo coloured community's dominance of coloured politics. The organisation had its core support and headquarters in Salisbury.[43]

Once the EAPS had been formed, political relations between the two competing groups became increasingly polarised. Divisions within the coloured community deepened, as both organisations battled to score points off one another and to win support from the government and the public.[44] Only from the 1950s onwards did internal divisions within the coloured community and tension between coloureds of South African origin and their locally born counterparts begin to diminish.

Towards a more cohesive identity in the 1950s

A number of social, economic and political developments contributed to the making of a more cohesive coloured community in the latter half of the 20th century. Firstly, there was the issue of the reshaping of migrants' identity as they adapted to their country of residence. Having lived in Southern Rhodesia for a number of decades, some of the older-generation Cape coloureds set down local roots. They stopped looking to South Africa for political and cultural inspiration or as a place they could call home. For instance, Dorothy Louw, the daughter of William Pretorius, who was one of the early Cape coloured leaders in Bulawayo, says that her family lost contact with their relatives living in South Africa by the 1940s. The apartheid government's increasingly hostile attitude towards coloureds also led some of these Cape coloureds to cut ties with South Africa. Because of apartheid, coloured workers who came to Southern Rhodesia during the Federation (1953–1963) were reportedly more interested in settling in the country than staying temporarily. As the immigrants sought to establish themselves, they gradually began to shed their South African identity and to develop a local one. This meant discarding some of the attitudes and cultural values brought from South Africa, such as an attachment to Afrikaans culture and adopting certain aspects of British colonial culture which prevailed in Southern Rhodesia such as the use of English in public discourse. As Virginia Pinto, whose family migrated from the Cape and settled in Umtali around this period, remembers, her mother and all her siblings could only speak Afrikaans when they arrived but they had to learn English in order to adapt. Eventually, she lost her fluency in Afrikaans. Adapting to Rhodesian life also meant developing a sporting culture that emphasised soccer and cricket rather than rugby, as was the case in South Africa.[45]

The adoption of these cultural aspects by immigrant workers and their dependants did not necessarily lead to the immediate abandonment of all the values and attitudes brought from outside. Nor did they automatically lead to the development of a common identity between immigrants and local coloureds. In Bulawayo, for instance, Afrikaans cultural values continued to have a strong influence on a significant proportion of Cape coloureds. The cultural divide between these coloureds and Eurafricans also continued to govern relations between the two groups until the late 1970s. Nevertheless, the socialisation of immigrants into the prevailing culture helped to foster the development of a common identity with locally born coloureds who, like most Southern Rhodesians, were disdainful of both Afrikaans culture and language.[46]

Secondly, increased socialisation among coloureds in segregated residential areas helped to bring greater social cohesion among coloureds. In the case of Salisbury, for instance, Julia Seirlis argues that the creation of Arcadia in the 1940s 'offered Coloureds something of their own, somewhere to belong – a home', and a place where people's feelings of belonging helped to shape their sense of identity. Because of the community's small size, it also did not take much time for residents to get to know one another, and soon they began to bond and to develop an identity as a community. For the younger generation of Rhodesian-born coloureds, shared experiences in segregated schools, such as Founders High School and Morgan Secondary School, particularly among boarders, were important in fostering a sense of commonality.[47]

This younger generation also began to redefine their identity in their own cultural terms. They began to develop a slang of their own, called Kabid. A variant of English that mixed English and Afrikaans terms, it challenged the dominant values within the coloured community and Rhodesian society at large by reinventing the meanings of terms and ignoring grammatical correctness in speech.[48] This new dialect, Seirlis explains, helped to give them something in common, both as youths and coloureds. Kabid had the potential to exclude outsiders, and marked the cultural distinctiveness of those who used it. It represented a different outlook on life and a youthful desire to assert their freedom from parents and tradition. Kabid was also an expression of defiance in that it disregarded the formalities of colonial culture and formed one of the elements of an emerging culture of protest among the youth in the 1960s. Kabid was widely used in the 1970s, a time when a growing number of coloured youths were turning to protest politics.[49]

Continuity and change in the 1960s and 1970s

From the 1960s onwards, coloured identity was influenced by a resurgent African nationalism, the Black Consciousness Movement in South Africa as well as the Civil Rights and the Black Power movements in the US. Because of these changes, the ideologies of the coloured youth, particularly the educated, urban sector, gradually shifted towards a culture of protest. As Eugene Raftopoulos explains, 'the Black Power movement … created an identity for the guys … They looked on the telly and saw a guy winning the Olympics and getting up there and saying yeah man, I am black and I am proud of it'. A significant number of coloured youngsters began to identify with the cultural aspects of Black Power – the Afro hairstyle, the Black Power salute and Malcolm X's speeches and writings.[50]

Partly influenced by the American Civil Rights Movement, politically conscious coloureds stressed the need for self-pride, and rejected white tutelage. They began to affirm the beauty of being black and the idea of racial equality. It was in this spirit that they opposed the Arcadia Gardening Scheme, a coloured self-help project financed by white sympathisers, which they described as paternalistic and stifling the development of a spirit of self-determination among coloureds. Their ideas were also significantly influenced by the works of writers and activists such as William du Bois, Martin Luther King and Malcolm X. The influence of these ideas on Herbert Thompson, one of the most fiery coloured communal leaders and nationalist activists of the time, was so profound that in 1964 he changed his surname to Foya-Thompson, a practice associated with the followers of Malcolm X. 'With my political convictions I cannot use a European surname,' Thompson had asserted when he announced his name change, 'we are Africans, born of African mothers, although some of us have European fathers.'[51]

Especially from the early 1970s onwards, according to Thomas Shoppo, the coloured world view was also being shaped by the ideas of the Black Consciousness Movement of South Africa which were beginning to filter into coloured schools and churches. Indeed, as in South Africa where the Black Consciousness Movement's influence spread mainly among intellectuals, in Rhodesia its influence also remained confined to a literate minority. But for these few, the Black Consciousness Movement became a major ideological influence, and some coloureds began to identify, at least culturally and symbolically, with its ideas.[52]

Local influences such as frustrations arising from conscription, growing hardship as a result of the liberatory war and the resurgence in African nationalism were beginning to shape coloured political behaviour. A significant number of coloureds were being radicalised and aligning themselves with the nationalist movement. More and more coloured people joined the national protest movement as the war progressed, the socio-economic situation deteriorated and the Rhodesian Front government seemed to be losing the initiative. Some leaders of the dominant political force in coloured communal politics in the late 1960s and early 1970s, the National Association of Coloured People (NACP), such as Herbert Foya-Thompson (the organisation's founding president), Gerald Raftopoulos (the chairman), Eugene Robinson (the secretary), and Cecil Smith (a member of the national executive) openly supported the African nationalist struggle, and urged their followers to do the same. Having assumed leadership positions in nationalist organisations, such as the United African National Congress (UANC) and Zimbabwe African People's Union (ZAPU), they tried to foster political unity between coloureds and Africans. Speaking at the NACP's annual conference of November 1975, chairman Gerald Raftopoulos not only warned his audience of 'future changes which are on the horizon' but also urged coloureds to uproot all traces of racial prejudice against Africans and to work with them.[53]

Partly responding to these organisational efforts, a small but growing number of coloureds were more willing to support the nationalist struggle. A survey carried out by the *National Observer* towards the end of 1978 reported that there was 'growing evidence of Coloureds joining African nationalist parties where they were also warmly received'. In the previous year, a spokesman of the Arcadia branch of the UANC, in a bid to gain political mileage for both his party and branch, exaggerated that 'about half of the coloured community in Salisbury belonged to the UANC, while another large section belonged to other African nationalist organizations'.[54]

The shift to new ideologies and changes in the political behaviour of coloureds was neither dramatic nor all-encompassing. As in the past, coloured identity continued to provide the basis for mobilisation within the coloured community, and the number of coloureds who embraced African nationalism or formally joined African nationalist organisations remained limited. Most coloureds remained poorly informed about the ideologies of the leading African nationalist organisations and suspicious of their political intentions. Reminiscing about his days as an activist in the 1960s, Gerald Raftopoulos points out that there was a 'genuine fear' among some coloureds that an African government coming to power would lead to an erosion of their social and economic position, and that coloured workers were going to be replaced by African labourers. Most coloureds were particularly disturbed that African nationalist organisations mainly spoke the language of African rights and not more inclusively of black rights. Equally disturbing was the African nationalists' emphasis on 'majority rule'. To some this meant replacing white supremacy with an African domination. To others it meant that coloureds would remain an intermediate minority with limited rights and privileges. For some, political developments in neighbouring states such as Malawi and Zambia, where the coloured racial category had been abolished in post-independence constitutions, were enough evidence of African nationalists' prejudice against coloureds. Given these fears and suspicions, a significant proportion of coloureds, particularly the older generation, could not easily be convinced that they had anything to gain from African majority rule. They also felt a closer racial and cultural affinity with whites than with Africans, and that their interests were intertwined with those of whites rather than Africans. For many of these coloureds, particularly the less educated and unskilled who faced being displaced from their jobs by Africans, the prospect of African rule and the deracialisation of society was highly unsettling.[55]

African nationalist leaders and their organisations also did little to allay coloured fears or to bring them on board the movement. Both the Zimbabwe African National Union (ZANU) and ZAPU were unambiguously Africanist in their ideologies and not particularly receptive to non-Africans. As Brian Raftopoulos who joined ZANU in the mid-1970s, explains:

ZANU was less tolerant of non-blacks, there was no doubt about that ... It was considered a more strictly African movement ... Coloureds and even whites were not considered to be part of that ... Even when I joined ZANU in London in 1974–1975 I had problems. It was a slow process, there was this fear that I was not black.[56]

Nationalists' underlying suspicions about coloureds who joined their organisations militated against the widespread involvement of coloureds in the liberation movement. So strong were some African nationalists' suspicions of coloureds that there were times when coloureds who tried to join African nationalist guerrilla armies were either turned away or executed on suspicion of being spies.[57]

From its birth in the 1890s, the relationship between coloured identity and other black identities was complex, and its place within a broader black identity was never defined. As second-class citizens who enjoyed a status of relative privilege, coloureds came to be seen as both instruments and beneficiaries of colonialism. The contradictory experience of coloureds as a subject minority group meant that they were identified with colonial rulers in spite of their political experience being marked by both collaboration and resistance. They collaborated with the colonial regime in the exploitation of Africans and aligned with the masses in resisting their discrimination. In the eyes of African nationalists, coloureds thus increasingly came to be viewed as a suspect 'other'.[58]

When coloured, Asian and African leaders tried to form a united political front in the 1940s, problems and contradictions arising from the ambiguities of coloured identity and the intermediate position of coloureds in the Rhodesian colonial system had created tension and uneasiness in the movement, and led to its demise by the late 1940s. Only in the 1960s and 1970s, when further attempts were made to mobilise coloureds into the mass-protest movement, was there any degree of success. Even then, the position of coloureds in the national movement of the 1960s and 1970s was never fully defined. In fact, coloured identity increasingly came under siege from a resurgent African nationalism, which treated the coloured community as an adjunct to African nationalism rather than as an integral part of the political movement.[59] Most coloureds were disturbed by the African nationalists' denial of the validity of a distinct coloured identity. In the eyes of these nationalists, coloured identity, like any other identity, was a 'false consciousness' invented by colonialists complicit with the black elite. As such, coloured identity had to subject itself to African nationalism, while coloured political activists could only organise and express themselves through African nationalist organisations.[60]

In their attempt to speak to coloured identity and coloured people, African nationalists thus not only failed to relate the political behaviour of coloureds to prevailing socio-economic and historical conditions, but also failed to address what Brian Raftopoulos has termed 'the central problem of relating nationalist hegemony to difference, and discourses of unity to the contradictions born out of the struggles and the varying perspectives of subordinate classes'.[61] Because of these and other factors, throughout the 1970s coloureds who had joined nationalist organisations had difficulty justifying their position.

Adaptation to the coming of independence

Coloured identity has always been a highly fluid and adaptable phenomenon, its dynamism sometimes being denounced as 'shameless opportunism'. Coloured identity's fluidity was demonstrated in the late 1970s when it was faced with imminent changes in the Zimbabwean power structure. With the advent of independence under African majority rule, some politicised coloureds readily realigned their political allegiances. Coloureds from this group increasingly identified themselves with African nationalism, and urged other coloureds to support African nationalist aspirations. For instance, while conceding that, through the educational system and their language, coloureds espoused Western values and culture, Gerald Raftopoulos, who had risen to become a member of the ZAPU national executive by 1978, argued that the coloured people's political future was intertwined with that of Africans. He also argued that there was no further need for separate coloured organisations and that only the major African nationalist parties could fully represent coloured people's interests. Other leaders of the NACP also urged coloureds to support majority rule.[62]

These calls for support of African demands for independence were mainly heeded by the younger generation of educated coloureds, who had been exposed to the radicalising influences described earlier. A growing number, especially those who had gone through university, saw themselves as part of the oppressed African majority and identified with the liberation struggle. They saw coloured identity as an artificial construct imposed by the state to divide blacks, and regarded themselves as 'African first … [and] Coloured … [as] a label tagged on'. Rejecting the validity of a separate coloured identity, a growing number of this generation assumed African names and identities, and called for the adoption of the Zambian and Malawian constitutional models, where coloureds were treated as part of the African community.[63]

Some politicised coloureds were also able to use family links with Africans to negotiate and to legitimise their claims to resources in the post-colonial order. David Kilpin, a coloured political activist, argued that coloureds should not be identified with whites but were 'children of the majority and should thus be identified with them'. He further appealed to notions of indigeneity, and argued that coloureds were, unlike other minorities such as whites or Asians, truly Zimbabwean because they 'have no other country besides that of their birth'. Jack Malhakis, a resident of Arcadia interviewed by the *Herald* in 1979, also argued that the word 'coloured' was not only unacceptable, but that coloureds could not be 'separated from Africans who brought them up'.[64] In the same vein, a memorandum sent by members of the coloured community to Lord Soames, the British governor overseeing the political transition to independence, portrayed coloured people as products and victims of the 'sexual exploitation of the African woman by the white man' who were defined as coloured from their infancy and 'stigmatized to attend separate schools, separate hospitals and were denied employment in the civil service … on the grounds of our African origin'. The memorandum castigated African nationalist leaders of ZANU, ZAPU and the UANC for agreeing to categorise coloureds in the same group as whites at the Lancaster House constitutional talks. This unilateral decision, the drafters of the memorandum further protested, 'not only negates our sovereignty as an integral part of the indigenous people, but also aligns us conspicuously with the criminal past of the white man'. They categorically asserted that coloureds were 'bona fide Africans, authentic Zimbabweans born of African parents in Africa'.[65]

Conclusion

This chapter examined the origins of coloured identity in Zimbabwe and argued that the growth of a distinct coloured consciousness was shaped by the complex interaction of both internal and external factors. The Rhodesian state and its agents, which set up parameters through which the process of self-identification occurred, were among the more important external influences. Yet, despite the important role played by the state in the creation of coloured identity, notions of group identity among people who came to see themselves and were seen by others as coloured were not simply imposed from above. The dynamics of coloured group creation were instead negotiated within a process of self-definition which occurred among Rhodesians as they defined themselves in opposition and in relation to one another in their day-to-day social relations.

The meaning and content of coloured identity has always been highly contested, not only by groups who made up the culturally diverse coloured community but also by outsiders. Because of these contestations, coloured identity continued to be redefined. In the very early stages of colonial rule, for instance, coloureds tended to express their group consciousness mainly in terms of their assimilation to Western culture and non-indigenousness. They also emphasised a historic connection to the coloured community in South Africa, and largely saw themselves as a community in diaspora. By the beginning of the 1930s, this view of coloured identity was challenged by other groups, particularly the first generation of Rhodesian-born coloureds, who felt excluded by such a definition. Confronted by these challenges, which were a major cause of disunity in the coloured community for the greater part of the 1940s, coloured identity underwent a process of redefinition. By the 1950s, Cape coloured identity had been subsumed under a broader, more inclusive identity that sought to accommodate both coloureds of South African origin and their Rhodesian-born counterparts. The new sense of coloured group consciousness that was emerging emphasised local roots, and many of the older generation of Cape coloureds stopped looking to South Africa as home.

The fluidity of coloured identity in changing social situations was also demonstrated in the late 1970s, when coloured people had to deal with the imminent changes in the political and economic structures under African majority rule. Many coloured people struggled to come to terms with looming socio-political changes, while others experienced difficulty dealing with their multiple identities as black, as African, and as coloured. Because of the dynamic and hybrid nature of their identity, some politicised coloureds were, however, able to use their family links with Africans to negotiate and realign their identities in the post-colonial order.

Endnotes

1   This is not entirely surprising, as coloured people never formed more than 0.5 per cent of the population and today number approximately 32 000, which is 0.3 per cent of the national population.

2   The role of the colonial state in the construction of racial identities in Africa in general and southern Africa in particular has been well documented in influential studies such as Ranger T O. 1995. *The Invention of Tribalism in Zimbabwe*. Gweru: Mambo Press; Vail L (ed). 1989. *The Creation of Tribalism in Southern Africa*. London: James Currey; Marks S & Trapido S (eds). 1987. *The Politics of Race, Class and Nationalism in 20th Century South Africa*. London: Longman; Adam H & Giliomee H. 1979. *Ethnic Power Mobilized*. New Haven: Yale University Press; Mandaza I. 1997. *Race, Colour and Class in Southern Africa: A Study of the Coloured Question in the Context of an Analysis of the Colonial and White Settler Racial Ideology, and African Nationalism in Twentieth Century Zimbabwe, Zambia and Malawi*. Harare: Sapes Books; Goldin I. 1987. *Making Race: The Politics and Economics of Coloured Identity in South Africa*. Cape Town: Maskew Miller Longman; Erasmus Z (ed). 2001. *Coloured by Place, Shaped by History: New Perspectives on Coloured Identities in Cape Town*. Cape Town: Kwela Books; and Gilroy P. 2000. *Between Camps: Nations, Cultures and the Allure of Race*. London: Penguin Press.

3   Southern Rhodesia (hereafter SR). 1912. *Statute Law of Southern Rhodesia, from the Charter to 1910*. Salisbury: Government Printer, 270, 321; *Rhodesia Herald*, 25 January 1895.

4   Palley C. 1966. *The Constitutional History and Law of Southern Rhodesia, 1888–1965*. Oxford: Clarendon Press, 122, 144; Yoshikuni T. 1989. 'Black migrants in a white city: a social history of African Harare, 1890–1925'. PhD dissertation, University of Zimbabwe, 39; Muzondidya J. 1996. 'The state, local government, local capital and the residential segregation of minorities: the case of coloureds and Indians in Salisbury, 1890–1945'. MA thesis, University of Zimbabwe, 70–86.

5   SR. 1928. *Report of the Director of Census Regarding the Census Taken on the 4th of May 1926, Part 3*, 11; Dorothy Pinto, interviewed by James Muzondidya, 21 January 1998.

6   *Rhodesia Herald*, 31 May 1902; 24 September 1900.

7   Seirlis J. 1999. 'Urban space and "coloured" identities in Harare, Zimbabwe'. PhD dissertation, University of Oxford, 112; Mandaza, *Race, Colour and Class*, 218–239.

8   *Rhodesia Herald*, 24 September 1900; Sykes F W. 1897. *With Plumer in Matabeleland: An Account of the Operations of the Matabeleland Relief Force during the Rebellion of 1896*. Westminster: A Constable, 155; Hyatt S P. 1914. *The Old Transport Road*. London: Andrew Melrose, 70, 92. Mandaza, *Race, Colour and Class*, 42; Van Onselen C. 1976. *Chibaro: African Mine Labour in Southern Rhodesia, 1900–1933*. London: Pluto, 101–103.

9   *Rhodesia Herald*, 15 March 1895; 11 April 1903; B S A Co, *Reports on the Administration of Rhodesia, 1900–1902*, 176–78; Van Onselen, *Chibaro*, 81, 102; Yoshikuni, 'Black migrants', 32. For a more comprehensive discussion of popular stereotyping of coloureds in South Africa, see Adhikari M. 1992. 'God, Jan van Riebeeck and the coloured people: the anatomy of a South African joke'. *Southern African Discourse*, 4, 4–10; Bickford-Smith V. 1995. *Ethnic Pride and Racial*

Prejudice in Victorian Cape Town: Group Identity and Social Practice, 1875–1902. Cambridge: Cambridge University Press, 67–83.

10 For extended arguments on this point, see Adhikari M. 2005. *Not White Enough, Not Black Enough: Racial Identity in the South African Coloured Community*. Athens: Ohio University Press, 1–32; Bickford-Smith V. 1995. 'Black ethnicities, communities and political expression in late Victorian Cape Town'. *Journal of African History*, 36, no. 3, 445; Alexander J & McGregor J. 1997. 'Modernity and ethnicity in a frontier society: understanding difference in Northwestern Zimbabwe'. *Journal of Southern African Studies*, 23, no. 2, 201.

11 Adhikari M. 1992. 'The sons of Ham: slavery and the making of coloured identity'. *South African Historical Journal*, 27, 107–110; Adhikari M. 1993. *'Let Us Live for Our Children': The Teachers' League of South Africa, 1913–1940*. Cape Town: University of Cape Town, 1–4; Lewis G. 1987. *Between the Wire and the Wall: A History of South African 'Coloured' Politics*. Cape Town: David Philip, 7–20; Bickford-Smith, *Ethnic Pride*, 201.

12 Hyatt, *The Old Transport Road*, 288.

13 Ranger T O. 1970. *The African Voice in Southern Rhodesia, 1890–1930*. London: Heinemann, 45–46; Keppel-Jones A. 1983. *Rhodes and Rhodesia: The White Conquest of Zimbabwe, 1884–1902*. Pietermaritzburg: University of Natal Press, 420–421; Van Onselen, *Chibaro*, 102.

14 Ranger, *The African Voice*, 45–46; Keppel-Jones, *Rhodes and Rhodesia*, 450, 453, 455, 466–468; Van Onselen, *Chibaro*, 103, 287, note 146.

15 National Archives of Zimbabwe (hereafter NAZ), S824/68/1, Education, correspondence and other papers, Mrs E M Walters, Bikita, oral evidence presented to the Committee of Enquiry into the Education of Coloured and Half-caste Children in Southern Rhodesia, 29 August 1933; *Parade*, August 1999, 17.

16 *Rhodesia Herald*, 31 May 1902; Parry R. 1999. 'Culture, organization and class: the African experience in Salisbury, 1892–1935', in *Sites of Struggle: Essays in Zimbabwe's Urban History*, eds B Raftopoulos & T Yoshikuni. Harare: Weaver Press, 56; Van Onselen, *Chibaro*, 102; Keppel-Jones, *Rhodes and Rhodesia*, 420; Dotson F & Dotson L. 1968. *The Indian Minority of Zambia, Rhodesia and Malawi*. New Haven: Yale University Press, 162–166; Hyatt, *The Old Transport Road*, 70, 92; Mandaza, *Race, Colour and Class*, 70.

17 Muzondidya, 'The residential segregation of minorities', 70–86; Yoshikuni, 'Black migrants', 27–28; Zinyama L. 1993. 'The evolution of the spatial structure of greater Harare: 1890–1990', in *Harare: The Growth and Problems of the City*, eds L Zinyama, D Tevera & S Cumming. Harare: University of Zimbabwe, 11–12; Kosmin B. 1974. 'Ethnic and commercial relations in Southern Rhodesia: a socio-historical study of the Asian, Hellenic and Jewish populations, 1898–1943'. PhD dissertation, University of Rhodesia, 82.

18 NAZ, S1227, Police Criminal Investigation Department, Immorality Policy reports, Detective Sergeant I Smith, to the assistant superintendent, CID, Salisbury, 26 September 1916; W Parke's statement to CID, Mvuma, RCA33/3/16.

19 Parry, 'Culture, organization and class', 57; Tanser G. 1974. *Sequence of Time: The Story of Salisbury, Rhodesia 1900 to 1914*. Salisbury: Pioneer Head, 163–166.

20 *SR, Second and Final Report of the Director of Census Regarding the Census Taken on the 3rd of May 1921*, 5, 11; Kosmin B. 1977. 'Ethnic groups and the qualified

franchise in Southern Rhodesia, 1898–1922'. *Rhodesian History*, 8, 36, 37; Gann L H. 1969. *A History of Southern Rhodesia: Early Days to 1934*. New York: Humanities Press, 121; Keppel-Jones, *Rhodes and Rhodesia*, 377.

21 For a more detailed discussion of this urban and industrial ethnic hierarchy, see Yoshikuni, 'Black migrants', 68; B S A Co, *Reports on the Administration of Rhodesia, 1900–1902*, 176–178; Van Onselen, *Chibaro*, 81, 93; and Ranger, *The Invention of Tribalism*, 10–14.

22 NAZ, E2/10/7, Education, correspondence, S McAdam, principal, Salisbury Coloured School, to Director of Education, 12 April 1916; E2/3/1, Education, correspondence, Mrs S M Williams to Administrator, 25 May 1911; Cecil Smith, interviewed by James Muzondidya, 6 February 1998; Virginia Pinto, interviewed 20 January 1998; Thomas Shoppo, interviewed by James Muzondidya, 11 February 1997; Mandaza, *Race, Colour and Class*, 78.

23 Hall S. 1996. 'Politics of identity', in *Culture, Identity and Politics*, eds T Ranger, Y Samad & O Stuart. Aldershot: Avebury, 132. For more elaborate discussion on the identity dialectic in colonial society, see also Wilmsen E, Dubow S & Sharp J. 1994. 'Introduction: ethnicity, identity and nationalism in southern Africa'. *Journal of Southern African Studies*, 20, 3; and Markakis J & Fukui K. 1994. 'Introduction', in *Ethnicity and Conflict in the Horn of Africa*, eds J Markakis & K Fukui. London: James Currey.

24 NAZ, E2/10/2/3, Education, correspondence, Inspector of Schools, Bulawayo, to Director of Education, 1 February 1928; E2/3/1, Education, correspondence, Mrs S M Williams to Administrator, 28 May 1911; E2/10/7, Education, correspondence, C L Hendrickse to Advisory Committee, Salisbury Public School, 9 March 1916; secretary, Acting Director of Education, to C L Hendrickse, 20 May 1916; Mandaza, *Race, Colour and Class*, 35–37, 77–79.

25 NAZ, S824/667, Ministry of Education, general correspondence, CID, Umtali, to secretary, Umtali School Advisory Committee, 22 October 1925; minutes of Umtali School Advisory Committee, 4 December 1925; secretary, Umtali Coloured School Advisory Board, to Colonial Secretary, 5 January 1926; secretary, Department of the Colonial Secretary to Coloured School Advisory Board, 23 January 1926.

26 NAZ, S482/188/39, Prime Minister, general correspondence, A J W McLeod, REVA, to PM, SR, 9 January 1928; memorandum of a meeting between the PM and the executive committee of REVA, 11 January 1928.

27 Minutes of REVA meeting, 9 March 1928, as cited in Mandaza, *Race, Colour and Class*, 96–97.

28 NAZ, S1227/3, Police Criminal Investigations Department Headquarters, Immorality Policy reports, detective sergeant, CID, to chief superintendent, CID, Bulawayo, 10 September 1929; letter from the chairman of the Umtali branch of the CCSL, 12 April 1935, cited in SR, *Legislative Assembly Debates*, 15 April 1935, cols 1048–1049.

29 NAZ, S482/188/39, Prime Minister, general correspondence, A J W McLeod, REVA, to PM, SR, 30 March 1931; minutes of deputation from CCSL, 28 February 1933; *Rhodesia Tribune*, August 1945; August 1946.

30 NAZ, S245/1094, Internal Affairs, general correspondence, EAPS memorandum, nd, 1946; *Rhodesia Tribune*, September 1947; December 1947; January 1948.

31 NAZ, S482/188/39, Prime Minister, general correspondence, minutes of deputation from CCSL, 28 February 1933.

32 NAZ, S482/188/39, Prime Minister, general correspondence, A J W McLeod, president, CCSL, to Attorney General, Southern Rhodesia, 28 November 1931; Gaston Thornicroft, interviewed by Ibbo Mandaza, 1 March 1974, cited in Mandaza, *Race, Colour and Class*, 512.

33 NAZ, S824/68/1, Ministry of Education, correspondence and other papers, Aaron Jacha, to the Committee of Enquiry into the Education of Coloured and Half-caste Children, 5 December 1933; B J Mnyanda, to the Committee of Enquiry into the Education of Coloured and Half-caste Children, 20 November 1933.

34 For a more detailed discussion of this movement, see Muzondidya J. 2005. *Walking a Tightrope: Towards a Social History of the Coloured People of Zimbabwe*. Trenton: Africa World Press, 94–99.

35 *African Weekly*, 21 May 1946; 22 May 1946; ZBZ1/2/1, Salisbury African Vigilance Association, 14 February 1948, cited in Phimister I. 1988. *An Economic and Social History of Zimbabwe, 1890–1948*. London: Longman, 269.

36 *Rhodesia Tribune*, March, September & November 1946; *Sunday Mail*, 29 February 1948; *African Weekly*, 17 March 1948.

37 NAZ, S245/1094, Internal Affairs, general correspondence, EAPS memorandum, no date, 1946; S824/667, Ministry of Education, general correspondence, minutes of Umtali School Advisory Committee, 4 December 1925; secretary, Umtali Coloured School Advisory Board, to Colonial Secretary, 5 January 1926; secretary, Department of the Colonial Secretary to Coloured School Advisory Board, 23 January 1926; *Rhodesia Tribune*, October 1949, November 1949; Dotson & Dotson, *The Indian Minority*, 285–291; Seirlis, 'Urban space and "coloured" identities', 198.

38 *Rhodesia Tribune*, May 1947. S245/1094, Internal Affairs, general correspondence, EAPS memorandum, no date, 1946; *Rhodesia Tribune*, April 1946; January 1948.

39 NAZ, S824/430, Ministry of Education, general correspondence, S M Stodart, headmaster, Sinoia Coloured and Indian School, to chief education officer, 11 June 1946; MS1082/2, memorandum of evidence presented by Garfield Todd to the Social Welfare Commission, nd, 1945; S245/1094, Internal Affairs, correspondence, 'Unpublished Report of the Committee Appointed by the Government of Southern Rhodesia to Look into Questions Concerning the Education of Coloured and Half-caste Children in the Colony, 1934'; S824/650, Ministry of Education, general correspondence, minutes of first meeting of the Bulawayo School Advisory Committee, 23 February 1932; SR. 1928. *Report of the Director of Census Regarding the Census of Population taken on the 11th of May 1926, Part 3 and Final*, 38; Gaston Solomons, interviewed by James Muzondidya, 19 January 1997.

40 SR, *Report of the Census of May 1926*, 16, 40; NAZ, S482/188/39, Prime Minister, general correspondence, President, CCSL to PM, 28 October 1938.

41 NAZ, MS/ORAL/TRI, Sir Robert Tredgold, notes of interview with R Challiss, Salisbury, 16 September 1970; S482/188/39, Prime Minister, general correspondence, EAPS Conference, 8 December 1944.

42 NAZ, S245/1094, Internal Affairs, general correspondence, EAPS Memorandum, no date, 1946; S245/919, Internal Affairs, general correspondence, anon.

'Extraordinary special', 16 January 1946; *Rhodesia Tribune*, April 1946; January 1948; Mandaza, *Race, Colour and Class* 771–772.

43 NAZ, S245/919, Internal Affairs, general correspondence, undated and anonymous letter written in 1946; S482/188/39, Prime Minister, general correspondence, J E Jones, chairman, 'Euro-African Patriotic Society: social and cultural report', vol 1, 944; *Rhodesia Tribune*, April 1946; November 1946.

44 See Muzondidya, *Walking a Tightrope*, 86–93, for more detailed discussion of the political battle between the EAPS and the CCSL.

45 NAZ, F119/IMM6, Home Affairs, general correspondence, notes of meeting held in the conference room, Ministry of Home Affairs, 21 August 1958; Dorothy Louw, interviewed by James Muzondidya, 13 January 1997; Virginia Pinto, interviewed 20 January 1998; MacLaren I. 1981. *Some Renowned Rhodesian Schools*, 1892–1979. Bulawayo: Books of Zimbabwe, 136.

46 Bob Kickens, interviewed by James Muzondidya, 6 July 2000; Jimmy Adams, interviewed by James Muzondidya, 12 July 2000; Gaston Solomons, interviewed 19 January 1997; Thomas Shoppo, interviewed 11 February 1997; Hodder-Williams R. 1983. *White Farmers in Rhodesia: 1890–1965: A History of the Marandellas District*. London: Macmillan, 70–71, 103, 215.

47 Seirlis, 'Urban space and "coloured" identities', 223–224.

48 In Kabid, women were referred to as 'chiks' or 'cherries', mothers were called 'queens' while men were called 'blokes'. Whites were referred to as 'whitey', the British as 'britz', Afrikaners as 'japies', and Africans as 'houties'. See Seirlis, 'Urban space and "coloured" identities', 290–294, for a more detailed discussion on Kabid. Paul Hotz's (1990) historical novel, *Muzukuru: A Guerilla's Story* (Johannesburg: Ravan Press), is a good example of a text which extensively uses Kabid, while the coloured diaspora website, http://www.goffal.com, has a rich glossary of terms used in Kabid.

49 Brian Raftopoulos, interviewed by James Muzondidya, 6 February 1997; Thomas Shoppo, interviewed 11 February 1997; Seirlis, 'Urban space and "coloured" identities', 290; Moorcraft P. 1977. *A Short Thousand Years: The End of Rhodesia's Rebellion*. Salisbury: Galaxie Press, 230; Gann L & Henriksen T. 1981. *The Struggle for Zimbabwe: Battle in the Bush*. New York: Praeger, 69.

50 NAZ, MS 536/14/6, Julie Frederikse, transcribed interview with Gerry, Brian and Eugene Raftopoulos, Harare, 1981; Frederikse J. 1982. *None but Ourselves: Masses vs the Media in the Making of Zimbabwe*. Johannesburg: Ravan Press, 237–240.

51 *Daily News*, 5 May 1964; 7 May 1964; B Machine, 'Herbert Foya-Thompson', 7; Mandaza, *Race, Colour and Class*, 685–686, 733.

52 Thomas Shoppo, interviewed 11 February 1997; Price R. 1991. *The Apartheid State in Crisis: Political Transformation in South Africa, 1975–1990*. Oxford: Oxford University Press, 49–90.

53 *Rhodesia Herald*, 9 November 1975.

54 *Sunday Mail*, 20 November 1977; *National Observer*, 14 December 1978.

55 NAZ, MS 536/14/6, Julie Frederikse, transcribed interview with Gerald, Brian and Eugene Raftopoulos, Harare, 1981; Brian Raftopoulos, interviewed 6 February 1997; Mary Pretorius, interviewed 13 January 1997; *Illustrated Life Rhodesia*, 7 December 1978; *Rhodesia Daily Mail*, 4 February 1980; 8 January 1979.

56 Brian Raftopoulos, interviewed 6 February 1997.

57 Thomas Shoppo, interviewed 11 February 1997; Robert Brown (nom de plume), interviewed by James Muzondidya, 16 August 2000; Chung F. 2005. *Re-living the Second Chimurenga: Memories from Zimbabwe's Liberation Struggle*. Harare: Weaver Press, 175–178. Nyagumbo M. 1980. *With the People: An Autobiography from the Zimbabwe Struggle*. London: Alison & Busby, 215.

58 NAZ, F377/A/51/, Public Service Commission, correspondence, report of the subcommittee appointed to investigate the conditions of service of coloured and Asiatic employees, 1956–1957; Simon Indi, interviewed 14 January 1997; Mamdani M. 2001. *When Victims Become Killers: Colonialism, Nativism, and the Genocide in Rwanda*. Princeton: Princeton University Press, 27–28.

59 *African Weekly*, 1 May 1946, 17 March 1948; *Sunday Mail*, 29 February 1948; James Chikerema, interviewed by James Muzondidya, 24 January 2000; Cecil Smith, interviewed 6 February 1998.

60 Nyangoni C & Nyandoro G (eds). 1979. *Zimbabwe Independence Movements*. London: Rex Collins, 22; Mkandawire T. 2005. 'African intellectuals and nationalism', in *African Intellectuals: Rethinking Politics, Language, Gender and Development*, ed T Mkandaire. Dakar: Codesria, 12; Mandaza, *Race, Colour and Class*, 469, 560–574.

61 Raftopoulos B. 1999. 'Problematising nationalism in Zimbabwe: a historiographical review'. *Zambezia*, 26, no. 2, 116.

62 NAZ, MS536/14/6, Julie Frederikse, transcribed interview with Gerald, Eugene and Brian Raftopoulos, Harare, 26 April 1981; Sam Hendrickse, interviewed by James Muzondidya, 22 January 1998; Cecil Smith, interviewed 6 February 1998; *Illustrated Life Rhodesia*, 7 December 1978; *Sunday Mail*, 24 May 1981; 4 April 2001; Mandaza, *Race, Colour and Class*, 570–573; 790.

63 NAZ, MS536/14/6, Julie Frederikse, transcribed interview with Gerald, Eugene and Brian Raftopoulos, Harare, 26 April 1981; *Illustrated Life Rhodesia*, 7 December 1978; *National Observer*, 22 March 1979; *Zimbabwe Times*, 29 February 1980.

64 *Rhodesia Herald*, 14 March 1979.

65 NAZ, MS36/7/5, Julie Frederikse, general memoranda, memorandum to His Excellency Lord C Soames, Governor for the Administration of Southern Rhodesia, nd, 1980; *Rhodesia Herald*, 14 March 1979.

CHAPTER 8

Absent white fathers: coloured identity in Zambia[1]

BY

JULIETTE MILNER-THORNTON

GRIFFITH UNIVERSITY

Colouredness in Zambia, formerly the British colony of Northern Rhodesia, needs to be understood within the context of a racist ideology that portrayed it in pathological terms as an identity fragmented between conflicting positive traits derived from its European ancestry and negative traits derived from its African lineage. Coloured people were thus viewed as racially degenerate, and despised as illegitimate. These attitudes were not exclusive to Zambia but common to the entire subcontinent, especially South Africa with its substantial coloured population. The Zambian experience differs from that of South Africa, however, in that the majority of Zambian coloureds are the descendants of colonial British men and African women, and that colonialism arrived relatively late with Zambia being colonised only towards the end of the 19th century.[2] The Zambian coloured population is much smaller than South Africa's. Zambia's Population and Housing Census form for 2000 did not include a separate coloured classification. This exclusion by Zambia's Central Statistics Office makes it difficult to evaluate how many people in Zambia currently identify as coloured.[3] However, according to James Muzondidya, Zambia's coloured population represents only 0.3 per cent of the national total.[4]

The coloured presence in Zambia is a legacy of British colonialism and what I term the 'absent white father'. The latter refers to the absence, or ambiguous presence, of white fathers's names in public documents relating to their 'mixed-race' children. Historical records reveal the absence of white fathers's names in public records relating to coloured children was, to a certain extent, encouraged by the Northern Rhodesian colonial administration. This is clearly demonstrated in a letter Tom Page, Member for the Eastern Electoral Area, wrote to the Secretary for Native Affairs advising him as follows:

> Compulsory registration of births of coloured children with the names of the alleged fathers is open to serious abuse. I think that Native Authorities might be instructed to note and keep a record of the births of coloured children without any reference whatever to the fathers and also to keep a record of the deaths. Here again the enquiry might be made as to whether anything in this respect is being done in other countries which are faced with this problem.[5]

The 'mixed-race' presence in Northern Rhodesia and other parts of the British Empire was considered a source of great embarrassment and shame that needed special treatment.[6] The absence of their fathers' names in the public record meant that their coloured children were branded as illegitimate. This stigma resonates down to the present day and continues to have repercussions for Zambian coloured people. It, for example, creates difficulties for 'mixed-race' descendants of absent white fathers to claim political, social and legal rights – including the rights of inheritance and citizenship in the homeland of their European ancestors.

My interest in the nature of Zambian coloured identity was initially sparked by curiosity about my own family history because I am the descendant of a British adventurer, Dr Sidney Spencer 'Kachalola' Broomfield, celebrated as one of the pioneers of Northern Rhodesia. In the late 1920s, Broomfield mysteriously left Northern Rhodesia, abandoning his mixed-race children, who never learned why their father left or his fate. Broomfield's behaviour was not uncommon, though. It reflects the experience of many Zambian coloured families.

The disavowal of mixed-race children by European fathers is a common characteristic of colonisation in other parts of Africa, Southeast Asia and Australia.[7] In the Australian context, Fiona Probyn makes the point that '[w]hite fathers were disavowed and often the subject of public and legal censure … and at the same time, they were in a sense protected, monitored and sponsored by government policies which surrounded them'.[8] By these means, she explains, 'white fathers were both agents of assimilation … and irritants to segregation'. Probyn suggests that white fathers' only contribution to their Aboriginal families was sanguineous, through the provision of their 'blood'. Yet this act of miscegenation contributed to their own invisibility, their children's visibility and, for many, their subsequent removal from Aboriginal society.[9] By contrast, in the Zambian context, the visibility of white colonial fathers as pioneers, administrators and officials rendered their Anglo-African descendants invisible. Their children have been erased from the public record, history books and family genealogies. My interest in Zambian coloured identity was piqued by the way the original denial of paternity, or the abandonment of their families as in the case of Broomfield, by absent white fathers, impacted on the lives and identities of subsequent generations of their descendants.

In this study I use auto-ethnography as an analytical tool to situate my family history within the social experience of Zambia's coloured community. Discussing auto-ethnographic films, Catherine Russell explains that 'autobiography becomes ethnographic at the point where the film-maker understands his or her personal history to be implicated in larger social and historical processes'.[10] Essentially, an auto-ethnographic text reveals the doubling coexistence of the collective and individual experience. Mary Louise Pratt (1992) makes the point that:

> [i]f ethnographic texts are a means by which Europeans represent to themselves their (usually subjugated) others, auto-ethnographic texts are those the others construct in response to or in dialogue with those metropolitan representations.[11]

In other words, auto-ethnography is the autobiographical response of the subjugated to European or metropolitan representations.

Accordingly, I compare my family history to Broomfield's autobiography and the archival and historical record of Zambia as a way of exploring the complexities of coloured identity in Zambia.

Broomfield's life

When I first read *Kachalola or the Mighty Hunter*, the autobiography of Dr Sidney Spencer Broomfield,[12] it was with the expectation that I would discover both my ancestor's background and his special legacy to me. It came as a surprise that he did not acknowledge his family, and made no mention of his children, white or mixed-race. Although in his private life in Northern Rhodesia Broomfield openly acknowledged his Anglo-African children, he did not do so in his public life. They do not appear in his autobiography or even in his last will and testament.[13]

Broomfield is my great-grandfather and his son, Stephen, fathered my mother Nellie.[14] Our family has limited information about my grandfather Stephen's mother, and my mother Nellie told me that her father never spoke of her. Apparently, Kachalola removed his children from their African mothers and took them to live with him on his farm. My siblings and I were born, and lived the greater part of our lives, in Zambia. My father, Francis Japhet Milner, was born in Nyati, Southern Rhodesia in 1934. He was the offspring of a Lithuanian Jewish man, Joseph Milner, and a Zulu woman, Esther Cele. My father migrated to Northern Rhodesia in 1951, where he met and married my mother in 1956. We lived together in Zambia until his death and subsequent burial in Chingola in 1986. In 1994, I migrated to Australia having married an Australian national, Robert Thornton, whom I met in Zambia. Ten months after arriving in Australia we relocated to Bangkok, where we lived for four years. In 1998 we returned to Australia and settled in Brisbane. Shortly after that, I solved the 70-year-old family mystery of what happened to Broomfield – he died at the Royal Brisbane Hospital on 24 October 1933 and was buried at Toowong Cemetery in Brisbane.

Broomfield states he was born in the south of England in July 1847 and that his mother died in childbirth on the day he was born. His death certificate states he was born in Hampshire, England. Broomfield reveals that when he was nine years old he was sent to London to live with his father. He does not state with whom or where he lived until then. In his writing, Broomfield presents himself as an intrepid transcontinental traveller and adventurer. He claims that, after his first trip – to Africa in 1868 as a 21-year-old – he continued to travel, trade and explore the world for an additional 66 years. His exploits took him as far afield as South America, Southeast Asia, India, Ceylon, China, Australia, the Dutch East Indies, New Guinea, and East and South Central Africa. After extensive travels in Australia, including a two-year-long overland trek from Victoria to the Northern Territory, Broomfield's decades of adventure and travel abruptly ended with his death from pneumonia and cardiac failure.[15]

Broomfield's book provides a sparse family account. He does not mention any siblings, though he claims he inherited money from his mother when he came of age. He also states that he was estranged from his father. Broomfield presents himself and his family as wealthy. He implies that he studied medicine at Edinburgh University.[16] After contacting numerous universities in Scotland and England, I have been unable to find any evidence to support this claim. However, W V Brelsford, a Northern Rhodesian administrator and academic, alleges that 'he first appeared, as Sydney Spencer, in Southern Rhodesia in 1892 … There was a Dr Broomfield also in Southern Rhodesia who was an entomologist. He disappeared and somehow Spencer took his title and name. One version of this happening is that the real Dr Broomfield left his estate to Spencer who took the name of his benefactor, and that as Broomfield he got an American doctorship for five dollars following some correspondence course'.[17] I have not been able to confirm Brelsford's allegations, and there is no record of birth for a Sidney Spencer Broomfield. However, I have been able to obtain a birth certificate corresponding to Broomfield's date of birth for a Sidney Edgar Spencer of Oxford Street, London and a copy of my great-grandfather's death certificate stating his name as Dr Sidney Spencer Broomfield.

According to Broomfield's Anglo-African granddaughter, Mavis Burt, her mother Dolly, Broomfield's daughter, often spoke of his great wealth.[18] Documents at the Brisbane City Council Cemetery Administration Office state that Broomfield died bankrupt, and was buried in a pauper's grave in 1933 in Toowong Cemetery. However, five years after Broomfield's death, records at Toowong Cemetery reveal that a person identified only as 'Broomfield' purchased his grave and erected a headstone.[19] The person who purchased Broomfield's grave was most probably a family member, who demonstrated his or her familiarity with him by inscribing his headstone with his epithet, 'Kachalola'.

Throughout his autobiography, Broomfield maintains that he was a doctor, big-game hunter, abolitionist and entomologist. He claims that, as he travelled in the various tribal lands of Northern Rhodesia, he became known for his prowess as a hunter. He exhibits great pride in his epithet 'Kachalola'. He wrote: 'But I think it was a later trip that the name Kachalola was first given to me, because I had a lot to do with bringing the tribes together. I have been told by some natives that it means "to bring together" and by others "the great hunter"'.[20] Brelsford suggests that the origin and meaning of 'Kachalola' is unknown, and provides the following explanation: 'Chiripula Stephenson, a Northern Rhodesian administrator and contemporary of Broomfield's whose etymology was often suspect, states it meant 'rumbling in the belly', while P H Selby, a colonial official, claimed it meant 'woolly and unkempt'.'[21] A granddaughter of Bruce Gray, a contemporary and associate of Broomfield's, explained that in Nsenga 'Kachalola' in its crudest sense is used to describe a man who 'likes women'. Unfortunately, our family oral history is unable to provide any further insight, apart from the fact that Broomfield was always referred to as Kachalola by his family and friends, and a town in the eastern province of Zambia is named 'Kachalola' in his honour.[22]

Colouredness in Zambia

It is important to recognise the significant role of colonial sexual relations in the creation of Zambia's coloured community. According to Ronald Hyam, sexual desire performed many functions in British colonialism. Hyam states that British men initiated sexual relations with indigenous women in Africa and Asia for their mental well-being, the alleviation of loneliness and boredom, and because they could indulge in their sexuality in a way they could not at home.[23]

Brelsford describes Kachalola Broomfield as 'one of the most colorful characters … of Northern Rhodesian history' and implies that he was notorious for his sexual exploits with African women. He mistakenly writes that 'Kachalola had at least eight or nine wives in the Feira district alone and he left thirty-six half-caste children … Descendants still alive today call themselves Bloomfield and not Broomfield'.[24] Broomfield justifies his and other male settlers' sexual relations with indigenous women by citing the scarcity of white women in the colonies. This, together with the expense of keeping a white woman in a place like Northern Rhodesia, meant that many white men found it more practical to form sexual unions with indigenous women. Such alliances, he asserts, established white men's sexual virility, thus commanding the respect of the colonised. He contends that the advantages for white men of establishing sexual alliances with native women far outweighed the disadvantages, as white men benefitted both sexually and financially. According to Broomfield, indigenous women were useful for establishing congenial relations with African chiefs and as intermediaries through whom white men could gain political and trade concessions. They were also an effective and pleasant way in which white men could gain access to vital knowledge and learn the local languages and customs. In Broomfield's words, African women were white men's 'feather bed dictionaries'.[25]

Contrary to Broomfield's assertions of the value of interracial sexual alliances, he denounced indigenous women because of the social and sexual retrogression they produced among white settler men, who were supposedly defenceless in the face of their charms. Broomfield reproached African men for offering indigenous women and girls as gifts or bribes and as commodities that could be purchased by white men. Broomfield's opinion about indigenous women exemplifies the consensus of white men in Northern Rhodesia.[26]

Furthermore, Broomfield shows no compunction about claiming that 'native girls were only too eager to take on a white man' and that since 'the contract was not binding they could be discarded at any time'. Broomfield exonerates himself from criticism by arguing that '[native women] are plentiful and easy to get, and they have a charm of their own, a good many white men of all classes fall to them'. His allegation is supported by the existence of coloureds who are acknowledged locally in Zambia as the descendants of former Northern Rhodesian pioneers, colonial administrators and officials. The list includes prominent men such as E H Lane-Poole, described by Brelsford as a 'Balliol man who had rowed bow for his college and whose father was a professor at Oxford', and Sir Alfred Sharpe, whom Gann and Duignan identify as Rhodes's emissary. Others were J E Chiripula Stephenson, colonial administrator; Dr Alan Kinghorn, a medical doctor who arrived in Northern Rhodesia to research sleeping sickness; Sir Percy Sillitoe, a police officer based in Lusaka who was later appointed Director General of Britain's Security Service, MI5; and Dongolosi Thornicroft, District Commissioner at Old Petauke. Broomfield's observation reveals the impunity with which certain white men abandoned their coloured children.[27]

In contrast to some of these men, Broomfield's frank disclosure of his attitude towards African women is exceptional. According to Gann and Duignan, colonial white men who openly admitted to consorting with native women were rejected as reprobate. Chiripula Stephenson experienced this when 'his open and unashamed marriage and cohabitation with native women enforced his resignation from his prestigious colonial posting by his senior colonial officers'.[28] The open secret of colonial white men having mixed-race children confirmed these children's shadowy existence.

As an eight-year-old, my late grandmother, Eliza Maria Broomfield, was forcibly removed from her African mother by Jack Cowie, an associate of Broomfield's. Cowie would later tell her that he did this because she was half-caste and as such she should not live with 'natives'.

My grandmother often told me that it was not uncommon for white men to live openly with their indigenous or coloured wives and children in black society, but they would not do so among their fellow white settlers. If a white settler unexpectedly visited such a family, the African wife and 'half-caste' children were not permitted to show themselves. They had to hide. Such women were known as a 'kitchen wives' or 'cooks women'. My grandmother's observation is supported by Gann and Duignan, who write about white men in Northern Rhodesia putting 'away their African mistresses'. These women's status within such family units, as preparers of food and providers of sex, was regarded as insulting, shameful and humiliating within African society.[29]

In colonial archival records, mixed-race progeny and their African mothers, where acknowledged, typically remain nameless. This is the case with my paternal Zulu grandmother Esther Cele and her mixed-race children, my father Japhet and his three siblings, Aaron, Michael and Rebecca. The children's father, Joseph Milner, a Lithuanian Jew by birth and British subject, died in Southern Rhodesia in 1939. Joseph's death certificate, dated 18 February 1939, states that at the time of this death he was 'unmarried', that he was survived by four 'illegitimate' children whose names were unknown and that his children's mother was 'native'.[30] Joseph Milner's children remain nameless in archival records and, until recently, their existence was unknown to other Jewish family members. After many years spent searching for my Jewish family, I discovered them in South Africa. I contacted them, informed them of our relationship and naively expected an affirmation of our common ancestry. Their initial excitement turned to perplexity and dismay when I informed them of my ethnic and cultural multiplicity.

White paternity greatly affected coloureds' lifestyle in Northern Rhodesia. Fathered by white men and mothered by black women, mixed-race progeny were seen by colonial society as an affront to race, nature and God, and as such were not considered the rightful heirs of white men. This is confirmed by my paternal uncle Aaron Milner, a former Home Affairs Minister in Zambia:

> Northern and Southern Rhodesia colonial laws did not allow white men or women to marry a black person. Such marriages were performed under the tribal African tradition … [C]hildren, born under such arrangements were then called 'illegitimate' having no paternal rights to the inheritance of their father's property … Some white fathers, as mine did, took

steps to register the birth of their children with the Colonial Native Commissioner's Office ... under their surnames. It was not uncommon for the remaining white relatives to force the native mother and her mixed-race offspring to change their surnames through coercion and bribery.[31]

Euro-African children, such as my father and his siblings, Aaron, Michael and Rebecca, were acknowledged by their Lithuanian Jewish father but not by other white relatives. The Rhodesian government classified them as illegitimate. Joseph Milner's children were denied the status of being born in a legitimate union by the colonial office and their Jewish family, and this ensured their painful stigma of illegitimacy and poverty. My father and his siblings were sent to Embakwe, a Catholic missionary school in Plumtree, Southern Rhodesia, which Hugh Macmillan and Frank Shapiro describe as 'effectively an orphanage'.[32]

The coloured presence in Northern Rhodesia instigated public debate among colonists about their social and political status in the territory. The prevailing attitude was one of contempt for coloureds, and identifying with their fathers or associating with settler society was discouraged. A few colonists, however, had sympathy for coloureds and saw them as deserving of full acceptance into colonial society. For example Mr A W Edwardes-Jordan, a settler from Fort Jameson (present-day Chipata) felt sufficiently strongly about the issue to bypass the local administration and address his concerns directly to the Secretary of State for the Colonies in London:

> I have the honour to bring to your notice the political status of the Euroafricans in Northern Rhodesia. These Euroafricans born of a European British subject, and an African mother, are graded by this government, sometimes as Natives, other times as Coloureds or halfcastes, and as British Protected Subjects. They claim, and I support the claim, that they are British Subjects, entitled to a British Passport, and the honour of British cityzenship [sic] Our Government has consistently postponed and evaded the issue...[33]

Settler society in Northern Rhodesia was scornful of white men who lived in concubinage with African women. Phillip Mason, founding director of the Institute of Race Relations in London, describes such sexual relations as 'a matter of physical gratification and no more'. Mason further contends that the arrival of white women in these colonies made white men realise the enormity of their sexual transgressions, and that they came to regard their colonial interracial exploits with indigenous women with 'horror, repulsion and deep remorse'. Mason reveals the sentiments of white women in Northern Rhodesia who seem to have been the bulwarks of racial segregation. He quotes the secretary of the [Northern] Rhodesia Women's League as follows:

> It is not generally known that in 1903 (before women of Rhodesia had the right to vote) the Immorality Suppression Ordinance was passed, making it a criminal offence for a white woman to cohabit with a native, while the reverse relationship of white men and native women continues to remain outside the cognizance of the law. All thoughtful people are agreed that such mixed intercourse was degrading to the white race and has a very evil influence on the black.[34]

Northern Rhodesian white settler society's displeasure about cohabitation between white men and African women was primarily because the relationships produced 'half-caste' children and this gravely concerned colonial society as coloureds were perceived to be a threat to white racial purity. Despite this attitude, miscegenation continued, as evidenced by the large number of coloured descendants of British men and African women who live within and outside Zambia.

In most conventional colonial narratives, coloured people are disparaged as illegitimate. Floyd and Lillian Dotson as recently as 1965 maintained that "Eurafricans' in Central Africa are products of casual and mercenary encounters'. The Dotsons, however, do concede that 'coloureds in Central Africa have customarily assumed the name of their [British] father, and among the most common names of the older generation of "coloureds" appear those of pioneer officials and administrators of the first rank'.[35] This acknowledgement goes against the presumption of casualness. The main point of reference for the majority of Zambian coloureds when it comes to obtaining information about their British ancestors is Brelsford's *The Generation of Men*. It highlights the significance and legacy of the absence of white fathers in the public record of their coloured children.

Northern Rhodesian interracial cohabitations between white men and African women were usually sanctioned with the payment of bride wealth, commonly known as *lobola*. This was not the 'sale of African women', as Sidney Broomfield implies.[36] *Lobola* should be seen within the context of African morality. For this reason, the children born within these marriages were not considered illegitimate by African society – most especially if they were in long-term, traditionally sanctioned marriages with African women.

The daughter of a prominent British settler in Northern Rhodesia agreed to speak with me about her childhood memories in Northern Rhodesia on condition that she remains anonymous. She informed me that *lobola* should be regarded in the same way as white people awarding a ring to their betrothed. The payment of *lobola* is a pledge made by a man to a woman and her family, a commitment to a longstanding relationship within the confines of marriage.[37] In Northern Rhodesia, traditional unions sanctioned through *lobola* were regarded as legal, both tribally and in 'native' courts of law. *Lobola* was in fact practised by Africans in accordance with their traditional moral codes.[38] In most instances, the long-term traditional marriages between colonial white men and African women included all the elements of conventional European marriages, except the sanction of Christian churches and the Northern Rhodesian colonial government. During the colonial era in Zambia, the practice of *lobola* between white men and indigenous women appears to have been the principal reason why the colonial government and settler society denied legitimacy and British citizenship rights to the children born in these interracial unions.

According to the Northern Rhodesian Marriage Ordinance of 1940, coloured children born in a union of a 'native' mother and non-native father were illegitimate. They could not claim British ancestry in spite of being born of British fathers. Instead, they were deemed 'British Protected Persons'. They were designated with the same social status as their African mothers.[39] African leaders in Northern Rhodesia, and most especially Kenneth Kaunda, resisted being classified as a 'British Protected Person'. They argued that, first and foremost, they should be given the dignity of being permitted to be citizens of their own country, Northern Rhodesia. In this regard, Kaunda appeared unsympathetic to their plight, accusing Euro-Africans of being 'misled' by British 'propaganda'. He expected the sons and daughters of African women and European men to renounce their European fathers, and thereby their European ancestry and any political privileges this way have entailed. Kaunda implied that it was necessary for Euro-Africans to do this in order to demonstrate their commitment to the African nationalist movement.[40]

However, it is important to recognise that a number of British men, particularly those who remained in Zambia, did not distance themselves from their Anglo-African children and grandchildren. This is evident from the way in which some British settlers defied government policy regarding the education of coloured children. From the late 1920s onwards, the Northern Rhodesian government refused to build separate schools for 'half-caste' children in the territory. The administration argued that separate schools would encourage 'half-castes' to think of themselves as separate from African society. They would then become an 'artificial' class of people that would not be accepted by either European or African society in the territory.[41] The government wanted coloured children to attend African missionary schools to encourage their being 'reabsorbed' into African society. This assimilationist strategy for resolving the 'half-caste problem' in the territory remained in place until the late 1950s.[42] Several British men, some of whom had formerly served as colonial officials, resisted this assimilationist scheme by building schools on their farms and employing teachers to instruct not only their own Anglo-African children and grandchildren but those of other settlers as well.[43]

Karen Transberg Hansen dismisses Chiripula Stephenson's romance with his first African wife as mere 'infatuation',[44] but romances between white men and African women were not as implausible as she implies, and many older coloured people speak about the loving relationships they enjoyed with their white fathers and grandfathers.[45] Recently in Australia, an elderly woman formerly from Zambia spoke to me about the loving relationship her British father shared with his African wife, who was the daughter of a prominent African chief. After paying *lobola*, her father swooped down from his horse, picked up his bride and carried her on horseback to his home. The marriage produced nine Anglo-African children.

This woman also spoke to me about the public debates which raged in colonial Zambia about the social and racial classification of 'half-caste' people such as herself. She told me that, during the 1950s, there was much discussion in colonial Zambia about what status and categorisation mixed-race people should hold. According to her, the term 'Eurafrican' was particularly controversial. The racial and cultural classification of Eurafrican or Euro-African was commonly used in the 1940s and early 1950s in Northern Rhodesia. John Grotpeter defines Eurafrican as people who have one parent who is predominantly European and one who is predominantly African.[46] The interviewee said the white settlers determined that the term 'Eurafrican' should be used to describe Europeans born in Northern Rhodesia. According to her, white settler society appropriated the term to eliminate any confusion with people like herself. Since then, Eurafricans in Zambia have been referred to by, and have subsequently adopted, the South African term 'coloured'.[47] In the late 1950s in Northern and Southern Rhodesia, the term 'coloured' became more commonly used to describe mixed-race people, who in turn adopted the term in preference to the derogatory and offensive 'half-caste' and 'darkie'.

Historical books and journals glorify British men in Northern Rhodesia as colonial trailblazers. Brelsford, numerous British contributors to the *Northern Rhodesian Journal*[48] and writers of other historical publications are biased in their reports about illustrious British colonial officials, administrators and farmers – men such as E H Lane Poole, H S Thornicroft, Frank and Jack Goddard, Dr Alan Kinghorn, Richard Thornton and Josilyn de Jong.[49] These reports deliberately avoided discussing the men's marital status and sexuality, choosing to ignore the long-term relationships many of them enjoyed with African women. They instead promoted these men as upstanding colonial citizens and glorious pioneers of empire in Northern Rhodesia. While a small number of historical texts do concede that 'half-caste' progeny in Zambia are the descendants of British men, they suggest that these children are evidence of the tarnished character of these men. In these historical narratives coloured people remain anonymous. These histories do not provide any insight into the social and political experiences of African descendants of British men.

Mixed-race child removal also occurred in Northern Rhodesia. One of its victims told me that because her mother was African and her father was British, the welfare department labelled her an orphan, which gave it authority over her life to dictate with whom and where she could live. She informed me that, during the school holidays, coloured children such as herself would either remain in St John's mission or, if the nuns permitted, they could spend their holidays at a fellow coloured student's home, provided that the student's parents were both coloured. These children were discouraged from going to their African mother's village. The informant told me that it was only in adulthood that she was reunited with her African mother, and then she found that she was unable to communicate with her as she had never learnt her mother's language.[50] The perpetrators of forced child removal believed they were acting in the best interests of the mixed-race children. They felt such action would enable the children to assimilate more easily into white colonial society.

In the social hierarchy of Northern Rhodesia, coloured children were left in limbo. British colonial administrators were split into two camps, one of which argued that it was necessary to create an intermediate status for coloured people, while the other did not agree. Ibbo Mandaza identifies H S Thornicroft and E H Lane Poole as two prominent British officials in Northern Rhodesia who supported a separate status for coloureds. It is commonly known that both men had fathered coloured children. Thornicroft initiated and supported the Euro-African Association, and Lane Poole, the provincial commissioner of Mongu, wrote to the Northern Rhodesian colonial government arguing that coloureds 'preferred' their own community rather than being assimilated into white or black society. Lane Poole further argued that to leave coloureds within their African kinship groups would corrupt them with an 'inferiority complex with almost inevitable complications in the future'.[51]

Many of the first and second generation of Zambian coloureds were abandoned by white fathers at the end of their colonial adventures and careers. Zambian coloureds originate from varying districts and ethnic groups. For example, in 1940 the largest number of Coloured persons lived in the eastern province of the territory closely followed by the northern province.[52] It was not an uncommon practice for white men to leave the district and not explain their true intentions to their African families. This seems to have been the case with Dr Alan Kinghorn, who 'dumped' his African wife and four coloured children, Andrew, Jean, Elizabeth and Meston, on his farm Kantenshi in Isoka in the Northern Province of Northern Rhodesia.[53] Kinghorn found employment in Livingstone, but did not inform his African wife. He instead married a European woman with whom he had one daughter named Jane, who later became a prominent magazine editor. Although the fate of Kinghorn's coloured children was sad, it seems that they were fortunate as they were well looked after by their African stepfather. Colonial administrators revealed that other abandoned coloured children were not as fortunate when their white fathers left them in their African mothers' villages. It was claimed that these children were often subjected to 'harsh treatment and abuse' by the native authorities.[54]

According to Tom Page, the treatment of coloured children depended on their mother's tribal affiliation and that particular tribe's customary laws. He pointed out that coloured children born to an Ngoni mother and white father who were subsequently abandoned by their white fathers in their mother's village were looked upon by the other villagers as 'an Ishmael (not the children of the covenant). Not wanted, despised as being without a father, very often neglected and badly treated, a possible obstacle to the subsequent marriage of his mother'. Page revealed that coloured children were subjected to ill treatment by their fellow Ngoni tribesmen because, according to the customary law, children belonged to their father. Therefore, the absence of white fathers had harsh social consequences for the children. On the other hand, Page noted, coloured children born to Achewa mothers and white fathers who were subsequently abandoned by their white fathers were accepted by their mother's tribe because, according to Achewa customary law, children belonged to their mother.[55]

In Northern Rhodesia, the legal and social status of coloureds was the subject of continuous debate in the 1940s. Page highlighted this to Sandford, the secretary for native affairs who was also chairman of the coloured status committee:

> There is first the general statement made in the Interpretation Ordinance which lays down that certain Coloured persons are, in the eyes of the law, 'Natives', all others being 'non-natives'. In the Marriage Ordinance a coloured person with only a trace of European blood is definitely excluded from being 'Native'. Finally there is the dictum that illegitimates take after the mother. As Coloured persons of the first generation born in N. Rhodesia are illegitimate they rank as 'Natives' irrespective of their manner of living. The offspring of Coloured marriages are still 'natives' after their fathers who are 'Natives'. They therefore come under the category of British Protected persons and not British subjects ... The child of illicit union contracted in Northern Rhodesia but who happens to have been born in S. Rhodesia or other British possession (not Protectorate) and who comes to live in N. Rhodesia is a full British subject even though living as a Native.[56]

In Northern Rhodesia, white paternity was not the only determinant of coloured identity. A person's lifestyle was an important consideration. In 1942, Sir John Waddington, the governor and commander-in-chief of Northern Rhodesia, set up a commission of enquiry to investigate land policy in the colonial territory. The report, sympathetic to the plight of coloureds, also revealed their unstable social and political status in the colony. The land commissioners informed the government that coloureds' racial classification and social status in Northern Rhodesia were too flexible, and recommended that they be re-evaluated:

> [T]he Coloured question is one of great complexity and we do not feel that the present definition of a Coloured person can be regarded as entirely satisfactory, based as it is, in actual fact, solely upon material possessions. No person without means, and little opportunity for employment, can live according to European standards but it does not necessarily follow that he wishes, or should be compelled, to adopt native standards and to be classed as native. We feel that this question needs further consideration.[57]

Financial criteria also determined coloureds' status and identity. This made their status unpredictable because it depended on an individual's material possessions and their maintenance of a European lifestyle. This emphasis on material possessions and lifestyle gravely concerned Northern Rhodesian coloureds, primarily because they had limited opportunities to find work and thereby maintain a European standard of living. Coloureds' economic disadvantages were a constant threat to their racial and social status in Northern Rhodesia.

Coloureds lived with the constant fear that their racial classification and status, along with the limited privileges these offered, would be taken from them and that they would be reclassified 'native' – like their African mothers. The 'native' categorisation and status in turn would assure further social, economic and educational disadvantage. In British colonial Africa, coloureds witnessed the debased treatment meted out by the colonial administrators to Africans, and it would seem that this greatly contributed to their dissociation from Africans. In addition, their European fathers who were in 'marriages' with their African mothers insisted that their children not associate with Africans. The coloured children, like my grandfather Stephen, were told they were *musungu*, which means 'white', or that they were 'half-caste' and coloured, but not African, which denoted blackness and inadequacy. My grandfather would call himself a '*musungu* half-caste', meaning he was 'white, half white and half black'. By calling himself a '*musungu* half-caste', he emphasised his white genealogy. The first and second generations of Zambian coloureds were constantly warned by their white fathers, black mothers, the ruling white minority, mission school teachers and fellow coloureds not to socialise with Africans, as it would contaminate and socially degenerate them. These conflicting ideas about their racial identity resulted in coloureds being culturally estranged and displaced – not belonging to either culture, African or European. Franz Fanon describes the phenomenon as 'an inferiority complex that has been created by the death and burial of its local cultural originality'.[58]

In Northern Rhodesia, it was common knowledge that fair-skinned coloured individuals who realised the predicament of institutionalised poverty were able to gain social mobility and attain a higher standard of living, but at great cost to themselves and their families. If they could pass as European, they did. 'Play whites', as such people were called, joined white social clubs, were promoted into managerial jobs which were reserved for white people and lived in white housing areas. Coloureds who played white had to reinvent themselves as white in speech and manner – which meant, in most cases, disowning their past, family and community.[59]

In the 1950s and 1960s, the intermediate status of coloured people in Northern Rhodesian society ensured feelings of conflict. They attributed their limited privileges to the white ruling minority to whom they felt indebted. Their privileged status contributed to an estrangement with their African families and also prevented them from establishing relationships with them. The aspiration of attaining a European lifestyle and the allure of a superior social status meant that coloureds embraced European culture. They hoped that Europeans would accept them, but they were often exposed to further humiliation and vulnerability, as their ambitions were frequently rejected. Coloureds' marginalisation and alienation contributed to their forming their own culture, an amalgamation of British and African cultures. Rejected and abandoned by white fathers, Northern Rhodesian coloured people formed their own social community. Elizabeth Robertson eloquently defined her experience growing up 'mixed race' in colonial Rhodesia as 'bonding in our abandonment'.[60]

Whereas in South Africa race laws upheld the privilege of whiteness, in Zambia the colour bar was imposed not by law but rather by custom. John Gunther points out that in Northern Rhodesia, white settler society, especially white South African immigrants, imposed an industrial colour bar and that this ideology eventually spilled over into every aspect of Northern Rhodesian Africans' social lives.[61]

In the 1950s, coloureds requested separate housing from the Northern Rhodesian government. The colonial government acceded to their demands and built houses specifically for coloureds. These housing areas became known as the coloured quarters. In most cases, they were situated on the margins of white society on the outskirts of industrial towns along the railway lines. In a recent interview, my mother Nellie Milner spoke to me about her colonial experiences. She described the houses in the quarters as small and in close proximity to one another. She also stated that, within the quarters, there was a social club and schools. In addition to segregated housing areas, coloured men were confined to specific areas of employment in the Public Works Department and Rhodesia Railways, with limited opportunities for promotion.[62] Coloureds' segregation and exclusion, although initially state imposed, evolved into a self-imposed separation, beginning with my grandparents' generation. They married within the Zambian and Zimbabwean coloured community. This preference persists among the present generation of Zambian coloureds both in Zambia and abroad. Such marriages ensure that the community remains a complex web of familial and kinship connections.[63]

Living within the confines of their own social group gave coloureds a sense of security and community, but it deprived them of far more. This segregated, alienated lifestyle was inherited by subsequent generations. From the segregated hospitals where they were born to the segregated schools for coloureds, the pattern persisted into adulthood in the segregated housing areas in which they lived, and their employment in racially segregated jobs. In this way the colonial government and coloureds themselves ensured their alienation and marginalisation from both white and black society.[64]

In Zambia, the memory of absentee white fathers such as Kachalola Broomfield may have started to fade. Their legacies can, however, still be discerned in the social, cultural, racial and political experiences of the current generation of their coloured descendants. The most notable manifestation of this heritage after independence has been the ongoing emigration of Zambia's Anglo-Africans to Great Britain. This exodus became pronounced with Zambia's economic decline from the early 1970s onwards. Anglo-Africans' dispersal from Zambia to the UK has also partly been prompted by the legacy of the absent white father. Cultural theorist Stuart Hall suggests that there 'can be no simple "return" or "recovery" of the ancestral past which is not re-experienced through the categories of the present'.[65] In other words, the Zambian Anglo-African social category and coloured identity are 'artefacts' of their colonial past, and many have felt the need to return and recover their ancestral past in order to make a coherent story of their current social and cultural predicament. They have experienced the diasporic described by Hall as 'not the so-called return to roots but a coming-to-terms-with our routes'.[66]

The migration of Zambian Anglo-Africans to Britain suggests that in the postcolonial situation they have come to see themselves as part of the British diaspora. The contemporary migration of coloureds from Zambia to Great Britain and other global destinations would indicate that they have not only crossed political borders demarcating nation states, but also crossed 'diasporic convergences across ethnicities, cultures, religions and nationalities' by reclaiming their British ancestry, which they were discouraged from asserting during British rule in Northern Rhodesia.[67] In contemporary times, these children's stigma of illegitimacy appears to be insignificant should they choose to claim British citizenship. British citizenship laws are sanguineous in that the children and grandchildren of British people who can irrevocably prove their British ancestry can claim 'right of abode' in the UK,[68] and many Anglo-Africans have done this. They have claimed their birthright – British citizenship. In the last 30 years, the British government has changed its earlier stance of not acknowledging the 'mixed-race' descendants of British men born in its former colonies, and awarded them equal access to British citizenship. Also during this period, social expectations changed. Today children born outside of marriage have equal rights to those born within marriages. Illegitimacy is no longer the stigma it was in the colonial era. Another factor is that during the colonial era, coloureds were not able to access British archival records. However, in the present these records are accessible, and coloureds have been able to retrieve and piece together their family histories through birth and death certificates, letters, wills and other such documentation relating to their British ancestors.

Conclusion

The fundamentals of the coloured phenomenon in Zambia are its 'Britishness', 'recentness' and 'separateness'. Zambian coloured people identify themselves in these terms primarily because of the commonality of their origins. They were born in Zambia as the descendants of colonial white men and African women. In colonial Zambia, coloureds lived as coloureds among coloureds – people like themselves – of African, Asiatic and European descent who shared their predicament of social alienation. The legacies of Anglo-Africans' colonial experience are their cultural displacement, migration and diaspora. In the Zambian context, the diasporic and return migration features further complicate colouredness. However, these two features are important in understanding the distinctiveness of the coloured experience in Zambia. Diaspora, in particular, deepens the complications and entanglements of colouredness in Zambia, wherein coloured is both white and not white. The visibility of whiteness, and particularly white genealogies of British ancestors, has currency for Anglo-Africans in Zambia. It enables them to 'return' to their 'imagined' homeland of Great Britain. Coloureds' return migration to Britain is partly a cultural repossession; it is a reclamation by those who have been culturally displaced and the creation of a coherent story of their Zambian past. More than a century after the onset of British colonisation, it has been estimated that as much as half of the total Zambian coloured population have retraced the footsteps of their British ancestors back to their 'imagined' homeland, Great Britain.

Endnotes

1   In loving memory of my father Japhet, my sister Alison, fondly remembered as 'Sukey', and my son Courtney. Mohamed Adhikari, my heartfelt thanks to you for your kindness, encouragement, extreme generosity, learned advice and friendship. Since a large part of this work is an outcome of my honours research project, a personal thank you to my BA (Hons) supervisors Belinda McKay and Fiona Paisley. For reading various drafts of this paper and for their encouragement and insightful advice I thank my present principal PhD supervisor Fiona Paisley, associate PhD supervisors Paul Turnbull and Sally Rickson, and my former PhD supervisor Felicity Grace. Many people shared their wonderful personal and family stories with me and I thank them all – in particular Mavis Burt, Caroline Goetzee, Judy Ethel Goddard, Elizabeth Robertson, Colin Kinghorn, Eric Wightman, Harry Sillitoe and Aaron Milner. In this regard I am particularly indebted to my late grandmother Eliza Maria Broomfield, and my dearest mother Nellie Milner. I thank my darling husband Bob for his continual love and support, and my children Lyle, Dianne, Lavinia (who is my sister and adopted daughter), Greg, Cameron and Dion, and my dearest son Courtney, who is no longer with me but whose memory lives on in my heart. Last but not least, I thank the rest of my family, the coloured community of Zambia, and the Zambian Anglo-African diaspora in the UK and wherever else I have met fellow Zambians.

2   Brelsford W. 1965. *Generations of Men: The European Pioneers of Northern Rhodesia*. Salisbury, Southern Rhodesia: Stuart Manning, 77; Dotson F & Dotson L. 1963. 'Indians and coloureds in Rhodesia and Nyasaland'. *Race*, 5, no. 1, 61–75.

3   Republic of Zambia. 2000. *2000 Census of Population and Housing*. Lusaka: Central Statistical Office, 57; Central Statistical Office of Zambia, http://www.zamstats.gov.zm/dload/cen.asp; Helen Rehin, deputy librarian, British Library for Development Studies, Brighton University, e-mail to author, 10 October 2006.

4   Muzondidya J. 2001. 'Sitting on the fence or walking the tightrope? A political history of the coloured community in Zimbabwe, 1945–1980'. PhD dissertation, University of Cape Town, 1; Janet Cooper, librarian, British Library for Development Studies, Brighton University, e-mail to author, 5 October 2006.

5   National Archives of Zambia, (hereafter NAZ), Status of Coloureds Committee (hereafter SEC1/581), T S Page to the Hon Secretary for Native Affairs, 24 September 1940.

6   See, for example, Sexton J. 1949. *The Half-Caste Problem: The Study of the Clash of Coloureds the World Over.* Adelaide: The Aborigines' Friends Association.

7   Haebich A. 2000. *Broken Circles: Fragmenting Indigenous Families 1800–2000.* Fremantle: Fremantle Arts Centre Press; Hyam R. 1991. *Empire and Sexuality: The British Experience.* Manchester: Manchester University Press; Mandaza I. 1997. *Race, Colour and Class in Southern Africa.* Harare: Sapes Books; Stoler A. 1999. *Carnal Knowledge and Imperial Power: Race and the Intimate in Colonial Rule.* Berkeley: University of California Press; Dotson & Dotson, 'Indians and coloureds in Rhodesia'.

8   Probyn F. 2003. 'The white father: denial, paternalism and community'. *Cultural Studies Review*, 9, no. 1, 63.

9   Probyn, 'White father', 63.

10   Russell C. 1999. *Experimental Ethnography.* Durham: Duke University Press, 276; see also Wallace M. 2004. *Dark Designs and Visual Culture.* Durham: Duke University Press, 4.

11   Pratt M. 1992. *Imperial Eyes: Travel Writing and Transculturation.* London: Routledge, 7.

12   Broomfield S. 1931. *Kachalola or the Mighty Hunter: The Early Life and Adventures of Sidney Spencer Broomfield.* New York: William Morrow.

13   Copy (in the possession of the author) of the last will and testament of Sidney Spencer Broomfield, 18 October 1930, Queensland Public Curator, Brisbane.

14   As far as my mother, her siblings and cousins, and their children and grandchildren are aware, they are the only surviving descendants of Broomfield. To date we have been unable to ascertain who, as Brelsford alleges, Broomfield's 'thirty-six half-caste children' or their African mothers were. See Brelsford, *Generation of Men*, 70.

15   Broomfield, *Kachalola*, 1, 299, 300; *Courier-Mail*, 26 October 1933; death certificate, Sidney Spencer Broomfield, 24 October 1933 (Register of Deaths, General Registry Office, Brisbane).

16   Broomfield, *Kachalola*, 3, 5.

17   Brelsford, *Generations of Men*, 65.

18   Mavis Burt, personal communication, 20 April 2003.

19   John Spiller, administrator of Toowong Cemetery, in personal communication to Juliette Milner-Thornton, 9 October 2000.

20   Broomfield, *Kachalola*, 154.

21   Brelsford, *Generations of Men*, 77.

22   Broomfield, *Kachalola*, 154; Brelsford, *Generations of Men*, 75–77; Caroline Goetzee, e-mail message to author, 18 January 2005.

23   Hyam, *Empire and Sexuality*, 89–91.

24   Brelsford, *Generations of Men*, 66, 70. Stephen Broomfield's children changed their surname from Broomfield to Bloomfield in the late 1950s while they were students at St John's School in Salisbury, Southern Rhodesia. Their fellow coloured students had relentlessly teased them about their surname 'Broomfield', saying it meant 'a field filled with brooms'. The family decided that the only way to stop the teasing was to change their surname to Bloomfield.

25 Broomfield, *Kachalola*, 18, 80–83.

26 Broomfield, *Kachalola*, 82; Dotson & Dotson, 'Indians and coloureds in Rhodesia', 61–75.

27 Broomfield, *Kachalola*, 18, 81–82; Brelsford, *Generations of Men*, 120; Gann L & Duignan P. 1978. *The Rulers of British Colonial Africa: 1870–1914*. Stanford: Stanford University Press, 226; Gelfand M. 1961. *Northern Rhodesia: In the Days of Charter*. Oxford: Basil Blackwell, 187, 240; http://www.kent-police-museum.co.uak/core_pages/pasttimes_early_days.

28 Gann & Duignan, *Rulers of British Africa*, 226.

29 Hansen K. 1989. *Distant Companions: Servants and Employers in Zambia, 1900–1985*. Ithaca: Cornell University Press, 87–89; Gann & Duignan, *Rulers of British Africa*, 242.

30 Joseph Milner, death notice, 13 March 1939 (in possession of the author).

31 Aaron Milner, interviewed by Juliette Milner-Thornton, 9 August 2003.

32 Macmillan H & Shapiro F. 1999. *Zion in Africa: The Jews of Zambia*. London: I B Tauris, 246.

33 NAZ, SEC1/581, Edwardes-Jordan to Creech-Jones (nd). Indications are that this letter was written sometime between 1946 and 1947.

34 Mason P. 1955. *The Birth of a Dilemma: The Conquest and Settlement of Rhodesia*. London: Oxford University Press, 240, 241.

35 Dotson & Dotson, 'Indians and coloureds in Rhodesia', 65.

36 Broomfield, *Kachalola*, 81.

37 E G, interviewed by Juliette Milner-Thornton, 6 April 2005.

38 For a discussion of traditional African marriage in Northern Rhodesia, see Chanock M. 1998. *Law, Custom and Social Order: The Colonial Experience in Malawi and Zambia*. Portsmouth: Heinemann, 192–216; and Rukavina K. 1950. *Jungle Pathfinder: Central Africa's Most Fabulous Adventurer*. New York: Exposition Press, 60, 61. For the practice and social obligations of lobola in South African society, see Ngubane H. 1987. 'The consequences for women of marriage payments in a society with patrilineal descent', in *Transformations of African Marriage*, eds D Parkin & D Nyamwaya. Manchester: Manchester University Press, 173–182.

39 NAZ, SEC1/581, Page to Secretary for Native Affairs, 24 September 1940, 2. My grandfather Stephen Broomfield's passport indicates that he was classified as a British Protected Person, the same status as his African mother. Stephen Broomfield, Northern Rhodesian Passport no. 16138, 1954 (in possession of the author).

40 Kaunda K. 1962. *Zambia Shall Be Free*. London: Heinemann, 158.

41 NAZ, SEC1/576, 'Education of coloured children general', Mr John B Clark, the Director of European Education, Mazabuka to Chief Secretary Lusaka, 19 July 1937.

42 NAZ SEC1/575. See also Ellinghaus K. 2006. *Taking Assimilation to Heart: Marriages of White Women and Indigenous Men in the United States of America and Australia 1887–1937*. London, University of Nebraska Press, xvii.

43 NAZ SEC1/575; Africa Studies Centre, Leiden University, Leiden, the Netherlands, ASC Afrika ke-301.185.12 (689.4), *Northern Rhodesia Report of the Committee to Inquire into the Status and Welfare of Coloured Persons in Northern Rhodesia, 1950*. Lusaka: Government Printer. Former colonial officials who did this include Messrs H S Thornicroft, R A Osborne and L W Gardner.

44 Hansen, *Distant Companions*, 91.

45 Personal communication with E G, April 2003, and Eric Wightman, July 2005.

46 Grotpeter J. 1979. *Historical Dictionary of Zambia*. London: Scarecrow Press, 76.

47 E G, personal communication, 27 June 2003.

48 The *Northern Rhodesian Journal* was published from 1950 to 1965. Journal articles were written by colonists, and were historical and anecdotal in nature.

49 Brelsford, *Generations of Men*, 77; Gelfand, *Northern Rhodesia*, 187, 240.

50 Elizabeth Robertson, interviewed by Juliette Milner-Thornton, 23 July 2003.

51 Mandaza, *Race, Colour and Class*, 392.

52 NAZ SEC1/581, 46/2, Page to Secretary for Native Affairs, 24 September 1940, 1.

53 E G, interviewed 16 August 2006; e-mail from Colin Kinghorn, 16 August 2006. The abandonment of African women and their coloured children was known locally as being 'dumped'.

54 NAZ, SEC1/581, 46/2, Page to Secretary for Native Affairs, 24 September 1940, 3–4.

55 NAZ, SEC1/581, 46/2, Page to Secretary for Native Affairs, 24 September 1940, 3–4.

56 NAZ, SEC1/3 278, *Report of The Land Commission on the North Charterland Concession Area*, 1942, 12, 13.

57 NAZ, SEC1/3 278, 12, 13; NAZ, SEC1/1 582, *General Questions Affecting Coloured People*, 30 August 1942, 12.

58 Fanon F. 1967. *Black Skins, White Masks*. New York: Grove Press, 18.

59 It is important to note that the current generations of Zambian coloureds – the fourth and fifth generations since initial sexual contact between Africans and Europeans – are rejecting the earlier ideology with which their ancestors grew up. They choose instead to re-establish a relationship with Africa and their Africanness, and it is now common practice for coloureds to marry into the African community.

60 Personal communication, Elizabeth Robertson, 23 July 2003; NAZ, SEC1/3 278, *Land Commission*, 12, 13. Elizabeth's father, retired British army officer Captain Robertson, was one of the white settlers who was commissioned by Sir John Waddington in 1942 to investigate land policy in Northern Rhodesia.

61 Gunther J. 1955. *Inside Africa*. London: Hamish Hamilton, 617–619.

62 Nellie Milner, personal communication, 23 February, 2003; NAZ, SEC1/3 278, *Land Commission*, 6.

63 NAZ SEC1/581, 46/1; 46/2.

64 NAZ SEC1/581, 46/1; 46/2.

65 Morley D & Chen K (eds). *Stuart Hall: Critical Dialogues in Cultural Studies*. London: Routledge, 448.

66 Morley & Chen, *Stuart Hall*, 443.

67 See Ifekwunigwe J (ed). 2004. *Mixed Race Studies: A Reader*. London: Routledge, xix, xx.

68 'Right of abode', British Home office: http://bhc.britaus.net/uploadedFiles/Visas/VAF4.pdf

'A generous dream, but difficult to realize': the making of the Anglo-African community of Nyasaland, 1929–1940

BY

CHRISTOPHER J LEE

UNIVERSITY OF NORTH CAROLINA, CHAPEL HILL

In April 1929, an unremarkable man – a local entrepreneur and defendant in a minor lawsuit – entered the High Court of Nyasaland and made a remarkable gesture. The son of an Indian immigrant and an African woman, Suleman Abdul Karim declared that he was a 'non-native' and that he should consequently be tried as such. The lawsuit brought against him by one Ernest Carr of Blantyre, Nyasaland, concerned the ownership of a Ford truck, for which he had failed to complete payment. Why he claimed this status is a mystery. Had he declared himself a 'native', Carr would most likely have been deemed guilty of transgressing the Credit Trade with Natives Ordinance of 1926, which restricted commercial loans and business transactions between European settlers and native Africans. The case would therefore likely have been rescinded with Carr perceived at fault under the law. Nevertheless, the court decided to accept Karim's claim despite the legal jeopardy under which it placed him. During his review, Judge Haythorne Reed accepted Karim as qualifying for 'non-native' status, given his 'non-native' paternal line of descent. The court case proceeded, and Karim was found guilty as charged.[1]

As a result of this ruling, the first meeting of what was to become the Anglo-African Association of Nyasaland was held in Limbe, a town neighbouring the commercial centre of Blantyre, on 28 July 1929.[2] Present were 19 men. As cited in the meeting minutes, the Association was created 'at the suggestion of the Blantyre District Commissioner' who mentioned that due to the *Carr versus Karim* ruling, 'our status was entirely changed'. Thomas Merry, secretary at the meeting, remarked that there were also

> [C]lauses in already existing Ordinances which would now apply to us, and certain of them may prove a hardship to parts of the community and some possibly an advantage and that the only way to overcome this difficulty would be to form an Association and select a capable Committee and meet the Provincial Commissioner and the District Commissioner.[3]

Motivated by the possibility of social advancement, this association attempted to define a new community unique to the colonial period.[4]

Because the area had only been colonised in the 1890s, the Anglo-African community of Nyasaland during the 1930s, for the most part, consisted of first-generation persons of 'mixed' racial descent.[5] This is reflected in their preference of the term 'Anglo-African' over 'coloured' and 'half-caste'. Although all three were used, 'Anglo-African' had the advantage of emphasising their partial descent from colonists. Not having the density of white settlement that characterised South Africa or Zimbabwe, the total size of Nyasaland's coloured population was commensurately small.[6] The European population of Nyasaland in 1931 numbered 1 975, the Indian population 1 591, and in 1934 the Anglo-African community numbered 1 202. On the other hand, the total African population was estimated at 1 599 888. This meant that the European and Anglo-African communities were respectively 0.12 and 0.07 per cent of the Protectorate's total population.[7] Nevertheless, Anglo-Africans comprised nearly a quarter of the total non-African population during the early 1930s. Their claim to separate status therefore was not insignificant.[8] Prior to the founding of the Association, it is difficult to determine with accuracy the size and character of the community. Beyond the conjecture that a semblance of 'group-ness', if not self-conscious community, existed beforehand, its contingent origins based on interracial relationships undermine any simple assumptions about its early history.[9]

This chapter is therefore concerned with the foundation and early challenges of the Anglo-African community of Nyasaland during the

1930s, before its activities and interests were transformed by changes ushered in by World War II. Questions of identity and status are explored with specific attention to the discursive manifestations of Anglo-African identity formation. Being a colonial subculture, the archival source base for such historical retrieval is limited, but not without local or comparative historical value. Indeed, a central contention of this chapter is the significance of such marginal communities and their complex, if historically nascent, intellectual traditions. Although 'Anglo-African' was the predominant term that people of 'mixed' racial descent used to refer to themselves in Nyasaland, the opportunities and challenges they faced as a group is indicative of broader patterns of coloured historical experience in southern Africa during this period, an experience characterised by a desire for racial equality with whites.[10] At the same time, the Nyasaland case also points to differences in how conventional notions of coloured identity, predicated largely on case studies from South Africa, might be reconsidered vis-à-vis Anglo-African conceptions of identity. In sum, the central concern of this chapter is to outline local rationales of self-understanding against this regional backdrop.[11]

The issue of separate education was of particular importance to the community during this period. To the Association, education not only offered the chance of economic betterment but also held out the possibility of eventual social equality with colonists. This emphasis is consequently significant in two key ways. Firstly, it firmly situates the making of Anglo-African identity within its era. In the 1920s and 1930s, Nyasaland was generally characterised by a colonial public sphere rich in aspirations towards forms of Western modernity, of which education was an element of central importance. The Anglo-African community of Nyasaland needs to be considered within this broader social milieu. Secondly, education also marks a significant point of thematic comparison with coloured communities within the region.[12] Such contextual and thematic elements underscore the coexistence of distinct variables for comparative analysis across the sub-continent.

Taken together, then, this chapter aims to walk a line between regional comparison and the specifics of local difference.[13] It is important to recognise that Anglo-African identity was discussed and debated on several fronts: by the colonial state, African officials, as well as the Anglo-African Association. A general conclusion of this chapter is that social identities must be understood as intersections of contending perspectives and interests.[14] In contrast to pre-existing approaches to identity in

Africa's historiography that have centred on notions of primordialism, instrumentalism or social constructionism, the contention here is that identities neither originate with state policies and action, nor are they entirely under the control of those who espouse them.[15] They do not 'belong' to any single entity or community. Rather, identities operate in contextually specific ways, existing between social structures and historical actors, rather than being located within, or in the possession of, one or the other. Their momentary meaning is consequently dependent on local contingencies of power and definition. Accounting for such conditions and the social practices and processes that create them is an important part of the historian's task. At the broadest level, this chapter proposes this revised approach of possession and dispossession to historicising identity formation, not only among coloured communities, but other ethnic and racial communities throughout the continent.[16]

Race, kinship and politics in a colonial subculture

The identity politics initiated by the Anglo-African Association during the 1930s had an impact at a number of levels. It became as much an administrative question of 'native' status in British Central and East Africa as it was a matter of individual self-reflection to members of the Association. Despite the High Court's initial emphasis on origin, defining the general category of 'native' or the more local identity of 'Anglo-African' were not simple tasks. The matter of separate education, which became a central concern of the Association, was an extension of these broader questions of identity and classification, and proved to be as intractable. Both issues became closely linked in the minds of government officials and African authorities, and particularly members of the Anglo-African Association.

Although the Anglo-African population was very small, institutional separation would complicate an ethnically based system of governance that was then being established through indirect rule. Indeed, it is important to note that the Association arose at a time when the colonial state, in consonance with British administrative practices elsewhere on the continent, was pursuing an ethnic, rather than a racial, option for rule. Though never entirely successful, this policy sought to avoid the perception of British colonial rule as racist. Instead, indirect rule proposed a 'dual mandate' of common interests and shared administrative tasks between British and African officials, thus mitigating the appearance of racial dominance.[17]

The Association's quest for racial privilege aggravated local colonial anxiety about racial tensions that had manifested themselves through the Chilembwe Uprising of 1915. Though short-lived, this revolt, led by John Chilembwe and his independent church movement, viewed British colonial rule as unjust and sought to end it.[18] Moving away from nakedly racist policies had therefore been an aim of the Nyasaland government ever since. In reference to this agenda, A T Lacey, director of education, argued in 1933 that he was not prepared to make any definite proposals on the matter of separate education since 'the whole question of the legal status of half castes bristles with difficulties'.[19] Until the question of status had been settled by the British Colonial Office, establishing separate education for Anglo-Africans would be premature and could be subversive to general policies of 'native' development under the British Dual Mandate. However, the need for separate education from the perspective of Anglo-Africans was entirely clear, as the community was growing and, in their view, formed a distinct and permanent stratum within the population. In the words of the Association: 'We are British Subjects and Citizens, and not mere non-natives … The marriages between non-natives and the black women, illegal as they may be, are bound to continue and increase, the number of the Anglo-Africans is also bound for certain to grow larger and larger as the years go along'.[20]

The main predicament of the Anglo-African community was therefore how to position itself in a context that was both racially and ethnically defined. The colonial state and African authorities alike wished to avoid the appearance of racial privilege, whereas members of the Association viewed their paternal kinship ties to colonists as a key advantage in the competition for limited social resources. This sense of connection in turn gave them a strong sense of entitlement. The upshot was that they found their racialised kinship background to offer a palpable advantage and strategy but one that was also limited given the context of indirect rule in Nyasaland. These competing perspectives on colonial priorities, African power, and senses of self and belonging help to illuminate the multifaceted processes of identification within this community.[21]

More broadly, the Anglo-African community of Nyasaland also demonstrates the contingencies and improvisations that mark racial and identity formation in marginal communities. As pointed out in recent scholarship in anthropology and cultural studies, marginal locations and subcultures are significant sites for such novelty, precisely because they are beyond the hegemony of mainstream patterns and practices.[22] Analytic significance and historical meaning therefore should not be dependent or measured by conventional notions of 'margin' and 'centre'. Rather, such locations should be reflected upon critically, with marginal sites and status embraced, not disparaged, which in most cases only serve to reproduce the problem of 'marginality'. Given their location and size, Nyasaland and its Anglo-African community readily fit into such an interpretive paradigm. The use of such a framework also enables a comparative dialogue to take place. Recent work on South Africa, for example, has used creolisation theory to understand coloured marginality and identity, though with little detail on the context, means and history of the process.[23] This chapter investigates such processes of creolisation – how a first-generation, racially 'mixed' community employed different resources and rationales to assert a hybridised identity. These demographic and spatial dimensions are therefore fundamental to understanding the shaping of Anglo-African identity in Nyasaland and help expand methodological possibilities for explaining the production of new social knowledge and identities in such spaces.[24]

From an imperial standpoint, the question of definition raised by the Reed ruling eventually took on a regional dimension, with Nyasaland officials looking to the experience and policies of neighbouring British colonies to inform their thinking. The significance of such discussion is that it points to the ambiguities of state power vis-à-vis coloured identity. Through their complex genealogical origins, coloured individuals and communities complicated existing views and policies that centred on racially pure notions of 'native' and 'non-native' status. Conventional colonial visions of rule were therefore interrupted and rendered illegible, if to a limited degree, by such subcultural formations.[25] This attribution of ambiguity to colonial states contrasts with conventional interpretations that have more often assigned ambiguity to coloured communities and their behaviour. The uncertainty of state policy during the 1930s allowed a degree of legal and social manoeuvrability for the Anglo-African Association and the community it represented. It created a discursive space for Anglo-African identity to insert itself into Nyasaland's broader civil society. The interwar years are consequently crucial for understanding the opportunities and challenges facing its establishment.[26]

To understand the place and predicament of the Anglo-African community during the 1930s, it is equally important to situate their interests and tactics within the broader social landscape of Nyasaland. As in other parts of the continent, a number of elite 'native' associations had emerged in Nyasaland since the early 1920s, their membership consisting mainly of mission-educated Africans. The concerns of these associations were primarily accommodationist in scope, seeking to revise rather than overthrow existing colonial policies, in sharp contrast with the armed struggle led by John Chilembwe. The history of the Anglo-African Association forms part of this civil activism.[27]

Like competing organisations, the Anglo-African Association sought certain privileges for its constituency through dialogue with the state. This strategy, more often than not, included written petitions, the submission of meeting minutes and transcribed speeches to government departments, as well as direct encounters with colonial officials. Such dialogue points to the interactive nature of Anglo-African identity formation from its inception. Minutes from the inaugural meeting of the Association, for example, were sent to the commissioner of the Southern Province within the Nyasaland government for consideration. This document stressed that:

> [T]he most important question above all was that of establishing our status ... [W]e humbly appeal to the Government that when framing any Ordinances concerning our community, especially with regard to our status, to kindly avoid, as far as possible, the scourge with which we have been initiated, namely, the term, 'HALF-CASTE'.

The Association further argued that there were 'millions of similar people' like them 'domiciled in various countries' and that the term 'half-caste' did not offer 'any compliment'. They wanted to 'replace this painful designation with something more appreciative' and felt it would help in establishing a 'kindly relationship with all sections of the communities of this country'. The other issues raised in their petition included welfare and education for children, taxation, higher wages and a census of the Anglo-African population.[28]

Initial government response at the district level expressed interest and support for the Association. 'In my opinion all their requests are reasonable. I believe that the formation of an Anglo-African Society would be useful', wrote one local official. He also noted that Anglo-Africans were 'not popular amongst the natives from whom they keep aloof and circumstances have cut them off from Europeans'. They were, however, 'very loyal to the British Government' and wanted 'to raise themselves and prove worthy of the citizenship they have inherited'. In his view, such a 'clean, law abiding, respectful community' deserved government attention and legislative consideration as 'a separate class'.[29] This early enthusiasm did not last, however. A brief handwritten note from the colonial secretary to the attorney general commented, 'I think this is likely to be a very difficult problem'.[30] This perspective proved prescient as debate over what to do about the Association's requests was to extend to the end of the 1930s.

Such official concerns did not deter local agency and voices. Ongoing ambivalence within the Nyasaland administration towards the Anglo-African community during this period created the space for Anglo-African interests to be expressed and the identity to be further entrenched. Separate education was of particular importance to the Association as it was regarded as necessary to the social advancement of the community. Anglo-Africans were not the only ones seeking such mobility through education, as other African communities in Nyasaland held similar aspirations. This competition only spurred the Anglo-African Association into striving even harder to achieve its goals.

The situation took on a particular urgency for the Anglo-African Association after 1933, the year that the Native Authority Ordinance and Native Courts Ordinance were promulgated. Both entrenched African interests within the system of indirect rule, thus representing their ongoing marginalisation in the eyes of Anglo-Africans. However, the passing of these ordinances was consistent with government policy of appeasing Africans after the Chilembwe Uprising. This historical moment also points to a key distinction between the situations in Nyasaland and South Africa. Anglo-Africans initially did not occupy a stable middle position within the racial hierarchy but were marginal to black and white interests alike. It is this subsidiary social position that further qualifies the community as a colonial subculture – what Ken Gelder characterises as a culture that is 'non-normative and/or marginal through [its] particular interests and practices'.[31] The passing of these ordinances did not dispel the Association's aspirations. Rather, they provided further impetus to their assertiveness. Two such instances, the first in 1933, the second in 1934, and both involving the drive for separate education, will be used to demonstrate the ways in which Anglo-African identity developed through a local process of creolisation.

Articulations of Anglo-African identity

On the morning of 30 July 1933, the Anglo-African Association held a meeting in Limbe to discuss ways of advancing the social interests of the community. They took as their guiding principle a statement made by then governor of Nyasaland, Sir Shenton Thomas, at a meeting held two years earlier on 13 July 1931 at which he stated that their community 'should be given every chance, opportunity and encouragement for their development'. There was agreement that this had not held true during the previous two years, particularly after Thomas's departure for the Gold Coast in 1932 and with the local economy hit hard by global depression. James Jamieson, a member in attendance, said his application for a job to the Agricultural Department was unsuccessful and claimed that little had been done by the government to recruit Anglo-Africans. It was recommended that the Association compile a list of unemployed to be circulated among district commissioners for any vacancies that might exist. They reiterated the opinion of the Secretary of State for the colonies that they should be given 'equal chances in life'.[32]

Closely connected to this short-term concern about employment was the issue of separate education. Henry Ascroft, a vocal member of the Association, argued that in light of Thomas's earlier statement, this matter be raised again.[33] With education a vital dimension of community development, two further meetings were proposed for 17 September and 1 October 1933.[34] Prior to the second meeting, Ascroft learnt from the head of the Blantyre Mission School, his alma mater, that education for the community was 'a general topic amongst the high Government Officials'. It was a matter being taken seriously, and the director of education for the protectorate was familiar with their concerns. With this encouragement, Ascroft made a speech to the Association at the October meeting entitled 'Education for the Anglo-Africans: a brief outline on education as a result of a meeting with His Excellency Sir Thomas in 1931'.[35] Ascroft's speech is important for the complex sets of connections it reveals regarding education, paternal responsibility and community development. Its argument that situated Anglo-African education in a context of identity claims, kinship and race evinces a sensibility that extended beyond the immediate issue at hand. It thus provides crucial insight into the social parameters and rationales that underpinned local notions of Anglo-African identity.

Ascroft began by emphasising the importance of education, and underscoring Anglo-African entitlement to separate education through notions of paternal responsibility. The Association had asked 'to make it compulsory that every non-native father-parent should deposit a certain sum of money with the Authorities ... to be used for fees for the child's elementary education'. With this funding, the Association believed 'there would be nothing more to worry about the child because at least there was something with which the child would secure his or her preliminary education; the father of any such child would then be free'. Governor Thomas, however, did not think this could be legally justified since in Great Britain such children could only make claims through affiliation laws, statutes that were not applicable in Nyasaland. Ascroft's response was to broaden the realm of paternal responsibility from strictly legal to more familial norms that, in metaphorical fashion, included the colonial state itself. 'The Government will find its way to the accomplishment of their duty to a people who so much need education for the means of their existence and comfort in this world,' he stated. 'It is the Government's charge and not the fathers' alone in every sense.' In this way, the failure of individuals to meet their paternal responsibilities was transferred onto the British colonial administration.[36]

With these personal and metaphorical kinship connections as a backdrop, the main argument of Ascroft's speech was that Anglo-Africans were fundamentally different from 'native' Africans. Ascroft hinged such claims not only on kinship but on what he perceived to be the general aims of colonial policy, namely the cultivation of loyalty among subjects. In his view, their intrinsic non-native status made it 'dishonest of any person so engaged to recommend our being educated together with natives for an indefinite period'. With rhetoric that was often infused with a racist tone, he justified this approach through personal experience: 'When later on the Anglo-african finds out the difference between him and his native classmates he is scorned, mocked, and abused in such a way that he never forgets until there is some suitable counteraction sooner or later'. He further asserted that their sense of inferiority towards African and white communities alike would inevitably be passed down to the next generation and would be intensified by 'mixed' education if a solution were not implemented. Ascroft closed his speech by emphasising their kinship with European colonists:

> We are children of non-natives; our thinking, living, [and] social life ... take after our fathers. We shall always stand by them and be of service to them. It is for this reason that Government should give us education to shape us into a respectable race and form us into useful citizens of the Government and the British Empire to which unhesitatingly we belong. If we are taught to know ourselves and what we should do there shall

be lacking no response on our side because we know what we are and what we owe the Government.

He also requested that a census and an assessment of the social conditions of the Anglo-African community in the Protectorate be taken.[37]

While agreeing that education was important, there were some sceptical voices in the Association. One member raised the case of South Africa, where there was separate education but 'there were some who [still] could not even get a job because of their colour'. He agreed there should be separate schools for Anglo-Africans, but felt 'there was no way of getting out of the fact that he was a Coloured man and that the same thing which affected the Coloured people in the South might become applicable in this country and that when the Coloured man failed to satisfy his ambition he became worried'. While Ascroft sympathised with such opinions, he re-emphasised that lack of education would be 'the end of our Community'.

Another opinion expressed was that separate education was necessary for circumventing the threat of Africanisation. A Mr King, for example, was 'very much grieved to see our people who lived in the villages drinking native beer, dancing with natives with only a blanket or a single cloth tied round their waists or hung over their shoulders ... and eating whatever the primitive native ate'. Their condition was 'intolerable and would only make one weep ... if these people had been brought up in a proper elementary school they would be of great service to the Government and would constitute a united Anglo-african Community'. Their kinship to colonists and the responsibility of the state entitled them to such education.[38]

Although copies of these meeting minutes were sent to the commissioner of the Southern Province and the governor himself as a petition for their cause, the government did not respond promptly to the claims made by the Association. The official view was that the legal status of 'mixed' race people was still under consideration for the east African colonies. The state could not make any formal policy decisions until this basic question was resolved. However, the temporary guiding principle was that 'no obstacle should be placed in the way of native half-castes being classed among members of a higher civilization where their standard and manner of life justified such classification'. It was also held that 'no obstacle should be raised to children, legitimate or illegitimate, of European or Indian fathers and native mothers being treated in accordance with the status of their fathers where they have been brought up in a manner suited to that status'. The government felt that this group was small and that there were 'comparatively few who would desire to be treated as other than natives' because the majority lived 'in exactly the same manner as natives', and it would be undesirable if these persons were prevented from 'taking their place in the life of a native village'. It was thus felt that 'any distinctive educational programme' would be 'premature' and potentially 'subversive of general policy'. These views were shared by missionary institutions in Nyasaland. 'Some people wish to make of the half caste children a middle class, between Europeans and African natives,' summarised one White Fathers missionary. 'This is a generous dream, but difficult to realize.'[39]

Negotiating modalities of race and kinship

It was not until mid-1934 that the government arrived at a clearer position on the issues raised by the Anglo-African Association. Though the Advisory Committee on Education viewed 'with great sympathy the plea of the Anglo-African Association with reference to children of mixed descent being "hidden in the villages"' and undertook 'to ensure that all such children have full opportunity of education', the official consensus was that 'there was no difference between the intellectual attainments of the African and the half-caste' and therefore no 'educational distinction should be made between them'. The Committee furthermore recommended that 'full consideration be given to the African point of view' regarding the issue, and concluded that any plan of separate education was 'undesirable'.[40]

Levi Mumba, the only African member of the advisory committee, provided the 'African point of view' as described in its report. Mumba's stance constitutes a meaningful contrast to both British and Anglo-African perspectives on the matter. Furthermore, his testimony confirms that Anglo-African identity rested at the intersection of three competing points of view, each of which had different rationales for the making or unmaking of this distinct identity.

Like colonial officials, Mumba considered the question of separate education for Anglo-Africans to be 'not only important but difficult and complex' because it entailed issues of racial privilege, separate legal status and novel notions of corporate belonging.[41] Mumba argued that the government should provide free elementary education to Africans and Anglo-Africans alike and supported its efforts in this regard. What he found problematic with the Association's request for separate education was that it was based on patrilineal lines of descent. He undermined its claims by asserting that a matrilineal kinship framework, as practised by African communities in the Nyasaland region, should also be applicable to Anglo-Africans.[42] Mumba recognised the tensions between this local corporate system and the aspirations of the Association. He saw the Association's claims not only as improvised but also as a form of cultural and racial subterfuge. The Association clearly identified more strongly with their British fathers than their African mothers, though not completely denying the latter. Their interstitial cultural position and first-generation status forced a creolised outlook and strategy upon Anglo-Africans, one shaped by their perceptions of social challenges and opportunities. Mumba also conceded that Anglo-Africans were not necessarily responsible for their predicament. He reasoned that they had access to educational facilities through mission schools, and believed that, should separate facilities be provided for them, their British fathers and not the government should bear the financial burden. Were the government to accede to the Association's request, it would in his view be guilty of 'wasting public revenue and for recognizing illegal miscegenation of races'.[43]

Mumba based his arguments on indigenous norms and practices and, like his British peers, embraced particular notions of protocol and cultural practice. For example, he contrasted situations of legitimacy and illegitimacy as conceived in Europe and Africa. In Europe, illegitimate children had no claim on their father even if social equality were attained through educational achievement. Similarly, he argued, '[i]n Africa among tribes who pay dowry the children belong to the father and have a claim on him. Among those who do not pay dowry, they belong to the mother and can [only] claim on the uncles'. With Anglo-Africans being, more often than not, 'the offspring of unions unauthorised by law, dowry, ankhoswe or other understanding', they should be considered under the guardianship of their African relatives, specifically their mothers' brothers or uncles. In terms of local customary law, Anglo-Africans were part of their African families, and their legal status thus needed to be determined by matrilineal lines of descent. To drive his point home, Mumba added that African families 'never grumbled when nursing or bringing them up, they care for them with a parental love which is lacking on the part of the civilized and rich father'.[44]

Mumba recognised the animosity to African values and culture inherent in the Association's position. In this regard, he perceived Anglo-Africans as not only ungrateful, but misguided. He described how many 'do not wish to see the sight of their mothers, much less that of their related uncles, for they think that if their identity is known it reduces their chance of passing as pure whitemen or Indians on account of their light colour and the father's name'. He also argued that Anglo-African claims to a new status were undermined by their diverse origins:

> They are not an independent race and the term Anglo African does not correctly describe them all, for it is not only the English who have children from African women. There are German, Italian, Portuguese, Indian, Greek, Arab and Somali halfcastes as well as Nyasaland African halfcastes (who are the children of African men and halfcaste women).

Mumba asserted that their desire for a separate status 'to avoid their growing among Africans in the villages and eating native food' was ultimately unrealistic. 'What force can unite all these diverse offspring into one solid mass when they are removed from the villages?' he asked. He was thus critical of the Association's use of race and kinship to try and set a 'civilization standard' since the community's paternal origins were so diverse. A higher standard of civilisation was the 'one avenue left through which they can push themselves up to higher positions and wages' though, as Mumba pointed out, this 'need not be a prerogative of any one single race'.[45] Mumba made it clear that their desire for education was 'reasonable and cannot be disputed', but that the request for separate education was not. Anglo-Africans in his eyes had no justification for claiming separate education for education should be available to all 'without distinction'.

In conclusion Mumba stated that Anglo-Africans were the 'children of wronged African women' who had carried the responsibility of raising them. He argued that:

> [t]hey may be non-natives but have no other home except as natives of Nyasaland. It would be a double wrong to the African woman, and no protection to the African race, if their halfcaste children are encouraged to look down on them by being given a higher educational status based on nothing except that they are the accidental children of some foreigner who is ashamed to own them.

He concluded that customary law which recognised matrilineal lines of descent should prevail in determining the status of Anglo-Africans:

In the absence of a law to the contrary the halfcaste child is bound to live with his mother and maternal uncles as hitherto and get his education together with other children. The removal of such a child from its African environment of village life is at present impracticable.[46]

Mumba's position is important not only for the cultural perspective he offers but also for the notions of cultural and racial purity evident in his thought.[47] The existence of such views and discourse within African society provides further evidence of the creolised nature of Anglo-African self-perception. If the Anglo-African Association spoke of patrilineal kinship and responsibility, Mumba drew upon an opposing local rationale for his position. These contrasts and tensions serve to locate the very site of creole identification processes in contestation over kinship norms and cultural practices. Mumba's interpretation shows that not only was Anglo-African identity the product of competing conceptualisations of corporate belonging, but also that African authorities and communities had a stake in maintaining control over such processes of identity formation. This concern over social and cultural boundaries served to reinforce pre-existing identities and local social relations of power.

The Anglo-African Association responded to Mumba's position with an extensive memorandum of its own, one frequently racist in tone. Their 1934 petition complained that their pleas for separate education were being 'criticised and attacked by a native instead of by a person of different status', and that no Anglo-Africans were given the opportunity to state their case to the committee. 'The fact that he is the first of the primitive stock to taste the blessings of European education was not considered,' lamented one member. The Association feared that Mumba's opinions would lead to:

… the doom of the whole halfcaste race of the country – [that] they must go down into the jaws of primitive life and its evil influences as if they were born by that inferior race alone without a drop of the blood of the advanced races in their veins.

The Association once again asserted their right, as descendants of European colonists, to privileged treatment. It claimed that they did not wish to be a burden to society but wanted to improve themselves and become useful citizens. They reasoned that free elementary education for the Anglo-African would lead to employment and enable him to follow the path established by his European forebears: 'for his fathers and forefathers, the Europeans, have led that very life and he must walk in their footsteps'.[48]

The Association furthermore rejected Mumba's claims that the matrilineal system nurtured Anglo-Africans for there was not one 'who has been educated by his "African uncle" who has reached any useful standard and who is now doing some work anywhere on such education and earning a decent salary'. In a similar vein, they did not see their petitions as an embarrassment to colonists or the Nyasaland government but as a matter of claiming their rightful inheritance which Mumba had no right to question:

> Who has found it embarrassing to do good to his own child, and why should an outside member or person or servant or slave be jealous and envious of the doings of a father to his child? Is it embarrassing for a prince to claim upon his blood father or his father's crown or kingdom? Will the king's servants and slaves have objections to his claims and will their objections be sound within the law?[49]

The petition further expressed concern that a decision had been reached before the question of status had been decided among the colonies of British East Africa. The Association consequently requested that their criticisms be sent on to the Colonial Office, in which it still held faith. They also expressed a desire to be allowed to participate in future policy making.[50]

In response, the Nyasaland administration shifted its position in October 1934, indicating that the question of Anglo-African status would be considered separately to matters of education, particularly since education was not under consideration at the east African governors' conference held that year. This change was intended to allow the administration to hold to its local policy of having a single education system for Africans and Anglo-Africans, whatever decision on the status of 'mixed' race people was reached.[51]

In the meantime, colonial officials in Nyasaland sought guidance on the status of Anglo-Africans from the policies implemented in neighbouring colonies, particularly Southern Rhodesia. Although the 1933 *Report of the Committee Appointed by the Government of Southern Rhodesia to Enquire into Questions Concerning the Education of Coloured and Half-caste Children in the Colony* was carefully reviewed by the director of education, it left several uncertainties as to how it might be applied in Nyasaland. The director, for example, perceived many of the recommendations for institutional improvement to be limited in nature and doubted that such institutions developed community identity and self-respect as the report claimed. He also expressed reservations about policy decisions that led to 'making distinctions, social and economic, between degrees of colour and race' where 'these distinctions must be more or less hard and fast'. The report in his view gave 'the idea of definite strata; below the African and the "African half-caste"; then the coloured and the "European" half-caste; then, though this is not quite so clear, the Indian; and then the European'. The appropriateness or utility of legislating for such a hierarchy in Nyasaland was not apparent to him.[52]

He concluded that there were fundamental differences between Southern Rhodesia and Nyasaland, largely centred on the density of white settlement. The education department in Nyasaland interpreted its own approach as one of 'bridging over' the gap between Africans and Europeans over time, not one of hardening racial distinctions and hierarchy. This policy did not take explicit account of Anglo-Africans, but neither did it exclude them. It did evince a concern for African interests, however. Segregation was not a priority for Nyasaland due to indirect rule being based on ethnic distinctions. The director of education felt that Anglo-African demands were out of step with this aspect of local policy, though they could be useful in the 'bridging over' process since they 'would and indeed do suggest that a bridge already exists in their comparative consanguinity'. He further concluded that 'the half-caste, no less than the African, shall, in Nyasaland, be accepted as eligible for any occupation for which he may prove himself to be fitted'.[53] Still, Southern Rhodesia's stark position only added to official uncertainty about how Anglo-Africans should be treated in Nyasaland. Uniformity of policy with the east African colonies was thus seen as 'the ultimate aim'.[54] However, regional considerations appeared only to complicate matters rather than simplify them.

Notwithstanding further petitions by the Anglo-African Association, the issues of separate education and acknowledgement of a privileged status for Anglo-Africans were rendered temporarily moribund a few years later with the advent of World War II, which put Nyasaland on a new trajectory towards political integration with Southern and Northern Rhodesia. As part of the Central African Federation, Anglo-Africans were placed in closer contact and dialogue with coloured communities in Southern and Northern Rhodesia between 1953 and 1963. Like the 1930s, this period provided an opportunity to stabilise and entrench the identity. By 1964, however, African nationalism had dissolved the Federation and undermined the salience of both 'Anglo-African' and 'coloured' as administrative or social identity categories. Today these terms have no legal or official standing, and their social currency, in terms of how people identify publicly, is greatly diminished. This is in large part due to the nationalist politics of Hastings Kamuzu Banda, who ruled Malawi from 1964 to 1994, during which he implemented an official policy of 'non-tribalism'.[55] In an interview conducted in 1999, Robert Jamieson, the nephew of James Jamieson, summarised his experience of the identity dating back to the 1950s in the following way: '[T]he term "Coloured" has been shifting considerably... There was a time when we were trying to get recognition as a people, as a separate entity, ... [though] during the thirty years of dictatorship our status was much reduced'.[56]

Despite having established an early foundation by the end of the 1930s and persisting in substantive form until independence, Anglo-African identity has had a tenuous existence since then because espousing a coloured rather than a Malawian identity has become a distinct liability. This contrast with the South African and Zimbabwean experiences emphasises the significance of local meanings of colouredness and again suggests fruitful ground for highlighting regional political contingencies and differences.

Conclusion

By the eve of World War II, the Anglo-African Association had failed in its efforts to secure an institutional foundation for its claim to 'non-native' status as determined by the Reed ruling. This failure was in part due to the administrative structure of indirect rule and the ethnically based, African-oriented priorities of the colonial government. Southern Rhodesia provides an example of how another colony with denser white settlement and a larger coloured community addressed the issue differently. Even there uncertainty existed about the benefits to be gained from separate education for the coloured grouping. The key point to be drawn from this comparison is that the interwar period constituted a time of transition throughout the region. Colonial policies under indirect rule were often contradictory, seeking to empower but within strict limitations. As illuminated by the struggles of the Anglo-African Association for separate education, even those social groups with the most collaborative of intentions met obstacles if they did not fit the agenda of the colonial state.

Though the Nyasaland government may have had the final word on the legal status of Anglo-Africans during this period, it is important not to hinge Anglo-African identity and welfare on this alone. Indeed, this chapter has pointed to the complex ways in which a distinct and durable Anglo-African identity was conceptualised and developed by members of the Association. An idiom of kinship intersected with race was used to situate the community between the racial and ethnic categories in place within Nyasaland society, and this hybrid identity was able to operate at multiple levels. It drew upon a sense of immediate familial history, and at the same time imparted a more broadly imagined sense of responsibility upon the colonial state for their welfare. Senses of loyalty and responsibility were invoked for both sides. These tactics also drew African perspectives into the discussion.

As Levi Mumba depicts, local idioms of kinship contrasted with the paternal approach used by the Association, evincing yet another layer of entanglement and meaning. Navigating such options demonstrates the kind of creole agency – drawing upon local and European cultural traditions of belonging – that Anglo-Africans had as a first-generation community building a new intellectual tradition and consciousness. And yet it also underscores the social limitations and competing perspectives involved in contestations over identity. As this example highlights, identities are rarely the product of a single origin or process, but instead represent an intersection of contending points of view, agencies and aspirations.

This case study also speaks to broader issues within Africa's historiography. Although a considerable amount of scholarship has been committed to understanding social and intellectual discourse about Africans as colonial subjects, a more recent complementary trend has examined the production of social, political and intellectual discourse by Africans.[57] To a large extent, such inquiry into the local production of social discourse is an extension of a longer-standing concern for recovering counter-narratives to Eurocentric histories through the use of African oral traditions and testimony.[58] Scholars who have studied such forms of discourse within African societies have been less concerned with their factual content and more attentive to their social utility and meaning. In short, recent work has argued that African voices should not necessarily be seen as a methodological means to an empirical end.

Instead, such testimony and its contours of inclusion and exclusion must be read as reflective and symptomatic of the modalities of power and identity transecting colonial and postcolonial social orders.

This chapter has similarly been framed within this broad concern for recovering the content, dimensions and meaning of local thought by offering an analysis of the political discourse expressed by the Anglo-African Association during the 1930s. Though small in size, this neglected community nevertheless provides a unique lens through which the local pathways and practices of racial discourse and coloured identity formation in southern Africa can be examined. There are limitations to the meaning that can be attributed to the organisational rhetoric discussed here, but it does provide significant insight into the ways Anglo-Africans conceptualised their position in Nyasaland's evolving colonial social order. Furthermore, given that the ideas embedded within its rhetoric drew from both African and European cultural realms with kinship suturing the two, this case study also helps to explain how concepts and categories of indigenous and Western knowledge were received and reconfigured at the local level by intellectuals, activists, and communities, even those considered marginal.[59] In sum, this case study points to the ways in which the concept of creolisation might be rendered more precise when applied to coloured identity. By extension, this essay has sought to elucidate the malleability and contingent social uses of 'coloured' as a category of identity and experience. Taken as a whole, the discursive production and interaction described here reveal the contingent and complex identification processes that were inaugurated and shaped by colonialism, events that demonstrate the intellectual and political creativity of local actors who at times entangled the colonial state in matters it wished to avoid.

Endnotes

1   Malawian National Archives (hereafter MNA), Judicial Record Collection, J5/2/73, 46.
2   Limbe is a commercial centre where Europeans, Indians and Anglo-Africans conducted business. The two towns are virtually conjoined today.
3   MNA, Native Secretariat (hereafter NS), 1/3/2, Folio 1, 1.
4   For a detailed discussion of these two moments and a general account of the community, see Lee C. 2003. 'Colonial kinships: the British dual mandate, Anglo-African status, and the politics of race and ethnicity in inter-war Nyasaland, 1915–1939'. PhD dissertation, Stanford University. For a more specific focus on the regional impact of the Reed ruling, see Lee C. 2005. 'The "Native" undefined: colonial categories, Anglo-African status and the politics of kinship in British Central Africa, 1929–1938'. *Journal of African History*, 46, no. 3, 455–478.

5   Europeans had traded and settled in the broader region, particularly the Zambezi River valley, as early as the 16th century, though such intrusions were small in scope. See Isaacman A. 1972. *Mozambique: The Africanization of a European Institution – The Zambezi Prazos, 1750–1902.* Madison: University of Wisconsin Press, chs 1–4, 7.

6   On black–white sexual relationships in Zimbabwe, see, for example, Kennedy D. 1987. *Islands of White: Settler Society and Culture in Kenya and Southern Rhodesia, 1890–1939.* Durham: Duke University Press; and McCulloch J. 2000. *Black Peril, White Virtue: Sexual Crime in Southern Rhodesia, 1902–1935.* Bloomington: Indiana University Press.

7   On the size of the Anglo-African community see MNA, Secretariat Files (hereafter s) 1/705¹/30, Folio 27, 4 January 1934. On population figures for the European, Indian and African communities, see the *Nyasaland Protectorate Census.* 1931. Zomba: Government Printer.

8   The Anglo-African community would over time decline significantly as a proportion of the national and especially the non-African populations. The 1962 census, the last before independence, estimated the community at 2 900 persons, the European community at 9 400, the Indian community at 11 300 and the African population at 2 960 000. See *Nyasaland: Report for the Year 1962.* 1964. London: Her Majesty's Stationery Office, 25.

9   The expression 'group-ness' is from Cooper F & Brubaker R. 2000. 'Beyond identity'. *Theory and Society,* 29, 19–21.

10   See, for example, Adhikari M. 2005. *Not White Enough, Not Black Enough: Racial Identity in the South African Coloured Community.* Athens: Ohio University Press; and Muzondidya J. 2005. *Walking a Tightrope: Towards a Social History of the Coloured People of Zimbabwe.* Trenton: Africa World Press.

11   For South Africa, see Adhikari, *Not White Enough;* Erasmus Z (ed). 2001. *Coloured by History, Shaped by Place: New Perspectives on Coloured Identity in Cape Town.* Cape Town: Kwela Books; Farred G. 1999. *Midfielder's Moment: Coloured Literature and Culture in Contemporary South Africa.* Boulder: Westview Press; Lewis G. 1987. *Between the Wire and the Wall: A History of South African 'Coloured' Politics.* Cape Town: David Philip; Goldin I. 1987. *Making Race: The Politics and Economics of Coloured Identity in South Africa.* Cape Town: Longman; Van der Ross R. 1986. *The Rise and Decline of Apartheid: A Study of Political Movements among the Coloured People of South Africa, 1880–1985.* Cape Town: Tafelberg; and February V. 1981. *Mind Your Colour: The 'Coloured' Stereotype in South African Literature.* London: Routledge & Kegan Paul.

12   On Western education and the discourse of 'civilization' and 'modernity' in Africa during this period, see, for example, Ranger T. 1965. 'African attempts to control education in East and Central Africa, 1900–1939'. *Past and Present,* 32, December, 57–85; Adhikari M. 1993. *'Let Us Live for Our Children': The Teachers' League of South Africa, 1913–1940.* Cape Town: UCT Press; Summers C. 1994. *From Civilization to Segregation: Social Ideals and Social Control in Southern Rhodesia, 1890–1934.* Athens: Ohio University Press; Summers C. 2002. *Colonial Lessons: Africans' Education in Southern Rhodesia, 1918–1940.* Portsmouth: Heinemann; and West M. 2002. *The Rise of an African Middle Class: Colonial Zimbabwe, 1898–1965.* Bloomington: Indiana University Press.

13   Though a full comparison is not pursued here, my thoughts on comparative history
     are influenced in part by Fredrickson G. 1997. 'From exceptionalism to variability:
     recent developments in cross-national comparative history', in *The Comparative
     Imagination: On the History of Racism, Nationalism, and Social Movements*. Berkeley:
     University of California Press.

14   On 'intersections' see Rosaldo R. 1989. *Culture and Truth: The Remaking of Social
     Analysis*. Boston: Beacon Press.

15   The literature on identity is vast. I draw in part on the following texts: Adhikari,
     Not White Enough; Erasmus, *Coloured by History*; Vail L (ed). 1989. *The Creation of
     Tribalism*. Berkeley: University of California Press; Ranger T. 1983. 'The invention
     of tradition in colonial Africa', in *The Invention of Tradition*, eds T Ranger & E
     Hobsbawm. Cambridge: Cambridge University Press; Spear T & Waller R (eds).
     1993. *Being Maasai: Ethnicity and Identity in East Africa*. London: James Currey;
     Mamdani M. 1996. *Citizen and Subject: Contemporary Africa and the Legacy of Late
     Colonialism*. Princeton: Princeton University Press.

16   This situational approach has been influenced, inter alia, by Hall S. 1990. 'Cultural
     identity and diaspora', in *Identity: Community, Culture, Difference*, ed J Rutherford.
     London: Lawrence & Wishart; Gilroy P. 1993. *The Black Atlantic: Modernity
     and Double-Consciousness*. Cambridge: Harvard University Press; and Cooper &
     Brubaker, 'Beyond identity', 1–47. On the expression 'subaltern', see, for example,
     Guha R & Spivak G (eds). 1988. *Selected Subaltern Studies*. Oxford: Oxford University
     Press.

17   On indirect rule, see Lugard F. 1965. *The Dual Mandate in British Tropical Africa*.
     London: Frank Cass; Mamdani, *Citizen and Subject*; Afigbo A. 1972. *The Warrant
     Chiefs: Indirect Rule in Southeastern Nigeria, 1891–1929*. London: Longman; and
     White L. 1984. '"Tribes" and the aftermath of the Chilembwe rising'. *African
     Affairs*, 83, 333, 533–536.

18   For a general account of the revolt, see Shepperson G & Price T. 1958. *Independent
     African: John Chilembwe and the Origins, Setting, and Significance of the Nyasaland
     Native Rising of 1915*. Edinburgh: Edinburgh University Press.

19   MNA, s1/705¹/30 (no Folio number given), 30 May 1933.

20   MNA, s1/309/33, Folios 22–27, 27a, 1 October 1933.

21   'Race' and 'ethnicity' as analytic terms have at times been conflated depending on
     the time period and social context. I use them somewhat generically here, with
     'race' referring to a 'pseudo-scientific' basis of difference and 'ethnicity' referring to
     culturally based notions of difference.

22   See, for example, Tsing A. 1993. *In the Realm of the Diamond Queen: Marginality
     in an Out-of-the-Way Place*. Princeton: Princeton University Press; and Piot C. 1999.
     Remotely Global: Village Modernity in West Africa. Chicago: University of Chicago
     Press.

23   Erasmus, *Coloured by History*, 'Introduction'.

24   Tsing, *In the Realm of the Diamond Queen*, and Piot, *Remotely Global* are key works
     on marginal communities. On subcultures generally, see Gelder K (ed). 2005. *The
     Subcultures Reader*. New York: Routledge.

25   On legibility and state vision, see Scott J. 1998. *Seeing Like a State: How Certain Schemes
     to Improve the Human Condition Have Failed*. New Haven: Yale University Press.

26   For a more extended discussion of this argument, see Lee, 'The "native" undefined'.

27   On native associations, see Van Velsen J. 1966. 'Some early pressure groups in
      Malawi', in *The Zambesian Past: Studies in Central African History*, ed E Stokes &
      R Brown. Manchester: Manchester University Press, 376–412; Chanock M. 1975.
      'The new men revisited: an essay on the development of political consciousness
      in colonial Malawi', in *From Nyasaland to Malawi: Studies in Colonial History*, ed
      R Macdonald. Nairobi: East Africa Publishing House, 234–253; and Tangri R.
      1971. 'Inter-war "Native Associations" and the formation of the Nyasaland African
      Congress'. *Transafrican Journal of History*, 1, 1, 84–102.
28   MNA, s1/705¹/30, Folio 1, 31 March 1930; s1/705¹/30, minutes section, no. 5, 24
      April 1930; s1/705¹/30, Folio 1a, 28 July 1929, 3; NS, 1/3/2, 1–8.
29   MNA, s1/705¹/30, minutes section, no. 5, 24 April 1930.
30   MNA, s1/705¹/30, minutes section, no. 6, 30 April 1930.
31   Gelder K. 2005. 'Introduction: the field of subcultural studies', in Gelder, *The
      Subcultures Reader*.
32   MNA, s1/309/33 (no Folio number given), 15 August 1933; s1/309/33, Folio 6,
      25 August 1933; s1/309/33, Folios 2, 3, 4, 30 July 1933.
33   The request for separate education was dropped due to the unsatisfactory response
      by Sir Thomas at the 1931 meeting. See MNA, s1/309/33, Folios 2, 3, 4, 30 July
      1933; s1/309/33, Folios 22–27, 27a, 1 October 1933.
34   These meeting minutes were forwarded to the chief secretary on 16 October 1933,
      with the hope that they would reach governor Hubert Young. MNA, s1/309/33,
      Folio 8; s1/309/33, Folios 9, 10, 11, 17 September 1933; s1/309/33, Folios 12–
      21, 1 October 1933.
35   MNA, s1/309/33, Folios 12–21, 1 October 1933; Folios 22–27, 27a, 1 October 1933.
36   MNA, s1/309/33, Folios 22–27, 27a, 1 October 1933.
37   MNA, s1/309/33, Folios 22–27, 27a, 1 October 1933.
38   MNA, s1/309/33, Folios 12–21, 1 October 1933.
39   MNA, s1/705¹/30, Folio 26, 27 November 1933.
40   MNA, s1/705¹/30, Folio 33, 29 & 30 May 1934; s1/705¹/30, Folio 34, 13 July 1934;
      s1/705¹/30, Folio 36, 25 July 1934. See also: MNA, s1/705¹/30, Folio 46, Copy 4.
41   For Mumba's testimony, see MNA, s1/705¹/30, Folio 31, 29 & 30 May 1934. See
      also MNA, s1/705¹/30, Folio 33a; Folio 46, Copy 7.
42   Matrilineal systems have long been recognised by scholars as fundamental to many
      Malawian ethnic groups. See Tew M. 1950. *Peoples of the Lake Nyasa Region: East
      Central Africa, Part I*. London: Oxford University Press; Phiri K M. 1983. 'Some
      changes in the matrilineal family system among the Chewa of Malawi since the
      nineteenth century'. *Journal of African History*, 24, no. 2, 257–274; and Vaughan
      M. 1987. *The Story of an African Famine: Gender and Famine in Twentieth-Century
      Malawi*. New York: Cambridge University Press.
43   MNA, s1/705¹/30, Folio 31, 29 & 30 May 1934.
44   MNA, s1/705¹/30, Folio 31, 29 & 30 May 1934.
45   MNA, s1/705¹/30, Folio 31, 29 & 30 May 1934.
46   MNA, s1/705¹/30, Folio 31, 29 & 30 May 1934.
47   For a contrasting African view, see MNA, s1/705¹/30, Folio 37. During a meeting
      between governor Young and local authorities held at Mzimba in the north on
      13 July 1934, the issue of relationships between African women and foreigners
      was raised. African authorities there wished for such 'marriages' to stop because

'the offspring introduced a foreign element into the tribe. These offspring were ill prepared to follow the customs of the land and other disturbing complications were bound to follow if these unions were not forbidden'.

48 MNA, s1/705¹/30, Folio 37.

49 MNA, s1/705¹/30, Folio 44a, 1–16. See also MNA, s1/705¹/30, Folio 46, Copy 9.

50 MNA, s1/705¹/30, Folio 44, 15 September 1934.

51 MNA, s1/705¹/30, Folio 45, 5 October 1934. See also MNA, s1/705¹/30, Folio 46, Copy 10; s1/705¹/30, 1a, 1–4; s1/309/33, Folios 22–27, 27a, 1 October 1933.

52 MNA, s26/2/4/5, Folio 16, 18 September 1935. For conditions in Southern Rhodesia, see Mandaza I. 1997. *Race, Colour and Class in Southern Africa*. Harare: Sapes Books, ch 5.

53 MNA, s26/2/4/5, Folio 17, 18 September 1935; s26/2/4/5, Folio 18, 18 September 1935.

54 MNA, s26/2/4/5, Folio 18, 29 September 1935; s26/2/4/5, Folio 19, 29 September 1935.

55 Despite this official position, many facets of postcolonial Malawian culture were based on Chewa culture, with Chichewa, for example, being made a national language. See Vail L & White L. 1989. 'Tribalism in the political history of Malawi', in Vail, *The Creation of Tribalism*, 182; and Vaughan M. 2001. 'Reported speech and other kinds of testimony', in *African Words, African Voices: Critical Practices in Oral History*, eds L White, D W Cohen & S Miescher. Bloomington: Indiana University Press, 55.

56 R Jamieson, interviewed by Christopher Lee, 15 November 1999, Lilongwe, Malawi.

57 For Africans as the subject of Western discourse, see, for example, Curtin P. 1964. *The Image of Africa: British Ideas and Action, 1780–1850*. Madison: University of Wisconsin Press; Mudimbe V. 1988. *The Invention of Africa: Gnosis, Philosophy, and the Order of Knowledge*. Bloomington: Indiana University Press; Vaughan M. 1991. *Curing Their Ills: Colonial Power and African Illness*. Stanford: Stanford University Press; and Burke T. 1996. *Lifebuoy Men, Lux Women: Commodification, Consumption, and Cleanliness in Modern Zimbabwe*. Durham: Duke University Press. For Africans as actively engaged in the production of forms of discourse, see Feierman S. 1990. *Peasant Intellectuals: Anthropology and History in Tanzania*. Madison: University of Wisconsin Press; Vail L & White L. 1991. *Power and the Praise Poem: Southern African Voices in History*. Charlottesville: University Press of Virginia; White L. 2000. *Speaking with Vampires: Rumor and History in Colonial Africa*. Berkeley: University of California Press; and Zachernuk P. 2000. *Colonial Subjects: An African Intelligentsia and Atlantic Ideas*. Charlottesville: University Press of Virginia.

58 For the practice of oral history in Africa, see Vansina J. 1985. *Oral Tradition as History*. Madison: University of Wisconsin Press. For critiques of this method, with particular attention to a more critical engagement with context in the shaping of oral history, see Cohen D W. 1989. 'The undefining of oral tradition'. *Ethnohistory*, 36, no. 1; and Cohen D W, Miescher S F & White L. 2001. 'Introduction: voices, words, and African history', in *African Words, African Voices: Critical Practices in*

Oral History, eds D W Cohen, S F Miescher & L White. Bloomington: Indiana University Press.

59 For the broader agenda from which this remark stems, see Stoler A & Cooper F (eds). 1997. *Tensions of Empire: Colonial Cultures in a Bourgeois World*. Berkeley: University of California Press.

Entries are listed in letter-by-letter alphabetical order. Numerical terms are filed as if spelt out.